TO:

_____

FROM:

_____

DATE:

_____

AMI McCONNELL & FRIENDS

Faithful Daughter

TRUE, INSPIRING STORIES CELEBRATING

a Mother's Legacy and Love

DaySpring

LIVE YOUR FAITH

Faithful Daughter: True, Inspiring Stories
Celebrating a Mother's Legacy and Love
Copyright © 2020 DaySpring Cards, Inc. All Rights Reserved.
First Edition, March 2020

Published by:

21154 Highway 16 East
Siloam Springs, AR 72761
dayspring.com

Written by Ami McConnell
Cover Designed by Hannah Skelton

Printed in China
Prime: J1595
ISBN: 978-1-64454-444-0

CONTENTS

Introduction

We met at Bricktop's in Franklin, Tennessee, for a business lunch. It's a genteel, white-tablecloth kind of place where the waiter hovers quietly in the background. A couple of our publishing friends stopped to say hello before tucking in to their own booth.

Once we ordered waters and salads, my friend and I dove into our usual book industry talk—which houses were having the most profitable year, which literary agents were misbehaving, which authors we enjoyed working with most (and least), and our current pet projects. I'd recently moved into a new home, and we talked about a bestseller that advised purging old things. My friend's mother had recently passed away. Going through her things to decide what to keep was harder, perhaps, than that book allowed. My friend teared up as she spoke about her time with her mom. "Don't wait," she said. "Book a plane ticket to go see your mom while she's well. You won't regret it. If you wait, you will." In that moment, we weren't just colleagues—she was my sister, offering advice that would no doubt ring true, like it or not.

After that lunch, I thought a lot about my mother. I'm as old now as she was when she came to see me in Nashville when I was a young newlywed. She told me she had breast cancer—stage four. Soon after, she was admitted to Duke University for experimental treatments: a bone marrow transplant, radical chemo, radiation, and regular chemo. She suffered. But she fought through, cheating death. She said she'd have given up except for one thing: she wanted to meet her first grandchild, my son Max, born later that year.

Mom handled that enormous challenge the way she has handled every other thing in life—with faith. She steeped herself in Scripture. She prayed and asked for prayer. She turned to her church community and found help and support in their care. Faith is what got her through it. She's not a particularly headstrong woman, just steadfast in her belief that she is a beloved daughter of God. She believes that about herself and about me. She even named me Ami, meaning "beloved," as a constant reminder of my core identity. Though we don't always think alike or live out our faith in the same way, my mother and I are fundamentally faithful daughters. Faithful to each other and to the One who holds us dear.

The truth is, my identity has largely been formed in the context of my mother. I learned so many of my behaviors and tendencies from her. As I mused on this after lunch with my friend, I thought about my friends. As daughters, we all look to our mothers as a sort of "true north," for better or for worse. We struggle to meet their standards or become exasperated that their standards weren't high enough. We make choices because of, and sometimes in defiance of, their choices. That's what my conversation with my publishing colleague at Bricktop's began to unearth in me.

Turning these thoughts over in my mind, I felt a hunger and a curiosity stirring. As a mother of four girls, I care deeply about this connection. I wanted to know what other women thought. How have my friends' lives been shaped in light of their mothers?

And what of their faith? I invited some of my favorite writers to muse about this subject with me. You hold in your hands the result of our conversations. It's a sort of literary exploration of women and their mothers' legacies. I hope you enjoy it as much as we have enjoyed creating it for you.

Don't Be Afraid to Go It Alone

BY MEGAN ALEXANDER

I was in the fourth grade. I was going through a difficult time with some of my friends. You know how kids can be. My two best friends had been ignoring me, and I was super lonely. I came home and said to my mom, "I have no one to play with at recess. I don't want to be alone. I try to tag along with other groups because I feel embarrassed standing alone, but I want real friends."

My mother said, "You know what, Meg? Don't be afraid to be alone. In fact, be proud to sit alone on that bench on the playground. You know why? Because I bet someone will look over, see you, and feel comfortable approaching you because you are alone. It's intimidating to approach someone in a group. But someone alone? Much easier. And I bet someone will be more inclined to approach you. You'll make a new friend soon—I promise!"

I had no idea how powerful and meaningful those words would become.

So I did what my mom suggested—I sat alone on the playground bench. And sure enough, eventually a girl named Kristy wandered over and asked if I wanted to join her and others in a game of kickball. I did, and I made new friends.

Years later, Mom's advice came into play again.

My first TV job was at the local CW news station in Nashville, Tennessee. I had been hired as a part-time morning reporter. I was so excited to be there! After I had been on-air for a few weeks, it was announced that the company was having a party. Everyone was invited. I knew very few people at the company and wasn't dating anyone. Some employees said they would not go by themselves. I was considering skipping it too. But my mother's words came to mind. And I decided to attend—by myself.

That night I walked into the hotel where the party was. Someone from the news station spotted me and came over to say hi. "Who's your date?" he asked. I smiled and answered, "No one. I came by myself." He looked surprised. "You came alone?" he asked. "Yup!" I responded and walked away confidently, even though I felt self-conscious. Soon I started chatting with people and making new friends. I met more people that night because I was alone and struck up conversations with a variety of people I would not normally have met.

I'll give you another example. I was invited to a women's business retreat in Washington, DC. It was a three-day event with women from all over the country, promising inspirational speakers and networking. I casually knew the director and another person speaking, but did not know anyone else attending. I went alone.

They held a cocktail reception the first night. I walked into the room all by myself. Many of the women were paired up, chatting happily, and the self-conscious feeling crept up. I stood alone for a few minutes, then squared my shoulders and remembered my mother's words. I made eye contact with one lady and smiled. She walked over and we started chatting. Later that night, at the formal dinner the conference held, I took my seat at my assigned table. I walked around the table, extending my hand and meeting people. One of the older women said she had traveled to the conference from Dallas with two friends. She asked, "And who are you here with?" I smiled. "Just me." She raised an eyebrow. "You came here alone? Wow—you are brave!"

I met some wonderful people and made some great business connections at that conference. I chatted with some ladies way more than I would have if I had attended with a friend and just talked to her the majority of the time. I am so glad I went alone!

These days, traveling or attending events on my own is not intimidating to me. In fact, I have come to really enjoy it.

What would my life be like if my mother hadn't encouraged me to be okay standing alone? What if she had rushed in to solve my problem for me instead of trusting me to handle it myself with poise and confidence? My whole life and career would have turned out differently. Thanks to my mother's relentless determination to turn uncomfortable situations into positive results, I get to interview celebrities and sports personalities on national television every week and travel the world. I owe her a great deal. Thanks, Mom!

Megan Alexander is a national news correspondent, host, emcee, speaker, actress, and producer. She's the author of Faith in the Spotlight. *Megan can be seen every evening as a correspondent on the top-rated national news magazine television show* Inside Edition *and has also been a special correspondent for* Thursday Night Football *on CBS. She was born and raised in Seattle, Washington, and graduated from Westmont College. Megan splits time between New York City and Nashville, Tennessee. She and her husband have two young sons.*

Courage

BY LAURI ARNOLD

I have this clear memory of my mother wearing a white dress with a wide belt accentuating her tiny waist. She has on white gloves, white high-heeled shoes, and white sunglasses, and is rounding up the four of us children. We'd just gotten off a plane in Michigan for a visit with our grandparents, her parents. In those by-gone days, people dressed to fly, so my three siblings and I were all dressed alike. We were all born within a five-year period. How tired my mother must have been!

Maybe this memory stands out because my mother only dressed up for special occasions. She was quite rebellious and headstrong in her ways. The youngest of three—a surprise—she learned early to do her own thing, no matter what my strong, opinionated grandmother demanded. Mom excelled at sports and won awards for her impressive athletic achievements in

high school. I didn't get that gene. I preferred reading, loved fashion, and played endlessly with dolls. I'd
spend hours rearranging the rooms in my dollhouse.
(No wonder I eventually started my own business dec-
orating and staging homes.)

Mom had no use for fashion, but I loved it. I rel-
ished shopping with her, talking her into buying things
she wouldn't normally buy. She didn't wear makeup—
except for just a bit of lipstick, the bare minimum for a
Southern woman of her time. She swam with dolphins
and loved spending time on the beach in the sun. I
guarded my skin from the dangerous rays and disliked
the feeling of sand between my toes. We seemed so
different to me back then! How could I be her daughter?

My mother was the "fun" mother who drove the
car pool. Sometimes she still had on her nightgown under her raincoat. My friends loved her. Me? I was both
in awe and afraid of her. Her personality could go from
funny to angry quickly, so I learned early to keep my
distance at certain times. One night, I heard my parents

fighting—the only time I'd ever heard them raise their voices at each other. When checking on my mother the next morning, I found papers on her bed beginning with the line "I am an alcoholic." I asked her what that meant. She responded with shame and defensiveness. She said it was a secret. There was no more discussion. Not long after that, my mother started going out alone on Monday evenings to a special meeting. She stayed sober for years until my father divorced her for another woman after sharing twenty-three years of marriage and four children together.

Mom was a "highly functioning" alcoholic. There were never any DUIs, wrecks, or embarrassing public displays of drunkenness. She never shirked her responsibilities. It was all very contained. But a child of an alcoholic figures out quickly how to spot the signs of drinking, signaling when to disappear. My mother's was the telling tone of her voice—a bit slurred and easily annoyed. I could hear it in a word whispered in person and even over the phone.

I watched my mother's sharper edges soften over

time. She remarried, went back to school, majored in theology, and impressively graduated *magna cum laude*. After moving to Chicago with my stepfather, she received her master's in theology. She became a pastoral-care counselor, volunteered with Hospice, got certified in infant massage, and became a lay minister serving communion in the Episcopal church and to men and women in assisted-living facilities. I was more than proud of the accomplishments and commitments filling the next chapters of her life story.

But here's the most important part. Somewhere along the line, Mom began drinking again. My three siblings and I confronted her with our concerns about it. My stepfather was equally concerned but wanted to avoid the conflict of bringing it to her attention himself. To her credit, Mom not only heard us, but she stopped drinking and began attending meetings faithfully. We got our mother back in ways we'd never thought possible.

I was afraid the drinking would start again when her second husband died. Instead, I watched as my mother thoughtfully put the pieces of her life back together yet again after being left alone. Daily she exemplified a bravery and competence I want to emulate now and in the days to come. She exudes confidence. She attends prayer circles and healing services weekly. She attended an intellectually and spiritually demanding Episcopal Cursillo weekend. She shows generosity with her friends, particularly those who are living alone, checking on them daily. She doesn't hesitate to reach out to complete strangers and share her good fortune. She actively cares for her physical health. She has carefully and considerately thought out her end-of-life directives and recorded them on paper, making their location in her home known to each of us. She is the consummate hostess to friends and family. She has taught me what it means to grow older gracefully and practice your faith in all things. Most importantly, she is now wholly present to her children, especially in their times of need.

My mother has taught me to value the precious things in life as I struggle to keep what Winston

Churchill always referred to as "the black dog" in his corner. I've had to learn to embrace as my friend the depression living on the periphery in my life instead of viewing it as my enemy. It is a part of me. Fighting it never produces a winner or helps assure my family I'm not to be feared in that state. If my mother can rise above being left behind by two of the most important people in her life and move on with such courage, I can certainly summon some of that courage to live in a state of gratitude rather than anxiety. Teaching me how to choose life and reimagine it has been the greatest of gifts she has passed on.

Lauri Arnold lives in Louisville, Kentucky, and Asheville, North Carolina. She was a regular contributor to Underwired *magazine and* NFocus *in Louisville, and was named a Face of Louisville in* StyleBlueprint. *She has recently retired from owning her own business, Optimal Surroundings, to enjoy being a grandmother, travel, and pursue her love of the arts in all venues.*

Confidence in Me

BY SARAH ARTHUR

When I was little, I thought my mother and the musical movie star Julie Andrews were basically the same person. Not only did Mom look remarkably like Andrews, but my mother seemed to have the same enjoyment of some of the characters she played—especially Maria von Trapp in *The Sound of Music*. Mom sewed our clothes, wasn't fazed by pranks, and managed roomfuls of students in algebra or Sunday school with apparent ease. She'd even studied in Austria as a young woman and knew a German word for everything.

As soon as I was old enough to pull a record from a jacket, place it on the player, and position the needle, I listened to *The Sound of Music* soundtrack relentlessly, memorizing not only the lyrics but Andrews's inflections. Over time it dawned on me that one significant difference between the celebrity and my mother was that Mom couldn't carry a tune. Oh, she'd sing along decently—in fact, even in church she could blend in when the main melody was carried by others. But when left to her own devices—say, humming "I have confidence in springtime . . ." while washing dishes—her song was likely to end up in a different key than it began. If anyone pointed this out, she'd acknowledge it with a grin and a shrug.

Meanwhile the annual airing of *The Sound of Music* on television was a family event. Mom would mark it on her tidy calendar, and we'd stay up late—till the commercial break after the wedding scene, anyway, at which point she'd announce, "Well, that's it! Time for bed." It wasn't until years later that I discovered the movie keeps going, into Nazi occupation and resistance and basically all the most harrowing, fascinating parts of the story. "Hey, what's this?" I exclaimed one night, coming back into the living room after brushing my teeth. "Wait: It's not *over*?" Mom glanced up from the screen with that familiar grin and a shrug.

As I got older, I began to look more and more like Mom, down to our shoe size. "Gosh, Peg," her friends would say. "She looks just like you!" I no longer listened to records; I was busy curling my hair and playing Amy Grant tapes and trying to decide if I wanted to become a teacher someday. ("Don't," Mom advised. "The bureaucracy will drive you nuts. There are other ways to help kids.") When I was assigned to write a paper on a hero of my choice, Mom suggested Dietrich Bonhoeffer, the German pastor who'd been imprisoned and executed for resisting the Nazis. This was what the von Trapps had escaped. This is what she'd shielded me from, sending me to bed early. I was old enough to understand now, to grasp the stakes. Resisting evil was costly.

I took her advice and wrote on Bonhoeffer—and didn't become a teacher. But I did have a blast with kids, serving at a summer camp after my freshman year of college and teaching campers the many goofy, mealtime prayer-songs in my repertoire. I was a horrible substitute teacher (itemize under "Things That Mom Makes Look Easy") but took a job as the youth director of a large mainline church after college. I picked up playing the guitar, carted vanloads of children all over the countryside, and taught them those goofy camp songs. And, like Maria, like Mom, I hoped they'd resist evil, whatever its form.

One morning I rushed into the busy church building to unload my car after a week of summer camp. I happened to be wearing a longish flared skirt and a wide-brimmed straw hat, my guitar case in one hand and a piece of luggage in the other. A woman I knew glanced up and exclaimed, "Gosh, you look just like Maria von Trapp!"

I hadn't thought of Julie Andrews in years. "I have confidence in springtime!" I belted out with a grin, marching down the hall.

Then it hit me. It wasn't Maria I resembled. It was my mom. This was her persona I had embraced: her love of children, her belief that music and joy are stronger than all the evil empires of the world. What I had thought were the qualities of a character from history were the enduring qualities of my own mother.

Now that I have children, I realize none of it was easy. What looked effortless takes, in fact, a great deal of energy. I will never sew anyone's clothes, but I can strive to delight in my kids and instill in them what matters, even when those skills don't come naturally. Those qualities I admire in my mother—in Maria, in Bonhoeffer, in all who resist evil—are possible. In my children. In me.

Sarah Arthur is a speaker and author of a dozen books ranging from popular devotionals to serious engagement with literature. She serves as preliminary fiction judge for the Christianity Today *Book Awards and speaks all over the country about the writing process. A graduate of Wheaton College and Duke University Divinity School, she served in full-time and volunteer youth ministry for over twenty years. She's a mother of two boys and lives in Lansing, Michigan, where her husband, Tom, is a pastor. Visit her website at saraharthur.com.*

An Inheritance of Blessing

BY JODIE BERNDT

I could hear him back there, bouncing his basketball. We were on our way home from elementary school, together and yet not. Thomas, the coolest boy in the whole third grade, walked twenty feet behind me. I didn't look back.

Suddenly the bouncing stopped. A split second later I felt the breath leave my body. Thomas had thrown his ball, and—since he was also the most athletic boy in third grade—it had hit me, square in the back.

I took off running.

Three blocks later I burst through my front door. "Mom!" I cried through my tears. "Thomas Mayfield [not his real name] just hit me in the back! With his *basketball*!"

My mother has never been known for her nurturing personality. She could tell I wasn't seriously hurt, and so, rather than letting me wallow in self-pity, she pointed me toward the door.

"Jodie," she said, "Thomas will be walking past our house in about one minute, and when he goes by, I want you to say, 'Have a nice day, Thomas.'

"And then I want you to curtsy."

I know what you are thinking. You're thinking that my mom sounds a little bit crazy. And she is, in a mostly good kind of way.

Like, when my sixty-one-year-old dad was battling brain cancer and lacked the strength to get from the car to their condo, and my mom told him to sit on the sidewalk. "Stay right there," she said (as if my father had another option), and then she disappeared into the building. Five minutes later she returned, carrying the cushions from their lanai, a bottle of Pepsi, and a bag of Doritos.

Which is how my parents wound up spending an entire afternoon sunning themselves in a parking lot until my dad found the strength to begin again. Crazy, right? Yeah. Crazy good.

But back to Thomas.

Per Mom's instructions, I went out to the street

and saw him coming my way. Thomas didn't acknowledge me, but as he drew abreast of our house, I spoke up: "Have a nice day, Thomas." And I curtsied. (Having seen *The Sound of Music* at least three times before I turned eight, I knew how.)

If Thomas was surprised, he didn't show it. If anything, he looked a bit worried. He probably figured my mother had called his mom—and that he'd have to face the music when he got home. That's what most moms would have done back in the day: called and tattled. But not mine.

Claire Rundle may have been short on maternal compassion and sympathy, but she was long on the Bible. She knew what it said. And whenever anyone tried to hurt her or one of her kids, she always found a way to pay them back.

With a blessing.

"Do not repay evil with evil," the Bible says, "or insult with insult. On the contrary, repay evil with blessing, because to this you were called so that you may inherit a blessing."

That's I Peter 3:9. And it worked. Thomas never bothered me after that day; in fact, we became friends. And my mom's crazy counsel—to repay insults with blessings—has stood me in good stead over the years. Because what I've found is that the more I try to extend kindness to people who hurt or offend me, the better life gets. It's as if grace finds a way to get rid of the sting.

I have four children. They're all grown up now, but I tried to raise them in the spirit of I Peter 3:9. I'm sure there were times when they thought I was as crazy as I thought my mom was. I'm sure there were days when they thought I was worse. One year, for instance, they gave me a homemade Mother's Day card where they'd picked a word to go with each letter of *MOTHER*. Next to the *e* they wrote EMBARRASSING.

Honestly, though, I didn't care if they thought I was nuts. I just didn't want them to miss out on a blessing. And so I encouraged them to invite the mean girl to their party. To bake cookies for our grumpy neighbor when he complained about the noise they made. To pray God's richest favor over the middle-school bully.

I did not, however, ever ask them to curtsy. So there's that.

But here's the thing: repaying meanness with kindness almost never makes sense, nor is it usually easy. Yet it opens the door to a life full of freedom and blessing—one that refuses to take up an offense—and for that wisdom nugget, I will be forever grateful to my mother.

She and my dad enjoyed their last parking-lot picnic back in 2001, the year that my father went to be with the Lord. Mom got remarried several years later—her name is Claire Gilman now—and I love my stepdad. John is just as generous and crazy as she is.

They downsized recently, moving from a big house to a small condo, taking only their most beloved possessions. As John pushed his favorite stone bench into place outside their new front door, a neighbor approached.

"That is the ugliest thing I have ever seen," the neighbor said, inclining his head toward the bench. "Where do you plan to put it?"

John straightened up. "Well, I guess I will put it wherever you like," he said with a smile. And then he invited the man and his wife over for dinner.

Which is not, to be perfectly frank, what I would have done. But it's the sort of thing I *want* to do when someone gets under my skin. And so, even as I pray for my children to "repay evil with blessing," I pray for myself.

Lord, make me willing to return kindness for cruelty. Let me meet meanness with love.

Lord, make me more like my mom.

Jodie Berndt is the author of nine books, including Praying the Scriptures for Your Children *and* Praying the Scriptures for Your Adult Children. *A speaker and Bible teacher, Jodie encourages people to pursue joy, celebrate grace, and live on purpose. Find her writing at JodieBerndt.*

com or on Facebook, Twitter, and Instagram. Jodie and her husband, Robert, have four grown children and two sons-in-law. They live in Virginia Beach but can often be found up the road in Charlottesville, Virginia, cheering for their beloved U.Va. Cavaliers.

I'm a Survivor

BY KARLI BUTLER

If you're looking for a perfect happy ending, *spoiler alert*: you won't find it here. I waited a long time for the perfect happy ending, imagining that someday my life story would have a neat, tidy, happy resolution. It'd be wrapped up like a treasure in a Tiffany-blue box, trimmed with a perfect bow. Then I'd reveal it to the world like a gift. "Here's my story. Enjoy!"

Things didn't work out that way. Even so, I'm proud of my life. I look into the eyes of my little boy, and I'm proud of where we are and how we got here. I'm proud of my growth, my resilience, and the way I've chosen to live my life after drama, trauma, and scars.

Isn't that how God works? We make plans, and with love in His eyes, He laughs. He probably thinks our naivete is so adorable.

At twenty-three years old, I was absolutely sure I'd be some big-time entertainment publicist living it up

34

in New York City—and the truth was, I was so close to getting there. After successfully completing internships in the public relations departments at Harpo Studios, CBS New York, and BET Radio in New York, I was on my way. A dozen years later, I'm now a social-services provider and single mother of one, living a modest life in the suburbs of Chicago. Who knew? I didn't know that I was built for this.

Truth is, becoming the woman I am today nearly killed me. Literally. In 2006, I was the victim of a violent crime that I talk about as I travel and speak. I call myself a survivor of violent crime.

Anyone initially affected by violence or crime finds the offense doesn't stop when the violence ends. No, immediately you find you've been slapped with a label. Suddenly you're a "victim." The police refer to you as a victim. The state refers to you as a victim. Your power has been stripped away and you feel very much a victim.

But once you move past the hurt, sadness, and shock of it all, you might discover a new label that feels more appropriate. Right somehow. That label? *Survivor.* That one word makes all the difference. Where *victim* implies loss of power, *survivor* is empowering.

When I share my story, it's not to shame anyone or to ask for pity. I don't ever want anyone to feel sorry for me. I tell my story to declare that I am a survivor. It reminds me that God is real and that there is always a way. A way to faith, courage, optimism, and love.

I knew I was a survivor years before I was violently assaulted. That's because my mother was a suicide victim. She took her own life.

I'll never forget the moment I found out. I felt physically sick. The entire day is a blur. Anytime I think about it, my breathing slows and my eyes well up with tears. She left me motherless at just twenty-two. The woman I adored and loved more than anyone was suddenly gone.

Practically speaking, I was an adult. I'd graduated from college, established financial independence, and purchased a car. Still, my mother's sudden death forced me to make decisions about caskets, funerals, and cemeteries long before most of my peers. The shift threw me into the complex world of adulthood. I was suddenly faced with my own mortality. It was if the world I'd lived in crumbled. My sense of safety, comfort, and stability was lost in the rubble.

I remember blacking out soon after her death. I was simply so exhausted that my body just had to shut down and sleep. When I woke up, I hoped it was all a bad dream. But it wasn't. The stress and bad news just kept coming. I lost nine pounds in two weeks. Stress will do that to you. I soldiered on, trying to be strong for my sisters, even though I was shocked, lost, and scared.

I wish I could tell you that it's possible to get over the loss of a parent, but for me it hasn't been. And I don't expect to ever just "get over it." However, I have found ways to cope. My mother passed away thirteen years ago. When I have a rotten day or hit a milestone in my life, I think about her. Sometimes I feel anger . . . like she abandoned me. *Where is my mother when I need her? Did she think about me and my sisters when she pulled the trigger? What about us?* I try not to dwell in those feelings too long, but it's not easy. Loss and grief will turn your world upside down if you let them.

If I didn't "get over it," I'm grateful to say I survived it. And that's what people said about me: *You're a survivor.* It was true. I had life while she did not. And that felt like something big to me. Something worthwhile.

Turns out my mother had been preparing me my entire life. She had been teaching me, showing me, scolding me, all in preparation for the day she would no longer be there to help me. Although it's been difficult, I am so thankful for every lesson. And I am thankful for the twenty-two years I got to spend with her. Her death was a test of my strength; a test of my ability to use what I had learned and move forward; a test to rise to the occasion and be a good example for my sisters. At the time, I doubted my ability to do that.

Turns out I am as strong as I pretended to be.

Karli Butler is a writer, speaker, and social-services provider living in Evanston, Illinois. She holds a BA in Communication from DePaul University as well as a Master of Arts in Organizational and Multicultural Communication. Since the attack in 2006, Karli has spoken widely and played a major role in the passing of Illinois House Bill 2193, which requires anyone buying commercial-grade hydrochloric or sulfuric acid to have an ID, where they are entered into a monitored database. When Karli was attacked, she wondered if life could ever be good again. Now she loves her scars, pleased to know that her story has helped others. She lives with her son, Zailen, and loves to help others by sharing openly and dreaming big.

When One Becomes Two Again

BY KRISTY CAMBRON

The clock *tick-tocked* on the wall—a hollow sound competing for dominance with the beep of an IV machine, ringing phones at the nurses' station, and the soft fall of tears in the ICU.

In those last precious days of my dad's cancer battle, I watched her. My mom. Weary from restless sleep on tufted ottomans in the waiting room. Broken while she held his face in her hands, as leukemia forced them into a "goodbye for now." The red-letter words in Mark 10 came to mind: "A man will leave his father and mother and be united to his wife, and the two will become one flesh" (vv. 7–8). I watched as thirty-five years of oneness between my mom and dad split down the middle. When he died, they became two again.

Moms are proud of their kids. It's just what we do. We also make the school play costumes when we can't sew. We bandage about a thousand scraped knees in our tenure and bake six dozen cookies at midnight because we just heard about the school bake sale at bedtime. We drive them to every practice, cheer at their games, and wear our kid's numbered jersey like they're big-league MVPs. And only when those tangible pieces of our hearts are safe and slumbering in little beds—and we've checked the house three times over—do we lie down to rest.

I'd felt such pride at the births of my own children. And I thought I understood motherhood. But my lens shifted that day in the ICU when my mom handed my six-foot-four-inch cowboy hat–wearing, guitar–playing, booming laugh–owning dad over to God's eternal care. She did it with absolute trust. And faith. With dignity and beauty in spite of the gaping hole left in our small family tree. With a tender heart that bled tears for days, months, years afterward, but still kept it together for the sake of her daughters.

My lens of motherhood shifted, and I was proud—*of her.*

Pride spilled over as I watched my mom in the weeks after that ICU goodbye. Making funeral decisions. Cleaning out Dad's desk at the office when I could barely do more than cradle the framed family photo that he'd kept on the tabletop. She emptied closets of his shoes and ball caps. Thumbed through racks of ties and stacks of books with bookmarks still pressed in the middle, like he'd return to read them later. I think his favorite coffee is still in the cabinet, unopened.

She lives in the house that holds a lifetime of shared memories around every corner. But now the memories are snapshots of the new—holidays he won't be a part of, the birth of grandkids he'll never know, books published and lives so remarkably changed by Jesus that I wonder if he'd even recognize his own tribe now.

My mom tells us that when she was little, she wanted to grow up to have three sons and become an author. She had two daughters! We laugh now because her slightly wild, creative-minded daughter has three boys and writes for a living. I'm proud to get to live such a fun dream that began in her youth. And though her hero-sized dream was little boys and books, my dream is to one day be as strong as she is. I wonder, if I had to entrust God with the other half of the "one" that my husband and I made together, could I carry on? Could I turn to Jesus, trusting as I clean out closets and move stacks of books? And if I had to one day drink the coffee alone?

Grief and loss—they're not pretty. And they're certainly not our friends. But they're real. If anything, the lens with which I now see the world is realizing that truth. Troubles serve a purpose when they've crossed our path, if the walking we're doing is hand-in-hand with our Savior. Jesus matters more, loves more deeply, comforts more completely, and heals in ways my broken heart never could have imagined. Because though the one will become two again, we're assured that neither heart will ever walk alone. He comes alongside. Walks there with. Making us whole again through every journey.

On a quiet Friday morning years after that day in the ICU, I sat in my favorite local coffee shop. I'd dropped those three boys off at school and had scooted off to keep pace with the author dream, writing against a deadline. And she stepped through the door. My mom said hello, hugged me, and joined her Bible study sisters in the coffee-shop corner where they meet every week. I went to work, lost in story. But at one point, something told me to look up or I'd miss what God was doing.

And there it was—*her smile.*

Those ladies were laughing and loving and living together as sisters in the faith do. I realized then that pride and motherhood know no age. We start out as mother and daughter, evolve to co-mourners, and become sisters in the faith of Jesus, but we're forever bonded as daughters of the Most High.

The reflection I see staring back in the mirror, I pray, will one day have as much faith, and courage, and *fall-but-get-back-up* that she has.

My hero.

My mom.

Kristy Cambron has a background in art and design, but she fancies life as a vintage-inspired storyteller. She is the author of The Ringmaster's Wife, *named to* Publisher's Weekly *Spring 2016 Religion & Spirituality Top 10. Her novels have been included among* Library Journal Reviews' *Best Books and RT Reviewers' Choice Awards Best lists, and received 2015 and 2017 INSPY Awards nominations.* The Lost Castle *(2018) was her fifth novel. Her first Bible study DVD and study guides,* The Verse Mapping Series, *also released in 2018.*

Kristy holds a degree in art history from Indiana University and has fifteen years of experience in education and leadership development for a Fortune 100 corporation. She lives with her husband and three sons in Indiana, where she can probably be bribed with a coconut mocha latte and a good read. You can connect with Kristy in her Writing Desk *newsletter at KristyCambron.com.*

It's in the DNA

BY COLLEEN COBLE

I was at church a few weeks ago when my cousin brought over a book of family pictures. Seeing a picture of my mom as a child, I gasped, "Alexa looks just like her!" Until that moment, I would have told you our granddaughter looks like her dad (our son) and me, with a sprinkling of her mother, Donna. But she looks *exactly* like my mom. In that moment, I realized there was probably more of my mom in me than I'd ever thought too.

Growing up, everyone said I looked like my dad's side of the family with my dark hair and brown eyes. My mom has lighter brown hair and hazel eyes with much lighter skin than my olive tones, inherited through some strong Native American genes on my dad's side. But there she was, in the shape of my eyes, my hairline, and my mouth. I've looked at that picture many times over the past few weeks.

This resemblance pleases me because I grew up thinking she was the most beautiful mom out of all the moms I knew. She has daintier features than my strong bone structure, but she's anything but weak. A lot of who I am today is because she forced me to be strong. At the time, it seemed unfair that I had to do things my brothers didn't have to do, but I'm grateful for that training now.

As the oldest and only girl, she relied a lot on me to help with my younger brothers and with chores around the house. I remember ironing what seemed like endless shirts and dresses. I learned to cook, and my brothers looked to me for cocoa fudge nearly every night. Cleaning the house was a joint venture between Mom and myself, and to this day, I like to have a neat space. (Not perfect. I don't do perfect!) And I much prefer to clean house with my daughter or daughter-in-law than do it alone.

My mom grew up in the 1930s and '40s and brought the attitude that boys could do things girls couldn't. I railed against that notion, and still do! I might not be as strong as a guy, but my brain and common sense both function pretty well. Looking back, that desire to prove myself to be as competent as anyone else drove me on and helped make me who I am.

I have a nurturing spirit that came down directly from my mom—we both adore babies and children. My kids would tell you I'm a great mom, but I learned most of it by watching my own mother.

Seeing that picture of my mom made me take stock of who I am today in ways I hadn't thought of, maybe ever. I love my family with great passion and would lay down my life for them, just like my mom would. There were many times growing up when she would take a look at the bank account and get us kids what we needed, then leave that pretty new dress she'd been eyeing hanging on the rack. She would give her last dime to one of us and go hungry herself if it was necessary. She's much less likely to spend money on herself than she is on others. Case in point: she loves manicures, but she would never pay for one for herself. She'd give me the money for one if I needed it though, and I'm much more likely to get a manicure myself if I have a friend with me I can treat to one too. When I got married, Mom saw me looking at a dress that was much more expensive than I thought we could afford. She insisted I try it on, and she bought it on the spot. I did exactly the same with my daughter and daughter-in-law.

Maybe it was in the DNA. Or maybe it was in the experience. Either way, I see my mother's eyes looking back at me in the mirror.

USA Today *best-selling author Colleen Coble's novels have won or been finalists in awards ranging from the Best Books of Indiana to the ACFW Carol Award, the Romance Writers of America RITA, the Holt Medallion, the Daphne du Maurier, National Readers' Choice, and the Booksellers Best. She has nearly four million books in print and writes romantic mysteries because she loves to see justice prevail. Colleen is CEO of American Christian Fiction Writers.*

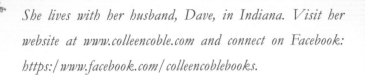

She lives with her husband, Dave, in Indiana. Visit her website at www.colleencoble.com and connect on Facebook: https://www.facebook.com/colleencoblebooks.

Precious Memories

BY SONJA CORBITT

Is it odd that my sharpest memory of my mother is the time she attacked me with a hairbrush? In the dark, wee hours of a school day, my younger sister and I bickered in the bathroom as we primped. I accused her of lollygagging and making us late for the bus. We hurled mean whispers at one another until I hit her with the hairbrush I was using. The retaliatory howl of injustice she let fly—full-voice—brought our mother lumbering, half-asleep, to my sister's defense.

Mom snatched the brush out of my hand and whacked me several times on my bony arm while my sister watched with smug satisfaction. It hurt so badly I threatened to hit my mom back.

Her pointed glare and offensive stance dared me to try it in a way that has prevented me from ever defying her again.

I remember that morning now with delight, perhaps

because it is a rare, vivid memory of us living together in familial normalcy. Unlike my father, my mother never punished unless to teach. So, even though she hit me once, with that brush, I wasn't afraid of her the way I was of my father. She was the glue of sanity that kept the dysfunction in our house from spiraling out into the cosmos.

She divorced my father when I was thirteen. Although it was like a bomb went off in our family, and particularly in me, I know now that she saved us from a long and certain death spiral.

Since then, I have spent my life working through the mushrooming fallout of my "father wound." That painful wound is the root of my predominant fault, and I reveal both the wound and the fault in my ministry, the way Jesus displayed the scars of His crucifixion.

Daily I peer into Jesus's open side, where mercy gushes forth. That mercy tells me my own wound is my path to sanctity and resurrection. My confidence and hope is that I, with this wound, will be raised through Him, in Him, and with Him through grace.

But Mom doesn't see my father wound as God's

triumph; she sees it as an indictment. Once, after hearing me speak on the father wound, Mom wished aloud that she had left Dad sooner. Hearing events from my point of view made her feel shame for leaving us all in the boiling stew of fear for as long as she did.

Not until I wrote a Bible study series on the Magnificat did I ruminate on my relationship with my mother in any depth. I was surprised and even discouraged at the lack of strong memories involving her, save that lone hairbrush attack. She seems faded somehow, and that bothered me.

Even now I struggle to remember her face or hear her voice in memories of my childhood. I just know she was there like my own breath. Everything I know of her as a presence in my life is soft around the edges and a little blurry. She is more of a feeling to me, as though I am still in her womb somehow.

How unfair that the pain I experienced in my relationship with my father seemed to eclipse consideration of my mother, as though his searing left me too numb to feel her strongly. I have memories of her, but every valley has been exalted, every mountain and hill made low, the crooked is straight and the rough ways plain, as the Scriptures say (Isaiah 40:4).

I asked the Lord about this. I felt my mom's presence in the background to be a disservice to her since she was the one constant in my young agony. She should figure more prominently in my memory, I thought.

Why does she seem so ambient to me? Occasionally I fingered the veil protecting the truth, but God left the question largely unanswered until recently.

The answer came over me, and in me, and through me like Ezekiel's prophetic river, flowing downward from beneath the altar in the temple. I was offering a Bible study called *Healing the Father Wound*, in which we entered our Gethsemane with Jesus, retraced our wounds with Him, crowned those after us with freedom and healing from generational sin patterns, carried the crosses of our predominant faults, and let ourselves feel the overwhelming darkness engulfing us as we allowed ourselves to be "crucified with Christ": "My God, My

God, why have You forsaken Me?" (Matthew 27:46)

In spiritual direction and therapy, the wounded are often counseled to ask God where He was in their woundedness, in the times when they felt abandoned and unprotected. *Where were You, God, in that agony?* Perhaps I was afraid to ask, but I had never done so until recently.

The answer gushed forth from the true and final temple: Jesus's torn body. Its realization first lapped at my ankles, then my knees. It swirled lovingly around my waist, healing me with every inch it rose, and suddenly I was swimming in the ocean of His mercy: Sonja, *I was with you, every second, in your mother.*

Sonja Corbitt is the Bible Study Evangelista, creator of the LOVE *the Word Bible study method, and author of the* Unleashed, Fearless, Ignite, *and* Fulfilled *Bible studies.*

Hernia Musings

BY JEANNIE CUNNION

I've birthed four boys, yet I still turn my face from the sight of a needle. I'll never get used to the idea—or the feeling—of a needle penetrating my skin. So, as you can imagine, when my doctor told me I'd be needing *another* hernia repair surgery, I ignored his advice for as long as possible.

I had my first repair not long after my third son was born, and I could still clearly recall how painful the recovery was. It didn't feel much different from the C-section recovery I'd just been through. But here I was, seven years later, after unexpectedly having a fourth son, needing another repair because the hernia returned with a vengeance. Ironically, I didn't much mind the peculiar look of a hernia protruding from my belly button. In some sense, I felt I'd earned it by carrying another child in my womb at forty-two years of age. I tried to view it as I did my C-section scar—a sweet reminder of the gift of life I'd been honored to carry.

But the hernia grew quickly, and with the growth came the pain and discomfort. I finally returned to my doctor. "Are you sure I can't wait a little longer?" I asked, already knowing what his answer would be. He didn't respond with words but with a look that allowed me just enough time to respond, "Fine. Put me on the schedule."

As he exited the room, my doctor turned to me and warned, "Just remember, you can't pick up your fourteen-month-old son for at least two weeks. You have to take this very seriously." And then he asked the question that brought a smile a mile wide to my face: "Do you have someone who can help you with him?"

"I do. My mom. She will fly into town to help me out."

"But be sure she knows she will have to stay for two weeks at a minimum. Or you will need to line up other help." My doctor knows I'm not great at following directions that include the word *rest*. What momma is?

"I know, doc. This I can promise you: she will stay as long as it takes for me to heal. That's the kind of mom I have."

"Well, you're a lucky girl," he responded.

I think my doctor was as caught off guard as I was when tears filled my eyes. "Yes, I am. I *really* am."

Two weeks later, my mom flew into town with her bags packed for two weeks. And she did what she always does. She serves so unselfishly. She loves so extravagantly.

She doesn't just cook the meals and wash the laundry and vacuum the piles of white golden retriever hair strewn across the hardwood floors. She asks my husband how she can be praying for him as he leaves for work. She gets up at the crack of dawn to snuggle with my fourteen-month-old, Finn. She plays board games with my seven-year-old, Owen. She tickles to tears my ten-year-old, Brennan. And the icing on the cake? She plays backyard baseball with my thirteen-year-old, Cal.

She is *everything* I want to be when I grow up.

But here's the thing. My mom would be quick to

tell you that she made a lot of mistakes as a mom when I was growing up. A lot. She remembers them well. She doesn't carry guilt; she just remembers the things she wishes she'd done differently. And she speaks about the faithfulness of God, whose grace has been sufficient for her weakness and whose mercy has freed her from shame over the things she wishes she could take back. But even "close to perfect" is not a title she'd be willing to accept.

The funny thing is, I don't remember all those mistakes my mom remembers so well. When I look back, I just remember that she was *always* there and I *always* felt loved. That's it. Well, no, that's not it actually.

I also remember a mom who was always willing to say "I'm sorry" when she got it wrong. And a mom who cheered me on but didn't find her worth in my success or failure.

I never carried the weight of being perfect for the sake of her self-worth. Oh, don't get me wrong. I felt the weight of trying to be perfect. But that wasn't placed on my shoulders by my parents. My mom—she loved me at my darkest. When my teen years brought her to daily tears and my hormone-induced words cut as sharp as a knife, she didn't withdraw. She came closer. She knew it would hurt to keep her heart open to me in those tumultuous years, but that didn't deter her. She was committed to loving like Jesus and pointing me to His grace. And as much as a sinful and flawed human can do that, she did. She gave me Jesus.

That gives me a lot of hope as I sit here in my backyard, stitches in my tummy still healing from my surgery, watching her play baseball with my boys. The same boys I often let down with my mistakes. The same boys I often need to seek forgiveness from. The same boys who see me at my worst. The same boys who, I pray, will get just a small glimpse of what it feels like to be known and loved by Jesus through my mothering.

Yes, watching her now, I have hope that the imperfect love I give them will be what they remember most and will lead them to the perfect love of Jesus.

Jeannie Cunnion is the author of Parenting the Whole-hearted Child *and* Mom Set Free, *as well as a frequent speaker at women's conferences and parenting events around the country. She holds a master's degree in social work, and her writing has been featured on outlets such as* TODAY, Fox News, The 700 Club, *and Focus on the Family. Jeannie and her husband, Mike, have four boys.*

Mom's Shadow

BY MELISSA D'ARABIAN

Getting my arms around my relationship with my mom is complicated because she has been gone for over half of my life. In quiet moments, I puzzle over the questions. *How would my mother parent the adult version of me? How would she grandparent my four daughters and their eight cousins?* I imagine her proudly watching Charlotte catch the critical ball as goalie, leading her team to victory. She'd marvel watching Valentine dance impossible routines, her hair slicked back in a feminine bun, feet wrapped snugly in pink toe shoes. She'd have cheered herself silly when I won *The Next Food Network Star* and boasted when I began my career in television. She'd have begged me to introduce her to Robert Redford, not because I actually know him, but because she had a theory that "all famous people know each other."

To use the word *suicide* in the same sentence as my mom's name feels like an injustice. Her death doesn't define her life; no one's does. So let me rewind and tell you about her life.

Her name was Cassie, but even at fifty, I still can't bring myself to call her by her first name (which is why I was unable to keep the promise I made myself after her death—to name a daughter after her—even though I was blessed with four chances). Mom was the smartest person I've ever met, and I've met some brilliant folks. She was bright and fun-loving and creative. She loved to host guests in our home. A mediocre cook, Mom found joy in cooking for others—a gift she passed on to me. She was insightful and deep. As a trained psychiatrist, Mom regularly probed the potentially juicy reasons for seemingly trivial life events, such as my forgetting to take out the trash (*Was I subconsciously angry at someone?*) or if I underperformed on a math test (*Was I feeling unworthy and sabotaging my own success?*). I inherited her inclination to analyze, which served me well in my pre–Food Network career as a financial analyst, though maybe a little less so in my interpersonal life.

By example, my mom showed me that with determination I could do anything. She was a single parent raising two daughters, but she put herself through college and then medical school. I grew up in a time when well-meaning adults commonly corrected me when I said my mom was becoming a doctor—didn't I mean she was becoming a nurse? Though these assumptions annoyed me, my mom would not be provoked. Instead, she redoubled her efforts, showing me what grace looks like on a daily basis. Money was always tight in those days, and I saw my mom stretch a dollar like nobody I've ever met, feeding our little family an entire dinner on a dollar or two sometimes. I brought that bargain mentality to my first big TV show, *Ten Dollar Dinners*, and it has never left me. And she was hilarious. Her sharp mind also gave her a sharp wit that attracted attention and admiration.

But even with all the positives, there was a darkness, a disconnection, to Mom whose momentum I didn't fully appreciate. Then, on April 13, 1989, I was in college and called home. A policeman answered the phone and told me Mom had died by suicide. I was blindsided. Mom was not a reclusive, mopey woman who sat in a dark corner watching life go by. Looking back, though, with the benefit of years of hindsight, there were signs. Enough signs that I know suicide is preventable, though I know I am not at fault for not preventing hers.

So while I can thank my mom for sharing with me her hospitality, her spunk, her sense of humor, her tireless ambition, and her work ethic, I believe she also shared with me her shadows. I don't relate to the vortex of despair that led her to believe that ending her life was her only option, but I know well her inclination to withdraw from the world and stop caring quite as much about it. I live my life with a healthy respect for the importance of mental and emotional health.

The lie of uselessness sometimes tugs at my heart, and when it does, I am careful not to let moodiness turn into something darker. Instead of listening to my inconstant heart, I've come to rely on my "smart feet," because my heart can't be trusted to take me to a place of self-care. But my feet? They are smart. They take me to talk to a friend or a therapist, or to the gym. I am intentional about connecting with people when I'm struggling even a little, because the shadows grow in isolation. I'm not alarmist, but I'm faithful to tell my husband if I'm in a funk—our code word for when I sense those looming shadows.

When the shadows recede, as they always do, I feel such joy and gratitude. I drink deeply from the pure pleasure of small things, such as the scent of my children's hair when I hug them first thing in the morning, breathing their scents into my very soul; the taste of a fresh tomato or rich butter on fresh asparagus; or the glimmer of sunlight off the Pacific Ocean. These shining moments of what Jesus called abundant life—I drink those in and think of my mom.

So, I got the bad with the good. The existence of the shadows doesn't obscure my ability to experience joy. In fact, maybe I feel it all the more because the darkness is also there, somewhere. I wonder if I wouldn't know how glorious a gentle breeze on my arms truly is if I didn't know about the lurking shadows.

My joy, my faith, and my God are big enough to house whatever sadness comes over me. I rest in that faith. I believe she's resting there too.

Melissa d'Arabian was a corporate finance executive before becoming the host of Food Network's Ten Dollar Dinners *and Cooking Channel's* Drop 5 Lbs with Good Housekeeping. *She also developed the FoodNetwork.com series* The Picky Eaters Project, *serves as lead judge on* Guy's Grocery Games, *and is the author of the* New York Times *best-selling cookbooks* Ten Dollar Dinners *and* Tasting Grace: How Food Invites Us into a Deeper Connection with God, One Another, and Ourselves. *Melissa has an MBA from Georgetown University and lives with her husband and their four daughters in San Diego.*

My mother stayed mostly silent.
She arrived at my door when
I miscarried. She perched a phone
between her shoulder and ear
to hear my cries.
She didn't give advice.
My mother practiced restraint,
and in doing so, she loved me well.

—CLAIRE GIBSON

Those Eyes

BY CLAIRE GIBSON

When I was a child, I rarely played with dolls.

Instead, I'd set up a chalkboard, place an unsuspecting friend in a chair, and start to teach. Sometimes my pupils were stuffed animals with unblinking eyes and sewn-on smiles. No matter. The youngest of three daughters, I was used to being told what to do. But in my pretend classroom, I was in charge.

It's no wonder that on the first day of kindergarten, my mother pulled my teacher aside.

"Keep an eye on her," my mother warned. "If you're not careful, she'll start teaching the class. And she'll do a good job too."

She wasn't wrong. But strong women aren't born in a vacuum, and if I had a tendency toward outspoken opinions, it's because I'd learned from the best.

To this day, my mother has an embroidered pillow that says: *I'm not bossy, I just have better ideas.* Most of my childhood memories include watching her in the kitchen, the white plastic telephone perched between her ear and shoulder. In long conversations with friends scattered across the country, my mother offered free advice. Her pseudo-therapy sessions stayed in high demand.

Her opinions weren't limited to acquaintances either. In the early 2000s, Abercrombie & Fitch circulated a catalog filled with topless models dressed in hundred-dollar jeans. In the photos, the models hung out the windows of an abandoned house, looking emaciated and cool. Appalled, my mother cut her store credit card into pieces and sealed it in an envelope along with a strongly worded letter to the CEO. Years later, I'm still impressed by the conviction of my mother's beliefs and the gall it takes to disappoint three teenage daughters, all of whom desperately wanted a pair of those A&F jeans. But I shouldn't be surprised. Once, a friend asked my opinion about a lamp. Two hours later, we'd rearranged all the furniture in her house. I am my mother's daughter.

And if I ever lose sight of that fact, I need only look in a mirror. Like my mother, I am five-foot-three. Our cheeks feature the same dimples. When I smile, two lines appear like parentheses around my mouth. (Her grin features the same punctuation.) Two deep horizontal lines recently appeared on my forehead, not unlike the ones my mother hides behind her bangs. My eyelids droop. My feet turn out when I walk. My fourth toe turns inward, like it's trying to hide from the others. Once, I offered my mother a foot rub and nearly gasped when I saw *her* fourth toe. It was an exact replica. Or perhaps, more accurately, I'm the replica.

Once I posted a photo of us together on Facebook. The comment thread went wild. *You two are twins!*

Poor Claire, my mother replied.

I suppose there's nothing to be done—about my wrinkles or my tendency to wield an opinion like a blunt instrument. It's simple biology. All of us are a product of the past, a mysterious mix of two family trees, a combination of love and DNA. Nature and nurture. When I look at my mother, I see my future. She sees her past.

There's a gift in that.

I would know.

Six years ago, my husband and I prayed for the elements of our biology to join and grow in the warmth of my womb. Months passed. A year. And then, on a Tuesday in early January 2016, my husband and I battled an ice storm, parked our car, and joined a sea of hope-battered couples in a beige waiting room. My mother had texted that morning. She wanted to know what the doctor had to say. Seated on a saggy couch, I read the text but didn't reply.

Eventually, a nurse called our names and took us to a tiny office where the clock ticked loudly. A plastic uterus sat on a shelf. So much time passed that I asked my husband to go in the hall and remind the nurse that we were waiting. When the doctor finally arrived, she never lifted her gaze from the file in her hands. My husband and I both go by our middle names—Patrick and Claire. She called us Beverly and Joseph. We never corrected her.

No one ever told me that hope would hurt so badly.

After that, doctors told me when to take the medicine, when to copulate, when to pee on a stick. I'd always thrived on authority, but suddenly I had none. I was the pupil, rapt with my beady, unblinking eyes and a sewn-on smile. What I learned in the classroom of infertility was the cycle of hope and loss. Hope lifted like a helium balloon in my chest, only to burst with every inevitable loss. Months of this. Years of this.

For her part, my mother stayed mostly silent. She arrived at my door when I miscarried. She perched a phone between her shoulder and ear to hear my cries. She didn't give advice. My mother practiced restraint, and in doing so, she loved me well.

One summer, Patrick and I went to Pawley's Island, South Carolina. We walked along the beach. We didn't talk about options, timelines, or hormones. We simply sat in the sun and read our books.

A few months later, we made a decision. Biology had failed us. And yet there were other ways forward. We would adopt.

"She looks just like you, Laura."

I was home visiting. My mother's friend gasped, looking at us. "You might as well be twins," she said.

By then our adoption was well underway. A birth mother in Florida had chosen us to be the parents of her unborn son. I smiled at my mother, at her friend. It was a common refrain—one my mother and I had both suffered for many years.

"You must get so sick of hearing that," my mother said later. She assumed I hated being told that I looked like a sixty-year-old woman.

We waited while coffee brewed. I cleared my throat. She'd taught me from a young age to speak my mind. And it was time.

"Don't say that."

She looked at me with wonder in her eyes.

"I don't know that anyone will ever tell me that about my children," I admitted. Tears sprang from my eyes. "And that's okay. I'm good with that now. But it's a privilege to look like you. It's a gift to look alike."

He is born in November. His mother has deep brown eyes and curly brown hair. As she hands him to my husband and me with my mother by my side, we all cry. Somehow, he grows into a boy. His eyes are ocean blue, the same shade as mine.

"I see where he gets his eyes," people say.

I don't always correct them. But I'm my mother's daughter. So sometimes I do.

Claire Gibson is a writer based in Nashville, Tennessee. Born and raised at the U.S. Military Academy at West Point, Claire went on to study political science and Asian studies at Furman University, where she was recruited by Teach for America to be a middle-school history instructor. In 2012, she left the classroom to pursue her lifelong dream of becoming a writer. Her work has appeared in the Washington Post, the Tennessean, Marie Claire, Entrepreneur, *and many other outlets.* Beyond the Point, *her debut novel, focuses on the power of female friendship and was a Book of the Month Club pick.*

Loving with a Broken Heart

BY SHERRI GRAGG

When I was twenty-two years old, I watched my mother's heart break. Until that moment, she had seemed invincible to me. I feel selfish when I admit this now, horrified that I was so completely oblivious to her obvious and profound physical challenges.

My mother contracted polio when she was just a small girl. One day she was running and playing with her sister and cousins; the next she was paralyzed. At the tender age of eight, she was taken to a polio hospital in Vicksburg, Mississippi, 221 miles away from home. She would spend the next three months in a ward filled with other children stricken with the dreaded disease. Her parents, too poor to stay in a hotel for that length of time, were forced to return home, leaving her there alone.

I can't imagine the terror and aching loneliness my mother felt that first night in the hospital. It was her first time to be away from home.

The doctors said she would never walk again. They were wrong. She learned to walk and even help out around the house, all while navigating a crutch to support her severely weakened right leg. Her body would never be the same, but she was determined it would not stop her.

Ultimately, she tossed the crutch aside and became the first person in her immediate family to attend college.

She left home as a young woman and went to Nashville, Tennessee, where she earned an undergraduate degree and then a degree in nursing. She became a pastor's wife and had three small children in quick succession. Somehow she balanced it all over the next twenty-five years: ministry, career, and full-time motherhood. She drove her broken body to the brink every single day, never taking its "no" for an answer.

She did it all so well that it never occurred to me that she was anything other than unstoppable, unflinchingly powerful . . . made of steel.

The year I turned twenty-two, everything changed. I watched in agony and horror as my mother stumbled for the first time. She fell under the weight of losing everything that seemed sure. In one swift stroke, her life as she knew it was gone forever, her *place* in this world irrevocably altered. The picture of how she imagined her future had been shattered beyond repair.

My father—the sun around which her world, *all of our worlds*, revolved—left.

I had a front-row seat in the arena of my mother's heartbreak and found she was both weaker and stronger than I had ever imagined. She was, in fact, human.

One image from that time, not long after my parents' twenty-five-year marriage ended, captures it all for me. It is a photo of my mother taken after my college graduation ceremony. She is standing on a beautiful lawn beneath a canopy of trees flamboyantly decked out in their spring blooms, her eyes rimmed with tears and her face traced with sorrow. She is skeletal because her broken heart has robbed her of the desire to eat.

It is painful for her to be at my graduation, painful beyond words to be surrounded by so many who know of her grief but do not love her well enough to be a comfort in it. But she is there. She is broken, grimly wading through the vulnerabilities of grief to navigate the social niceties the moment demands of her. She is gaunt and weeping and cannot imagine how she will endure the day or get up the next, but she is standing by my side, smiling through her tears.

She is there because her oldest daughter just graduated *summa cum laude*, and mothers show up for their kids.

Even when their own hearts are broken.

I have thought of that day so many times over the years as I, too, have loved my five children with a broken heart. I remember strapping them all into their booster seats when they were small, popping something cheerful into the CD player, and then proceeding to drive around town with tears silently streaming down my face. Years passed by. They grew. But some hearts take a long time to heal; some prayers are answered so slowly.

Now that my children are teenagers, I have discovered that the shower is really the perfect place to grieve. I turn the water on, let the tears flow, prayers rise.

How long, O Lord? How long?

Then I ask God to help me do it again. One more day. Be fully present for my kids. Listen attentively. Laugh when they are funny. Be strong when they push the boundaries. Comfort when they are hurting. Cheer their victories. Make sure that when they look in my eyes, they see delight there. I have learned to weaponize joy against the sorrow.

Day after day, year after year, I lean hard on the Savior so that I might love well with this broken heart.

One moment at a time.

Sherri Gragg is the author of Arms Open Wide: A Call to Linger in the Savior's Presence *and* Advent: The Story of Christmas. *She also partnered with author Sheila Walsh on her best-selling* 5 Minutes with Jesus *series. Sherri is currently working on a book of inspirational es-*

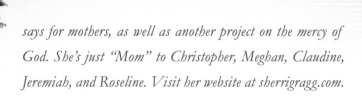

says for mothers, as well as another project on the mercy of God. She's just "Mom" to Christopher, Meghan, Claudine, Jeremiah, and Roseline. Visit her website at sherrigragg.com.

She Raised Me to Be Strong

BY KATIE SCHRODER HALL

My husband announced his choice to leave me on the morning Momma was coming for a weekend visit. I'd later find out—cleaning up the trail of debris he left in the house, including notated listings of divorce attorneys—that he'd been plotting this move for months. I don't know when he'd decided that October morning would be the one, but if for nothing else, I'm grateful he paid me the courtesy of the best safety net I can imagine.

She knew without a word, when I hugged her at baggage claim, that something was very wrong. Momma looked me in the eyes, confirmed the news, wrapped me to her chest, and charged through a rapid-fire progression of emotions. She wept with regret for my breaking heart. Hissed under her breath about what she'd do to him if she could. Then she planted her feet, holding her red-eyed, snotty-nosed, thirty-one-year-old at arm's length, just like she had when I was a child, and told me I was strong and brave and was going to be okay. Just like that. No discussion of a plan, but a statement of pure truth that came from the faith she'd prayed over my heart since before she'd given me life.

I remember studying her face that night as she laid open my Bible on the nightstand to a verse a friend had given her just a few years prior. "What do I do now?" I asked her. I was asking for the practical; the shock was starting to wear off, and I was disoriented.

She told me to climb into bed.

"Now what?" I asked again. She told me again that, now more than ever, we were going to have to take things a day, a moment, at a time. "I prayed you'd never have to experience this, but you are strong," she said.

She'd called me the morning her own world came crashing down a few years earlier. She'd been served divorce papers at her front door. And I failed her miserably. I had no file for comforting my mother while processing that my entire family was crumbling. She had been the constant—her very identity in my eyes was built on her ability to see to everyone else's needs without inconveniencing anyone with her own. Her hysteria scared me. But in the years to come, I'd have more chances. In her most tender moments, I've called her out on choosing to let fear rule instead of standing in the confidence of her faith. I've quoted verses and favorite authors, and she's studied my face and wondered aloud how I got to be so wise, so brave.

She was married for nearly a decade before I made her a mother and then never second-guessed her decision to stay home. She channeled her teaching degree into plans for mind-stimulating play: baking letter cookies, working jigsaw puzzles, crafting art projects. My brother and I snacked on cups of frozen peas between home-cooked meals. Dr. Spock encouraged Momma to trust her instincts and treat her children as individuals. Because raising healthy children was the biggest dream God had laid on her heart, she needed only to know that her sacrifices had mattered.

But the tales of my stubborn independence from

birth are the stuff of family legends. How I'd wailed until the nurses carted me down the hall in the middle of the night, only to refuse to eat. I bargained with the skill of a teenager before I started preschool, usually about underwear or socks. I pulled all-nighters in middle school because even the cardboard diorama had to be *just so*. While Dr. Dobson could offer plenty of strategies and prayers for parenting the strong-willed child, he never promised her a cure. Somewhere in the midst of mindfully raising a daughter, she'd fostered something that felt beyond her control. *You never really needed me*, she's told me more than once.

When I had healed enough to open my own heart again, it was a package deal. Loving my handsome new groom well meant agreeing to share him with his own daughter, a thirteen-year-old daddy's girl. More than one veteran stepparent friend encouraged me to *aim for neutral*, that for this child to view me as nonthreatening was the best I could hope for until much later.

My beloved and I continue to discuss at great

length how ill-prepared I often feel to step into any form of motherhood at this stage of my life. But it turns out I have a powerful capacity: a combination of instincts from my own not-so-ancient history as a clever teen and a lifetime of witnessing a mother's pure if complicated love. I hide finely minced spinach in the spaghetti sauce. I scour Pinterest to find lists of engaging questions for when school is *fine*. Recite a monologue I don't remember memorizing when the crusty scrambled-egg skillet is left in the sink. Forget that I have any other responsibilities in the world when she asks me to French braid her hair.

Momma and I don't speak daily as we did when faced with that first single-again year. And when we do talk, it's not often that I ask for her help. (I can also slip back into my own role of back-talking teen without much prompting.) But I sense pride in her laugh when I report my recent victories in battles of teenage wills and plans for new recipes and fun family craft projects. She couldn't be more thrilled to play honorary grandmother when we visit, filling my old bedroom with coloring books and teen magazines.

Though we've always leaned toward following each other's Christmas lists, Momma surprised me this year with a mother's necklace. A compliment, a reminder, and a warning to the world on a thick silver chain: *She is strong.*

Katie Schroder Hall is a marketing, fundraising, and events professional with a heart for authentic hospitality. She holds a creative writing degree from Agnes Scott College and lives with her family just outside Nashville, Tennessee. Visit her website at www.katieschroder.com.

Carrying Her Song

BY RACHEL HAUCK

When I was a wee babe in elementary school, my mother would wake my older brother and me up with a song. "It's time to get up, it's time to get up, it's time to get up in the morning."

It was her version of a reveille.

We'd moan and roll over, grousing that she should "stop it." But she sang on despite our protests and refused to let her song be stifled.

Fifty years later, I cherish the idea that my mother woke us up singing. A trained vocalist and pianist, she even participated in a national singing competition. Think the '50s version of *The Voice*.

She didn't win. People said she was "robbed." But she returned home to plot the rest of her life.

Instead of embarking on a national music career that could've led to who-knows-what, she met and married my dad. They had my brother and me within the first two and a half years. While my dad finished his degree at Ohio State, my mom worked, Grandma babysat us, and on Sundays we went to church.

Born again as a young girl, Mom's faith and personal relationship with Jesus brought her through tough times growing up. She forgave her abuser and went on with her life, not letting his actions have power over her. Instead, she carried a song of praise in her heart and connected time and time again to the vibrant heart of Jesus.

Growing up, I couldn't stand to hear her sing a solo. I would get so nervous for her. But watching her worship, heart wide open to the One she loved, the One who loved her, I saw there was something more to following Christ than walking down an aisle and saying a prayer. As a teen and, later, a college student, I'd arrive home to hear her singing. When her five children didn't command the TV so much, she'd have music on the stereo.

See, her music training wasn't ultimately about being a professional musician. Or a singer. It was about being a worshiper.

My parents were changed irrevocably by the Charismatic outpouring of the mid-'60s. Devoting their lives to Christ consumed their hearts. They gave up opportunities for wealth and position to follow a Holy Spirit–inspired passion.

Their passion trickled down to me.

Right after college graduation, I was in a funk. What was I supposed to *be*? My mother, in all her wisdom, confronted me. "What music are you listening to?"

She'd never before challenged my choice of Osmond-loving, bubblegum pop radio music. But that day she spoke from heaven.

She didn't commiserate with me or affirm my depression. She challenged me.

"I don't know . . ." was my answer. But I did know. I'd been listening continually to Van Halen's *5150*.

I understood in that moment the power of music. The power of words. The power of worship. What and whom was I worshiping?

I tossed the cassette tape and my attitude changed. My outlook brightened. I began to lift my gaze.

Without either of us knowing, Mom had given her gift of worship to me. And in ways I wouldn't understand until years later, the Lord was jealous for it.

Mom demonstrated a Mary of Bethany devotion all my life. The one kneeling at the feet of Jesus and washing His feet with her hair and tears. She modeled laying down her life to be more like Jesus. She demonstrated true worship and discipleship.

To this day, when I think of her, I see light and bright. And the music in her spirit.

Even though I have the equivalent of elementary-school music training, I'm now a worship leader. Incredibly, I'm in my seventeenth year.

I love God's economy. His trickle-down anointing. I gained my mom's treasure, and someone will gain mine. We stand on the shoulders of those who've gone before us. I'm blessed to stand on my mama's.

Thank you, Mama, for being a godly woman who chased the things that could not be taken away, and for waking us up with a song.

I carry your melody within me.

Rachel Hauck is an award-winning, New York Times, USA Today, *and* Wall Street Journal *best-selling author. Her book* The Wedding Dress *was named Inspirational Novel of the Year by* Romantic Times. *She is a double RITA finalist and a Christy and Carol Award winner. Rachel sits on the executive board for American Christian Fiction Writers and is the comical sidekick to Susan May Warren at the amazing My Book Therapy, a coaching service for novelists. She is a worship leader and speaker. A graduate of Ohio State University with a degree in journalism, Rachel is a devoted Ohio State football fan. She lives in sunny central Florida with her husband and ornery cat.*

The Last Blessing

BY KAREN DAVIS HILL

First came denial, then indecision. But eventually I dug down and found the courage to move my mother to assisted living. Such a big step signaled a life turn that I simply did not want to face.

This was Mama, after all—my sweet, smart, lovely, loving, incredible mother. The one who made our home lively and fun and caring. What a sweet childhood she and Daddy gave us kids!

Then we all grew up, and life started throwing big challenges our way. Together, Mama and I walked sorrow's valley, burying first Daddy, then my younger sister, and eight months later, my older brother. During that dark season, we survived a mountain of loss, held on to faith, and somehow not only kept going but allowed ourselves to see all the blessings that God had in store for us: great-grandchildren were born, estranged family members returned to the fold, books were written and published, Mama got to see her grandson perform on Broadway, the bounty of life was shared with friends . . .

Sorrow can never be vanquished, but Mama knew how to balance her sadness with joy. One day I asked how she found the will to go on and to experience so much joy. She said, "Honey, you can *will* or *wallow*. You can wallow in sadness. Or, you can will yourself to accept the joy that God still has for you. It's simply a choice."

And *will*, she did. *Enjoy* life, she did. She sat on the scholarship board at her church, mentored younger women, never declined an invitation, never missed a grandchild's school program or birthday party. When my daughter wanted to bring thirty-five college friends home to the family farm, Mama reacted like a kid anticipating Santa's arrival.

Then, in her early eighties, her memory began to fade. She lived alone, and my children began urging me to place her where she would be safer. Finally I saw that they were right. My children and grandchildren spent an entire weekend helping pack and move her to the best place we could find. Pictures hung, boxes unpacked, we stayed until bedtime to make sure she felt comfortable and content in her new home.

On my way to work the next morning, I popped in to check on her, fully expecting to find her chatting with new friends or taking charge of something or other. Instead, I found her sitting on a carton in the middle of her room, surrounded by packed boxes. Every picture, every curtain had been removed, bed linens neatly folded.

I pulled up a carton and sat beside her, trying to find my voice.

"Mama . . . what? What . . . is this?" I asked.

"You told me I'm moving, so I packed everything and I'm all ready to go to the new place!"

I couldn't bear to correct her. I just held her and cried. "Oh Mama . . . this . . . this . . . this is your new place. You're already here."

She tried not to cry, but there was no holding it back. "I'm so . . . sorry. I messed up, didn't I?"

No words could fix this. No words could change what we both knew in that moment. Our hearts spoke what no language could say. We both understood that we were turning a corner. From now on, I would be mothering my mother. I didn't feel up to the task. How could I be all that she had been? Comforter, caregiver, decision maker, life guide, friend. I was worried and overwhelmed.

About this time, a conversation with Christian singer Fernando Ortega recalibrated my thinking. He was guest worship leader at our church one weekend, and we visited backstage about our aging parents. He told me he was thrilled to live near his parents because, he said, "I don't want to miss one minute of their lives."

His words made sense. My mother had wanted to see my first steps, my first day of school, every scraped knee, every little victory, every little disappointment. Now it was my turn. *Yes,* I thought, *I don't want to miss a minute of her life!*

And so began the journey through the last season of my mother's life. It wasn't easy. But even in the valley of dementia, there was joy. We were together. Every day after work, I went straight to Mama like a little girl running home after school. She lived in a small care home with eleven other residents. Every day she would reintroduce me to her caregivers: "This is my darling daughter! Isn't she a wonder!" And the caregivers would smile as if hearing it for the first time.

Hard isn't a big enough word to describe dementia. Every day brings fresh pain, watching someone lively and bright become completely dependent on the kindness of others. But I allowed myself to just enjoy being in her presence, sitting beside her, holding hands. Even as her memory progressively faded, she always knew me. I begged God for that.

She began to speak less and less, and for the last two weeks of her life, she mostly slept. She no longer introduced "my darling daughter" to the caregivers, but she would wake and smile when I came in. And then God gave me an unexpected, amazing gift. About a week before she passed, Mama suddenly awakened and, for about half an hour, spoke with stunning clarity. She spoke as if she were giving the last speech of her life, and, in fact, that is what it was.

After she spoke, she drifted back into her foggy world and never spoke again. But for that one sweet moment, Mama was determined to give me a final blessing. Here is some of what she said:

I'm very proud of my four children. Children are the best part of life! We have such a special family. I treasure all our wonderful memories.

You've always been special. I have a very high regard for you. Your strength parallels mine.

You and I have such a strong faith! Faith is so important! We can handle absolutely anything because of faith!

I'm very, very proud of you. I love you and adore you. You are everything a mother could want in a daughter.

Like all mothers, mine saw me through the lens of love—dismissing my flaws, rejecting my failures and foibles, emphasizing any little kernel of goodness. But when she spoke of our mutual faith, she spoke truth. Early on, she planted a love of Jesus in my heart. She guarded and gardened that seed so it not only took root and flourished, it grew sturdy and reliable. Mama was right when she said our faith had enabled us to withstand any storm.

It has and it will. Thank you, Mama.

Karen Davis Hill is the author of more than twenty-five books. She has also served as Max Lucado's executive editor since 1992. Karen and her husband, Art, are the parents of two daughters and a son. They live in San Antonio, Texas.

I don't know how many years
my mother and I have left
on this earth, but one thing
I know is that if we both went
to heaven today, we'd have enough
memories for a lifetime—
some we wish we didn't have
and some we'd want to relive
over and over again.

—KARRIS HUDSON

How I Came to Live in Haiti

BY KARRIS HUDSON

I'm sitting in a Nashville park as the sun sets. Though this town is dear to me, I'm feeling lonesome for my kids back home in Haiti. As I struggle to share my heart in words, typing on a broken iPhone, I gaze at the cracked screen. Then God gently whispers three words: *This is life.* And I understand. Each of us carries broken pieces, and we're each trying to make sense of all of it. There is purpose in the brokenness.

I've spent the past seventeen years of my life in Haiti. It's been more fulfilling, more precious, and more challenging than I ever imagined. I've seen so much brokenness. So much beauty.

I wasn't born in Haiti, so when I come back to the United States to visit, people often ask me how I got there. I explain that my story didn't start with my decision to move there when I was twenty-one. It started decades before I was born. That's when a poor single lady in Greece secretly gave birth to a baby girl and left her to be raised in an orphanage. That girl was adopted three years later and moved to America. That little girl is my mother, one of the best gifts God has given me.

As a grown woman, my mom returned to Greece. When she arrived, she had no plans or desire to meet her birth family or visit that orphanage, but through a story only God could write, she arrived at the orphanage where she'd been left twenty-six years earlier. The nun who answered the door was the very woman who'd taken care of my mother as a baby. She told my mom that none of the other children had ever returned. Can you imagine? This dear lady had cared for hundreds of children year after year, never having the chance to see what had become of those children when they were grown.

I believe God brought my mom back that day to do something special in her own heart. I also believe that meeting was a special gift for the nun.

My mom went around and held every baby in the orphanage. She told them, "I'll never forget where I came from. One day I'll do something in your honor." And that's what she did. When she flew back to California, she quietly rented a storage space. She gathered food and furniture, worked with social workers and churches. Steadily, stealthily, she began to care for others. She became *love in action*. Like other families, we went to the homeless shelter on Thanksgiving and handed out toys around Christmas, but my mother also took me and my brothers to those places throughout the year. We visited foster-care kids and poor immigrant families. My mother never sat me down to say, "You need to serve others." Instead, she *showed* me. And that was an incredible gift.

My mother planted a deep desire in me to serve. I'd grown up with a strong desire to be a mom. I dreamed of being a missionary and believed that one day I would be a mom to orphaned children. I just never knew it would happen so soon. When I was eighteen, I moved to New York City to work with inner-city children and youth. Then, at twenty-one, I took a mission trip to Haiti to visit Danita's Children, an organization dedicated to the rescue, love, and care of orphans and the impoverished children of Haiti. I fell in love with it, and six months later, on September 9, 2002, I moved to Haiti permanently. That's where God granted my desire to be a mother in the most unexpected way.

Even though my mom had inspired my choice, she actually tried to talk me out of moving to Haiti. Deep down she knew this was my calling, but it was hard for her to let go of the dream she had of us living our lives close together. We've always been so close. It pained her to think I'd be so far away from her physically. But once she accepted it, she became my biggest cheerleader.

At the time, I didn't understand how hard it was for her. But in the past four years, I've helped ten of our kids move from Haiti to the United States to go to college. As much as I want them to do what God has called them to do, I know now how my mom felt all those years ago. Part of me wants to keep them close even while I know they need to go. I've done a lot in my short thirty-eight years of life, but being a mom to these amazing kids is the best gift God has ever given me.

I don't know how many years my mother and I have left on this earth, but one thing I know is that if we both went to heaven today, we'd have enough memories for a lifetime—some we wish we didn't have, and some we'd want to relive over and over again. We've stood side by side at my brother's grave site in Africa. We've walked the streets of London laughing. We've roamed the New York City streets and subways all day and night. We've explored the Vegas strip (side note: my mom has to be the only lady who's worn athletic shorts and a turtleneck to a pool in Vegas). We've celebrated as my brother married the most amazing girl. We've made lots of memories with my kids in Haiti. We are best friends . . . forever.

Karris Hudson grew up in the United States and moved to Ouanaminthe, Haiti, in 2002 to serve as a missionary with

Danita's Children, an organization dedicated to the rescue, love, and care of orphans and the impoverished children of Haiti. Today she serves as vice president and field director of Danita's Children and, most importantly, is "Mom" to more than one hundred kids.

Three Women Who Loved Me Well

BY MARSHA HUDSON

I had three mothers before I ever became one myself.

My birth mother left me on the doorstep of an orphanage in rural Greece. The nuns at the orphanage cared for me until I was adopted and became an American citizen. When I was twenty-seven, I traveled to Greece for vacation with my boyfriend (now husband) while he was studying premed. I wasn't thinking about exploring my past. I was just there for some rest and relaxation. But then, on the flight to Kalamata, Greece, I mentioned to my seatmate that I was born there. That conversation led me to a life-changing encounter that God used to shape my future.

Hours later, I stood on the doorstep of the orphanage where I'd spent the first three years of my life. Astonishingly, that door was opened by the same nun who'd found me there as a newborn twenty-seven years earlier. When I told her who I was, she burst into tears. She said, "No one has ever come back . . ."

I visited with every child in the orphanage. It was a holy thing. As I held each child, I whispered, "I will never forget where I came from. And one day, I will do something in your honor."

When we returned to America, everything seemed to go right back to normal. I kept my story to myself and continued my full-time nursing job. But deep inside I was changed by my time in Greece. I rented a storage unit and began to collect clothes, furniture, and food. I worked with local organizations and social workers to find families, foster-care children, and orphans in desperate need. Then I'd find a way to fill their needs. I became a mother myself and enlisted my three children in my efforts.

Fast-forward to when I was thirty-five years old. I wrote a letter to the *Live! with Regis and Kathie Lee* show, honoring my adoptive mother. Out of twenty-five thousand letters received, they chose my sweet mother for their "Mom's Dream Come True" contest. She'd won Mother of the Year!

Until that point, I had not shared my adoption story publicly, but once again, God was using my past to shape my future, this time on a national stage. That experience opened doors that led to even more families and children being helped. My story and subsequent work has been used by the Los Angeles Dream Center to help launch Foster Care Intervention, which is designed to keep families together, reduce the need for foster care, and minimize the orphan populations in America.

I've discovered that finding purpose often involves looking into the faces of pain. For many years I didn't remember being an orphan, so I lost touch with my own pain. When that door at my former orphanage opened, I saw pain in the face of the nun who had cared for me. I saw it in the faces of those orphans. And if you were to sit and get to know me and look closely at me today, you'd see it in my face after I lost my youngest child four years ago. I've learned to ask myself and others, "What faces of pain move *you* to action?"

Another face that showed pain was that of my birth mother, who I also met on that trip to Greece. Our meeting was brief but impactful. She wasn't a wealthy woman, but she had a precious gift that she handed over to me that day. It's a handmade tablecloth, and she asked me to give it to my adoptive mom in appreciation for raising me and giving me a happy life. When I did as she'd asked, Mom cried. The tablecloth is a tangible token, a "bridge," between the hearts of two mothers. One heart had to let go. The other heart had to accept that I had a past.

All three of the precious women who sacrificed so much for me have now passed away—my birth mother, the nun at the orphanage, and my adoptive mom. Beneath the surface of their hearts was a deep longing to know that I survived, that I was happy.

I still have that tablecloth. It's a reminder of a bond neither mother wanted or wished for. Neither wanted that bond because both would have rather not remembered. That tablecloth represents the unspoken fact that life isn't so black and white.

As my own body passed from one mother to another, now I will pass my birth mother's tablecloth to my daughter, Karris. For her it will be a reminder of the vulnerability of children and those who raise them. In a beautiful illustration of God's infinite mercy and grace, Karris has spent the past seventeen years of her life living in Haiti, being a mom to more than one hundred children who need her love and care. Karris is my daughter, but she's also my best friend. Our bond is something rare and sacred. If the measure of a bond is the sky, our love reaches the stratosphere. We both treasure it.

Karris is the epitome of love that my mothers' tablecloth embodies. Living out that love is how she has chosen to live her life. But the best part about her story is that Karris gets to raise the children in Haiti as her own. Never will she have to say, "No one ever came back." And one day, Karris will put my mothers' tablecloth in the hands of one of her daughters.

Marsha Hudson is the mother of three incredible children: Karris, Torry, and Brandon. She serves on the leadership staff at The Dream Center, a faith-based charitable organization based in Los Angeles that finds and fills the needs of struggling people from all over the United States. A former trauma nurse, Marsha lives in Nashville with her husband, Dr. Bernard Hudson.

Her Hand, Wrapped around a Church Pew

BY DENISE HILDRETH JONES

It was rare that we would even stand beside each other at church because she was usually playing the organ. She was a pastor's wife and the organ bench was her usual pew. But every now and then, my mom would make her way to my pew. When she'd stand, her dainty little hand would wrap around the rounded, wooden backrest in front of us to pull herself to standing. Then her veins would rise on her hands as if they were too delicate to hold all the life that flowed inside.

She would laugh gently at me as I pushed down tenderly on her veins, only to watch them rise again. I'd know those hands anywhere. The way each vein makes its trail from elbow to wrist to palm to finger, pumping life into those hands. Those hands that pulled my hand away from the hot stove when I climbed on top of the chair to help her cook, teaching me that sometimes attractive things can be painful. Those hands that had held my own fingers as she attempted to teach me how to crochet, only to learn that not everyone can do everything. Those hands that held the books she read to me each night, helping me fall in love with story. Those hands that hung pictures as an interior decorator and then hung them in my first apartment as I learned how to make a life of my own.

Those hands placed her antique watch on my wrist before I walked down the aisle to say "I do," marking the time behind me and the time ahead of me. Those hands brushed back my hair as I lay in her lap and wept when that very marriage hemorrhaged, leaving my heart broken. Those hands wrote hundreds of cards and letters, thanking me for the smallest things, loving me in the broken things. Those hands fold in prayer for my past and my present and my future.

I've watched them age and pat and hold and hug and cover her mouth as she laughs in that way that makes me love the beauty of laughter. I've watched those hands hold my dad's through fifty-two years of better and worse, richer and poorer, sickness and health, broken and not quite so broken. In fact, just recently I watched them as they walked down the beach together holding hands, those veins still pumping life into this woman who has poured hers out with selfless wonder.

Her hand was wrapped around a pew again when I noticed how alike our hands had become. At forty, I had no child of my own. No one to notice. No one to push. No one to share the history that those hands had lived. But then, that same year, I met a man with five children and married him, making me a bonus mom.

One day, in church no less, while I held on to the back of a pew trying desperately to hold on to the hope inside of the hurt that often coursed through my new life, my youngest bonus daughter noticed the veins in my hands. She touched them and looked at me. A curious look. A "Denise, do you realize you have really big veins?" kind of look.

I simply returned her look with a smile and said,

"I've got my mom's hands."

I hope in this life that is not the only thing people will see that I've gotten from my mom. Instead, I pray it will be what my hands have offered that will have them saying, "That girl, she is just like her mom."

My mom is beautiful. I am so glad she is mine.

Denise Hildreth Jones is an author and Bible study teacher. Her books have been hailed as "smart and witty" by Library Journal *and featured twice in* Southern Living. *With her husband, five bonus children, and her dog, she lives in Franklin, Tennessee, where she leads Reclaiming Hearts Ministries. Visit her at www.reclaiminghearts.com.*

Tea for Two

BY LORA JONES

When the sun rose high enough to shine in the living room windows, I curled up in my favorite chair and opened the Bible on my lap to prepare to teach Sunday school. The familiar passage came alive as I read. I jotted down an outline on my notepad until the sound of the old teakettle roused me from my comfortable seat to pour myself a cup of tea.

The gentle whistle of the teapot and the soft hum of the gas stove top always remind me of home and my dear momma. These days, nearly everything does. I miss her smile that lifted all the wrinkles of her soft face and crinkled them around her eyes.

Settling back in to my spot in the corner of my living room, I sipped my tea, watched the birds in the tree outside my window, and let my mind get lost in the memories.

Mom turned on the light. "Lora, time to get up," she said

as she walked quietly to my bedside, retrieved my eyeglasses from the nightstand, and disappeared. I turned over, stretched, and shaded my eyes from the sudden, bright intrusion.

In a couple of minutes, Mom returned with my sparkling-clean glasses and handed them to me. "Breakfast is ready," she said simply. My nose already detected the smell of bacon in the air. Oatmeal yesterday; scrambled eggs and bacon today; tomorrow, Cream of Wheat. The predictable pattern of alternating eggs with hot cereal kept us fed and happy, and Dad's cholesterol low.

After breakfast, I dressed in jeans and a sweatshirt. Glancing at the clock, I grabbed my books and keys and hurried toward the door for school. "I gotta work today, Mom. See ya about five thirty."

Mom sat in her usual study chair with her Bible open in her lap. "Have a great day!" she called after me with her characteristic quiet smile. Then she bowed her head to continue reading or praying—probably for me.

My reverie returned to the present when my pen fell to the floor.

Every. Single. Day. I saw Momma read her Bible and prepare to teach it to others. She taught the seventh-grade girls' Sunday school class for years, then switched to an adult class when she reached seventy. Her lessons were not hurriedly put together; she spent hours of study on each one. Every year she read the entire Bible systematically, always choosing a different version from the year before.

No wonder I trusted Jesus before I even learned to read.

The whole family loved and respected my momma, and trusted her Bible knowledge. If we played a Bible game (or any game for that matter), everyone wanted her on their team. Her presence ensured a win.

I once heard a preacher describe the word *meek* as a strong mustang willing to be under the control of a rein. I thought nothing could describe my momma better. Confident and strong-willed, she *chose* to be under the control of her Master, Jesus. Being near her seemed to calm storms in me. Her quiet faith taught me how to stand on His promises, no matter what life threw my way.

So, when I raised my children, I taught them to

love Jesus, like my momma taught me. I read them Bible stories on my lap and let them watch me study the Bible. I taught their Sunday school classes and answered their questions of faith. We visited Grandma and soaked up her love and peace. They snuggled with her in her favorite study chair.

The way Mom lived her life set the pattern for my own, but I believe her prayers in that old chair made the most difference in all of us. Momma's prayers rattled the gates of heaven on our behalf. I doubt she asked for material things, instead praying for peace, strength, and faith.

At eighty-nine, Momma decided to quit teaching Sunday school. For the next four years, her body weakened, her memory faded, and she needed us to fix breakfast and bring her a cup of tea. But she faithfully sat in her chair and prayed.

Every. Single. Day.

My teacup ran dry and my stomach growled. Smiling at the memories of the day, I glanced in the mirror as I washed my hands for lunch.

I stared at the reflection. The wrinkles crinkled around my eyes.

Momma smiled back at me.

Lora Jones was born and raised in Liberal, Kansas. She's a Kansas State University graduate and holds a master's degree in religious education from Midwestern Theological Seminary. During college she married J. L. Jones, and together they had two children, Janessa and Jayden. All three were tragically killed in a car accident in 2004.

Lora now serves as an inspirational speaker. Speaking to audiences of all sizes across the country, she encourages others to believe in the God who has sustained her. Her goal is to encourage people to open the Bible and hear from God.

Chariot of Fire

BY RIVER JORDAN

What saves us is our laughter. Our ability to look one another in the eye and laugh at ourselves. What a gracious gift God has given us in this.

We find ourselves these days in this boat called life. It's as if we have been put out to sea for the remainder of our days. I smile as I write this. As I imagine my mother and me in a tiny boat. We are casting off for what seems familiar but is really uncharted territory.

You may imagine me in the rear of the boat steering, but no. My mother steers because, even though she is older, she is larger than life, still in charge. I sit in the bow of the boat, eyes peeled for the unseen roots and logs hidden just beneath the surface. Those simple things that have so often upturned us in the past. The simple fact of us just being who we are in this world.

You would think to know us that my mother and I evolved from different species. She from the cold realities of winter's blush; stark, bare, and truthful to a fault. Me, full of summer's heat; awash in languid hopefulness.

"But you are not me," my mother says, casting stones to point out where I have done a thing and she would have done it better. Taken a different road. Achieved a preferred outcome.

"No, I am not you," I reply. "You are not me." Me, using a mirror to burn that image of imperfection where I find it. Casting fragmented glass, ripped images of imperfection.

There have been times when we both were burned and shattered by our words. Cut to the quick by the actions of the other, we have been full of righteous anger or fragmented pain. We were both younger then. But now, when there are curt sentences, angry words, the discomforts of disagreement, we are both quick to offer balm, to heal the wound. To strive to understand or be understood. We no longer hold the luxury of time. We are not innocent of this. We are in this boat because of love. Circumstance and love. We are both so brave to venture into these waters, to share this house.

Because—

This woman is ice. Her daughter fire. The two of us are capable of friction.

Yet—

We have our humor. It is our secret power. We wield it to survive.

I am a strange child. My mother told me so. She needed a kingdom to rule, not a daughter to raise, I told her. She agrees. Says, *I still do.*

Recently my mother had a flight to catch. A going-back-to-the-old-school to visit friends almost dear departed. I readied her. This was a job of military precision. It takes a tribe to prepare her. All is well, packed, prepared. The boxes and the bags, the medicines and the notes. The night has been long.

A notice comes across the phone. Her flight has been delayed.

"Great," we say in unison. In absolute agreement. In some things there is not a whit of difference. We

hate the now of going, both preferring one more moment of trees, of patter, of rest.

"Now, let's have coffee and a sit," I offer, "since
we have this gift of time."

"A conversation," she says.

We have coffee and a sit and a conversation, pleasant because it came as a surprise.

"Time to go."

En route, another text. The flight has been yet
again delayed.

"It's okay; we'll take our time to shop," I offer. "I
need some things for friends."

We enter this fortress of flight. I find a wheelchair
and roll her through security, past all the bells and
whistles. We make our way to the stores located at the
beginning of the C terminal. With so much time left
to us, we are rich in minutes that we spend looking at
T-shirts, and chocolate, and candles and books, buying
presents for this one and that.

Then we hear the loudspeaker calling her name,
adding the terminal words of "Final call for Mrs.

Thames." They continue, "We will be closing the gate in two minutes."

What fresh hell is this? What happened to our time? Where has it gone?

"Legs up, Mama!" I yell. "Hang on to your bags!"

"I got 'em!" she says. "Run like the wind."

"Last call for Mrs. Thames," they repeat.

Her gate is the last one at the end—C28. We are north of C1.

"I've got my bags. Run!" she yells.

In heels I run, yelling all manner of things at the top of my lungs to the people walking, wandering, meandering through life as if nothing is happening. As if I am not pushing my mother in a wheelchair at the breakneck speed of a full-on race. Me helping her reach the end of time where they are calling her name. Where she is bound for flight.

We have traded places. I am steering, and she is holding on tight. There is no slowing down, no going back. A sea of people part before us, stepping back and stopping to watch this strange aberration that is us. Me and Mama. We are flying, we are fire, we are flame. We are both seperate and the same.

River Jordan is a best-selling author, speaker, and broad-caster. She has published four novels and a nonfiction book, Prayers for a Stranger. *Her broadcast,* Clearstory Radio, *show-cases hundreds of authors including Pulitzer Prize–winning and best-selling writers of all genres. Ms. Jordan lives with her Big Dog on a hill just outside the Nashville city limits, surrounded by her wild, Southern family. Her latest book is* Confessions of an American Mystic: Stories of Faith and Fiction.

Pray for Me

BY AMI MCCONNELL

Marie had just brushed her teeth. "Tuck-in time!" she called from the hall upstairs. I dropped the laundry I'd been folding into the basket and made my way up. She climbed into bed and under her pink comforter, and we began the familiar ritual.

Glasses off? Check. Stuffed monkey? Check. Lullaby music? Check.

"Good night, sweet girl," I said, kissed her on the head, and stood to leave. There was laundry to finish, three more girls to tuck in—miles to go before sleep.

"Wait," she said, grasping my arm. "Pray with me?"

"About what?"

"My report."

And then I remembered. She'd told the family about this over dinner. This week my girl would present her report on Annie Oakley. She'd labored over the poster, the costume, and the script. She'd rehearsed it for us, and we told her it was bound to go well. But my girl doesn't like speaking in front of crowds—even classmates. She'd been facing this fear like a champ since second grade. Two whole years. And she was getting a little more comfortable each time. Even so, she was anxious.

So we prayed together. Prayers of thanks—for family, for restful sleep, for dinner, for cool supplies that made her report fun, and for past successes that would give her courage. And prayers of petition for God's supernatural presence and comfort.

When we finished, she smiled and snuggled into her covers. She was at peace.

In that moment, I sent up an addendum prayer of thanks, this time for my mother.

As far back as I can remember, my mother has been praying for me. Tuck-in time was our ritual too. Like me, she had a demanding job that required much of her time and attention. But each night, she'd tap on my door at bedtime. When I was little, she'd pray over me. As I got older, we'd pray together.

Prayer with my mom was no rote ritual. She rose early each day to spend time alone with God. In her journal and in the car—stashed behind the sun visor—she kept a list of who she was praying for, noting in loopy script when and how prayers were answered. She made decisions large and small only after talking to her Father. Those talks were peppered with Scripture she'd committed to memory and reminders of God's faithfulness. Her humble requests naturally blossomed out of this exchange. From her I learned the cadence of prayer—a conversation between intimates.

When I was newly single, parenting a rebellious, hurting teenage son and four young daughters, I'd fall into bed as soon as they were finally asleep. Even my toes were tired. Always a soft buzz sounded inside my head—I imagined it was adrenaline diluting in my blood, my pulse gradually subsiding. I'd will my body to be still, then sink into that familiar cadence with the Father: gratitude, shared conversations from the past, and thoughts about what was on my mind and heart. Restful peace descended—or was it rising? Assurance that even though it felt like everything was my responsibility, it wasn't true. He had us covered.

Just the other day I called Mom to check on her. She'd fallen and wasn't healing as well as she'd hoped. I wanted to encourage her. After we'd talked a bit, she sensed that I had a heavy heart and she asked about it. I told her. She didn't try to offer solutions. She just asked, "Can I pray about this with you now?" Of course I said yes!

There have been so many gifts my mother has given me, but the greatest by far is how she taught me to pray. When I face sadness, fear, nervousness, or change, I'm always hopeful. I talk about it all with my Father, and a supernatural peace floods me. That's why I'm forever grateful.

Ami McConnell is a Nashville-based writer and book editor. She founded and directs WriterFest Nashville, a conference for writers of books, songs, and films. Previously she served

as Simon & Schuster Publishing's VP and Editor-in-Chief of Howard Books and as an acquiring editor for HarperCollins. Her editing credits include dozens of USA Today and New York Times bestselling and award-winning trade books. Her writing credits include the USA Today bestseller Kind Is the New Classy with Candace Cameron Bure. She lives in Franklin, Tennessee, with her husband and children.

I see her with new eyes now
that I'm in my early forties. I see how
she faithfully and compassionately
cares for her aging mother and
handicapped brother. Every day
she puts her needs and wants
on hold to bring them a meal,
take them to a doctor appointment,
or just sit and visit with them.

—RACHEL MCRAE

When I Grow Up

BY RACHEL MCRAE

All children grow up wanting to be like someone else. Other than the brief stint in the sixth grade when I wanted to be Anne of Green Gables, I have always wanted to be like my mother. From a young age, I knew my mom was well respected. She was active in church and in our community, and people sought her out to organize and help with events. I also grew up with a generation of kids who only knew her as "Ms. Sandy" because she had been their preschool teacher. I saw the way she cared for our family, for people at church, and for many others in the community who she didn't even know. She just always seemed to be quietly serving and loving on people.

I didn't want to grow up to be famous. I wanted to grow up to be my mom.

It wasn't until I was an adult that I realized I had become my mother. However, it wasn't in the way I was intending. Several years ago, we discovered a black-and-white film of my parents' wedding from 1969. As the young bride came onto the screen, I said, "When was I in a wedding dress?" I could not believe how much I looked like my mom in that moment.

A few years later, I took a new picture for my work ID. Who was staring back at me? My mom.

After living in my new house for a few weeks, I was standing in the kitchen when the realization hit me. The cabinets, countertop, and flooring I had selected looked just like something Mom would have chosen.

When I see myself talking on a video, I notice the same facial expressions that my mother makes. Yes, Mom, we make fun of you for sometimes talking with your eyes closed, and I'm coming to terms with the fact that I do it too.

All this time, I had wanted to be the kind of person my mom is, but I was literally turning into her in every other way! I know that for some of my friends, this would have freaked them out. For me? I share a chuckle with the Lord, and I wholeheartedly own it.

I've had the privilege of meeting a lot of well-known people, thanks to my line of work. I have traveled to different parts of the world and have been introduced to many inspiring people who are making a difference where they live. After all of that, I still find myself wanting to grow up to be like my mom.

I see her with new eyes now that I'm in my early forties. I see how she faithfully and compassionately cares for her aging mother and handicapped brother. Every day she puts her needs and wants on hold to bring them a meal, take them to a doctor appointment, or just sit and visit with them.

After forty-nine years of marriage, I see her love my dad well, setting an example for many other couples.

She is well known to many homeless women because of the meals she provides, the prayers she says over them, and the phone calls she'll take from them.

I take pride in my mom when I see how people flock to her at church and how she quietly asks them about the things going on in their lives and how she can be praying for them.

I love seeing her expand her wings and try new things that she would have never dreamed of doing a few years ago. By following her ministry passion to support children around the world, my mom is a leader in our state and a source of encouragement for others in the work. At a time when most women her age are enjoying a quiet retirement, she's busy serving others. My mom is proof that you are never too old to try new things and to follow the call that God has put on your life.

When we were growing up, my sister, Leah, and I were known around our community as "Sandy's girls." After working twenty-eight years in our local middle school, our mom is known by countless students, teachers, and families. It was a regular occurrence for us to be out running an errand and be stopped by someone wanting to talk to Mom or asking Leah and me how our mom is doing. While it might have brought an eyeroll from us then, being known as "Sandy's girls" is something we both take pride in today. I strive to be the generous, compassionate, patient, and loving person that so many people know my mom to be. And as her daughter, I have the privilege of seeing even more of who God made her to be as we continue to go through life together.

So, as great as having fiery-red hair and a quick wit like the fictional Anne of Green Gables would have been to my sixth-grade self, I'll take being like my mom, Sandy McRae, any minute of the day.

Rachel McRae was born and raised in East Tennessee. Her mom, Sandy McRae, raised her and her sister in handmade dresses with a love of family and a reluctant love of chores. Rachel currently lives in Nashville, Tennessee, where she works for a national bookstore chain. When she's not working, she enjoys serving with a nonprofit that restores Jewish cemeteries in Poland. Sandy McRae is leading a busy retirement life in Knoxville, Tennessee, where she volunteers with church activities, a homeless women's ministry, and Samaritan's Purse.

Corn Silk

BY BETH JOHNSTONE MYERS

I was only four years old when Mom let me shuck the corn with the big girls. Shortly before supper was ready on a summer evening—the neighborhood lawn mowers finally silent—and before the front door banged because Daddy was home, the oldest would carry outside the brown grocery bag unevenly loaded with sweet corn, and the next oldest would carry out the pan, a big Revere Ware pot where the shucked corn would go. That day, I tripped after them, shouting, "I can help!"

We sat on the concrete back stoop overlooking the long, flat yard, our lawn a mix of dandelions gone to seed and overgrown grass. Across the way, our well-to-do neighbors' brick house with manicured hedges pained my mother, who longed for nicer things.

I had to dig in to the brown grocery bag to get started. Taking up an ear of corn almost as big as my leg (we lived in the famous corn country of central Illinois), I propped it between my little thighs and began to slowly peel off one pale, green, translucent leaf at a time, delicately seeking that inner core where all the mysterious silk surrounded the tiny yellow kernels. The silk put me off at first. The ends outside the leaves were dried, brown, and clumped together, but the ends inside were moist and fine; some blonde, some brunette, and some light brown.

My sisters had blonde hair; when they were little like me, they were a sweet pair of sisters. In all the black-and-white photos, they wore matching short, bright pixie haircuts and smocked dresses sewn by our grandmother. Now they were growing long legs and learning to dance with boys, and their blonde hair was in ponytails that gave every move they made a little sass.

My brother and I became the Other Pair, born a year apart and well after the older sisters. We both had dishwater-blonde hair, really light brown, inciting folks to think we were twins—the boy with blue eyes, the girl with brown. I was the most unremarkable in appearance, but I was too young to care. I thought I could run fast and do anything.

As I pulled the silk from the corn, the threads stuck to my little fingers until I could shake them off. I wonder if you have felt this, when the corn silk drifts down onto your legs and bare feet, a tickling sensation much like hair but more full of life.

Today, in Michigan, as I shuck the late-August corn at my sink, my sixty-year-old hands make quick work of this task. But when the silk gets away from me and falls at my bare feet, I am back with that little girl, trying to do the big girls' job. And along with that memory, I feel a crimp in my heart that my mother, with her Revere Ware pots, so proud of her children, is now gone. She who taught me how to quickly steam the corn in the frying pan and not to overcook it. Who, even before she was the age I am now, would rely on the help of her youngest daughter. She believed I could do anything.

So the corn silk feels like a touch of my mother, a tiny strand of her transported from wherever a mother is when she can't be with you. I bend to pick the silk from my feet, and I see it is white, which makes me smile.

Beth Johnstone Myers teaches creative writing at Adrian College in Michigan. Her family and her teaching are her life's great works. And after years of mucking around in prose and painting, she has also discovered that writing poetry is a swell marriage of her creative selves.

My Mother in the Mirror

BY DR. RAMONA PROBASCO

Sometimes as a woman, you don't understand the heart of your own mother until you become one. At least that has been the case for me. With my fiftieth birthday right around the corner, I have finally acquired a genuine and compassionate understanding of my mom. For this I am ever so grateful. Yet my understanding of her did not come easily, nor on my own accord. I now see God's faithfulness all over both of our lives, and it's beautiful.

Growing up, I felt very close to my mother. We spent a lot of time together and, in many respects, were more like friends than mother and daughter. Mom had me when she was very young, which I believe was the primary reason friendship seemed to trump parenting. Don't get me wrong: she parented (mostly from an "old school" perspective), but she would also confide in me like a friend, and I loved that.

Like my mother, I married very young and gave birth to my first child, a daughter, while still growing up myself. This is precisely when I began to notice the chasm growing between my mother and me. I was very confused about it and wondered what I was doing to "cause it." Now, as a grown, mature woman who has spent her fair share of time "figuring things out" in counseling, I understand what I didn't back then.

Catapult forward to ten years after my first daughter was born. I'm taking her to her friend's birthday party a few doors down from where we live. She's excited and can't wait to join the giggling girls. The birthday festivities include a hayride through the streets of our neighborhood. The mother of the birthday girl invites me to jump on the trailer and join the fun. Much to my surprise, my daughter gives me a look that clearly says, "Mom, pleeeease go away! I want to hang out with my friends!" Recognizing what this look means, I politely decline the invitation. As I turn to walk home, I cry. I feel hurt, confused, and rejected.

Like my own mom, I felt a kindred connection with my daughter. Her unspoken request to "go away" would be tucked inside my heart for years until God did what He does best: bring clarity to confusion, healing to our pockets of pain, and life to where life was lost.

Perhaps I'm a slow learner, but it would take another twenty years for me to see the overlap between my mother and me in this area. The connection between the hayride moment with my daughter and my own mother's sense of abandonment and loss when I moved away was something that eluded me for years. I had no clue how much my mother missed me when I married so young and moved thousands of miles from her. How I couldn't see it, I don't know. It's clear as day now but definitely was not in plain sight for many, many years.

As the saying goes, "Hurt people hurt people." Such was the case between Mom and me. In her pain, she would at times lash out at me. In my confusion, I would lash back. Around and around we went for years, not understanding that what we both wanted was to close the gap on the chasm and feel the kindred connection once again. I spent years asking the questions: "Why doesn't my mother love me anymore? Why doesn't she want to be my friend? Why does she push me away?"

Pain like this often comes with hidden treasures. In my case, this pain drove me to Jesus. I prayed, I cried, I sought counseling. The answer came in the most unexpected way. While reading Beth Moore's book *Praying God's Word*, I came across a passage where Beth encourages her readers who have experienced pain to take it to Jesus and ask Him to heal it. At first glance, I thought, *I've done this. It doesn't work!* But I reread her words more closely and found that she gently encourages her readers to pray this simple prayer: "God, please wrap *my wounded heart* in Your love, and renew *my mind*" (emphases mine). That was it! All those years I had been praying for my mom, which was a benevolent thing to do, but not enough to heal *my heart*.

Beth challenged me to pray that prayer for myself until I experienced a breakthrough. I gave it a go. I prayed it every day, multiple times a day, for months. This time of intentional prayer took place during one of the "dry spells" with my mom when we weren't talking to each other very much. Then it happened. My parents invited my family to dinner (we had since moved back near my parents). I was scared. I didn't want to feel that glaring chasm anymore between me and Mom. It was too painful. But I missed her, so I decided to go.

We all sat around my parents' dinner table, making small talk about mostly irrelevant matters to fill the silence. Then it happened. I put down my fork, looked up from my plate, and said to my mother, "I'm sorry for everything and anything I have knowingly or unknowingly done to cause you pain. Someday we are all going to be together in heaven. Surely we will get along then. But I want to start now. I want to live in peace with you now. Please forgive me for the things I've said and done that have caused you to retreat. Some things

I could control; some I couldn't. That's not what matters. What matters to me is that you know I love you, and I miss you. I want you back in my life again."

I waited. I was so nervous and could barely look her in the eyes. Mom is a person of few words.

Words were not necessary. Her eyes told it all.

In that moment, I felt her heart open back up to me. Where once was her pain from a sense of losing me, there now was an open door that said, "Come home."

Only God can perform miracles like that. First, He had to heal my wounded heart so that I could feel hers. Amazing how He does this. No wasted moves. Like mother, like daughter; both wrapped in His love, free once again to pick up where we left off. Friends.

As a marriage and family therapist, Dr. Ramona Probasco (Psy.D., M.F.T., N.C.C.) has dedicated more than twenty years to coming alongside those who are facing difficult life challenges or relationships that are causing them pain. She

holds a tender compassion for hurting people and a zealous desire to see broken lives mended and chasms closed. She draws from her own life and the lessons she has learned from her children, spouse, extended family, and clients throughout the years. She's the author of Healing Well and Living Free from an Abusive Relationship. *In it, she journeys with the reader down a clearly laid out path to healing well and living free from the trauma of an abusive relationship.*

Fighting Cancer with Courage and Kindness

BY APRIL RODGERS

Warm. Beautiful. Strong. Kind. Courageous. These are the words that describe my mother, Kathi.

Raised on a small farm with her eight siblings, she grew up sharing with others. It built character in her. You'll rarely find her in a moment when she's not sharing with others today—whether it be a meal, her money, or her faith in God. Sharing makes her happy.

However, my mother is no stranger to pain. She lost her son (my brother) in a car accident when he was only seventeen years old. It was earth-shattering and heart-wrenching for our whole family. She relied on her faith in the Lord to carry her through that awful time, and I can testify that she made it through the grief to tell of His goodness, ministering to others who have lost loved ones along the way.

Twelve years after losing her son, my sweet mother was diagnosed with an aggressive form of breast cancer. I was in disbelief. My mom? The one who eats healthy and exercises regularly? You mean to tell me that a bunch of cells coagulated into a lump and formed cancer inside her body, and now she has to have chemo, and surgery, AND radiation? Lord, no! Hasn't she been through enough already?

But it was true. So, I put on pink boxing gloves and jumped up and down in the corner, ready to knock this thing out. But that's not my mom's style. Hers is a gentle kind of strength.

Don't get me wrong. She's a fighter alright, but she's a different kind of fighter. She fights with courage and she fights with kindness, but most importantly, she fights on her knees.

From the very beginning, she put her trust in the Lord. When she met her oncologist, she said, "You're my doctor, and I am grateful for you, but the Lord is my Great Physician." What could he say to that but "Yes, ma'am"?

News spread of Mom's cancer. She was on countless prayer lists, and the notes and meals poured in as her treatment began. She told me, "April, I feel the peace of the Lord through every turn. He's been there, leading me to the right doctors, opening doors, showing me kindness through others. Oh, the kindness!"

Mom reciprocated the kindness by bringing treats to the oncologist's staff even when she could barely feel her hands and feet due to the chemotherapy's numbing effects. She would always befriend the person sitting next to her through each treatment, offering a prayer and a squeeze from her thin hand. The days that she was scheduled for treatment were always brighter in that office even though the drugs were ransacking her fragile body. She was a light in the darkness.

When the time came for Mom's lumpectomy, I traveled to MD Anderson in Houston to be with her and my father for the surgery. We prayed that the staff and doctors she came in contact with throughout the day would feel the presence of the Almighty. And wouldn't you know it, when the surgeon met with my dad and me later that afternoon, she called my mom an "angel." I believe that she was able to see Jesus in my mom that day.

The lumpectomy was deemed a success, and the two best words were uttered by the surgeon: "Cancer-free!" When I was finally able to see her in recovery and told her the good news, we both began to weep. Right away she pulled my hand in hers and we gave thanks to the Lord, right then and there. We spent the next several minutes just crying and praying. Mom prayed for everyone who had lifted her up in prayer throughout the process, and soon she was praying for the other patients in the recovery room because that's just her sweet heart.

That night as I gently readied her for bed, she asked me to put her iPad on a praise-and-worship play-list so she could listen as she drifted off to sleep. I did as she asked and quietly shut the door. When I heard her singing along to a familiar Hillsong tune, "Here I Am to Worship," I wept again.

The next day I asked Mom where she got her courageous spirit. She said, "It's a gift. Growing up the way I did makes a difference. When I start to lack faith, I rest in the assurance that God is in control and I don't have to be. He orchestrated everything, and He is the One who makes it livable, workable. The Lord is good. He holds me up and covers me."

To me, this is what it means to fight with courage and kindness. I'm so grateful for Mom's beautiful, selfless example. Her testimony of God's faithfulness inspires me. I hope that one day I can be just like her: a woman of kindness and courage.

April Rodgers is a speaker and Bible teacher. She holds a master's degree in theological studies from New Orleans Baptist Theological Seminary. April also serves as president of The Jeremy Barnhill Foundation for Christian Teens and as a contributing writer for LifeWay Women's Journey magazine. She and her husband, Adams, live in Monroe, Louisiana, with their daughters, Adelene and Ellanora.

I Choose Them

BY LISA JOY SAMSON

Driving down a dusty Texas road in a thirty-year-old RV, I realized that despite the facial features I so obviously shared with my mother, whose name was Joy, the features of character that she displayed were no longer evident in me. A two-year-old divorce had rendered me featureless, unable to find myself in a mirror framed by circumstances so new, so unrecognizable, I fled my life, taking my then eighteeen-year-old daughter with me.

Just after the new year, we'd vacated our town and set out in an old Jamboree that seemed to become less and less functional with every mile. But my daughter and I lived despite ourselves, despite the fact that we both felt as if we had been shattered into a million pieces.

My mother knew how to live. She always kept herself in community with one group or another—from political involvement to running a church office to playing bridge with other widows known as The Bridge Babes. My daughter and I played darts and joined in Texas barbeque potlucks at an RV park on the Gulf Coast. She spun flaming poi to delighted onlookers in parking lots. We talked with truckers at truck stops, searched for the Rio Grande, saw green jays and grackles for the first time. We learned how to trust that there would be a place for us to pull over in safety every night.

But one night, in the middle of the night, in the dust of a Texas winter, the propane ran out, the generator stopped for good, and we huddled together beneath two sleeping bags. I was tired, cold, and uncomfortable. I looked up and cried, "What have I become?" Words that used to flow onto the page failed to come forth from my fingers any longer, the roads were hard and mysterious, and I wanted to come home. But where was that? And wouldn't I take the same tired, confused, and shattered person there? What difference would that even make? The mess was my own, and ultimately had nothing to do with anyone else.

That was when I began to see what really needed healing—recognizing what could be restored, painful as it was to see my life with clarity at last.

I thought of my own mother, chronically and terminally ill, two weeks before being hospitalized for the final time before her death. I remembered her leaning heavily on a cart, shopping for Valentine's presents for her grandchildren. I don't know how she did it. But she did. My mother put her children first, no matter what.

I had fallen short in that regard so very many times.

After that long, cold night in the RV, I put my children up as my profile picture on social media and staked my claim in the one role I knew for sure. I was a mother, and my children would come first, no matter what. That changed everything. The world began to open up. My gifts returned, and I began to see in the mirror who I really was. The real person—the child of God—was loved and adored beyond imagining by her heavenly Father. I was not alone.

My mother had shown me my true north long ago. So I took her name as my own. I am Lisa Joy Samson, mother of three, friend of all, and beloved child of God. No longer shattered, no longer shamed, no longer lost. I was found by love beyond time and boundary, found by Love itself.

Lisa Joy Samson has been authoring stories full of hope in the love of God for His children for two and a half decades. With visual art and massage therapy, she promotes healing of body and mind. She lives in Colorado and is the mother of three grown, creative people, one senior cat, and a dog named Zeus.

Worry Warrior

BY AMY LEIGH SIMPSON

I was what you might call a miracle baby. Not because I was the result of a miraculous conception or traumatic labor, but because I grew very sick about six months into my life. The kind of sick that required experimental surgeries against seemingly insurmountable odds. Of course, I don't remember any of it. I can't imagine the fear and pain and heartache my parents must have faced in those days when their hopes hinged on a miracle.

It wasn't until I held my firstborn child in my arms that I understood not only the beauty and the wonder of the job I had just inherited but the paralyzing uncertainty winging toward me like arrows from every side. In that instant, with that wiggly weight on my chest, that fierce little grip holding my finger but anchoring my heart to his, I couldn't help but think of my mom.

How had she prepared herself for the onslaught, especially when my fragile existence hung in the balance? I replayed her words about how she'd armed herself with prayer and dreamt of me as a toddler with pigtails. She'd been battle-ready and proclaiming victory right in the thick of it. Those words came back to me right then, reminding me that motherhood isn't a meek calling for those who succumb to the biological urge to procreate. It's a long, arduous fight that will test your mettle in ways you couldn't have imagined. I vowed I'd be ready.

Big or small, our trials in parenting have the power to plow through all our best intentions and personal pep talks to poke at our deepest insecurities and fears. Am I failing my kids? Have I already ruined their lives? There are a million decisions to make on any given day, and some days, man, it sure feels like a swing and a miss over and over again.

Growing up, I never considered how hard those decisions had been for my mom. From those critical moments I spent in hospital cribs to the day my dad walked me down the aisle in a little stone chapel, did she think about all her missteps the way I often think about mine? I knew her to be something of a worrywart. I don't think she could help it. My mother was raised by a wonderful woman who also happens to be a world-class worrier. It seemed to be an inherited compulsion. Or perhaps a generational curse. I didn't exactly resent her for it, but I'd be lying if I said it wasn't, at times, tiresome. As much as I wanted to be like my mama, that was *one* thing I aspired to disinherit.

And then—wouldn't you know it?—I became a mom and, scary and wonderful as it was, I was shocked to discover how those worries I promised I wouldn't get caught up in were seemingly ingrained in my DNA. I can't tell you how many Bible verses I studied on the subject, determined to vanquish those pointless fears. After all, "Can any one of you by worrying add a single hour to your life?" (Matthew 6:27) and "Look at the birds of the air; they do not sow or reap or store away in barns, and yet your heavenly

Father feeds them. Are you not much more valuable than they?" (Matthew 6:26)

As much as I tried, that intrinsic need to protect, to nurture, to slay dragons and bullies, often comes at the price of a mama's sanity. I understand the nature of worry. It's because we care. We want the best for our kids. And we put a tremendous amount of pressure on ourselves to give them our version of the American Dream.

But why couldn't I seem to shake those ever-present fears sprouting like dandelions on every bump in our very bumpy road? Was my faith too weak? That didn't sound like the warrior I was trying to emulate.

I was drowning in the everyday madness of motherhood, losing myself to the perfect storm of exhaustion and tantrums and financial strain and unending laundry piles. I was mourning the loss of my free time, my hobbies, my friendships, my date nights, my pre-pregnancy jeans. My worries were snowballing. My love for my children, while big and bold, trembled beneath the weight of the responsibilities.

I had become battle-weary. My armor was drooping. My confidence shaken. I didn't recognize the person I saw in the mirror. She didn't look like me. And she sure didn't look like her mother. Her mama may have been a worrier, but she'd never been weak. She'd never let that fear change her the way it was overtaking me. She led with caution, but she never gave up. And all I wanted to do was crawl into the corner and have myself a good cry.

I confided my fears to my mom. Why wasn't my love stronger? Why did it feel like fear was always winning?

I'll never forget the words my warrior spoke to me that day. Words that picked me up, dusted me off, and put a sword back in my hand. She said, "The opposite of fear isn't faith. It's love."

Love. *His* love. Not my love.

I'd been falsely thinking my fear was a faith issue. Thinking if I'd drum up more faith, the fear wouldn't stand a chance. But the truth of it is, the world is a scary place. If I could, I'd swaddle my babies in Kevlar before they left the house and follow them everywhere they go, sword at the ready. But it's not my *faith* that wins in the end.

It's love that conquers my fears and calms my worries. *His* love renews my mind and gives me strength to keep fighting for my children. To keep training them up to be warriors who raise up warriors. My mother taught me that. She knew these days would come. She'd once fought on this very same front. And she equipped me for this battle. Now it's my turn to do the same. I may be a worry warrior. But I'm a warrior just like her.

Thanks for the sword, Mom.

Amy Leigh Simpson writes romantic mysteries with honesty and humor, sweetness and spice, and gritty reality covered by grace. When she's not stealing moments at naptime to squeeze out a few more adventures in storyland, she's chasing around two towheaded miscreants—ahem, boys—playing dress-up with one sweet princess baby, and being the very blessed wife

to the coolest, most swoon-worthy man alive. Amy is a Midwestern girl, singer, blogger, runner, coffee addict, and foodie. Her sports medicine degree is wasted patching up daily boo-boos, but whatever is left usually finds its way onto the page with fluttering hearts, blood and guts, and scars that lead to "happily ever after." Connect with Amy on Facebook or at her website, www.amyleighsimpson.com, to learn more about her USA Today *Happy Ever After "Must-Read Romance" novels,* When Fall Fades *and* From Winter's Ashes.

Styx and Engelbert Humperdinck

BY LEANNE W. SMITH

Our youngest was getting married. She asked my mother, whose yard and home would make for a nice piece in *Southern Living*, if we could have the wedding there. In the days leading up to the ceremony, some friends came over to help string lights under the reception tent. When one of those friends, Wendy, made the tour through the house and sunroom to reach the backyard, her eyes swept over the well-stocked bookcases, the family photos, the plants, the candles, the flowers, the fake bird's nests and watering cans. She looked at me and said, "This explains everything about you."

I wasn't sure how I felt about that. I may have even scrunched my face. After all, I have spent a lifetime stroking the *differences* between my mother and me. I didn't like to think I could be summed up from a quick tour through my mother's home.

When I was a child, people said I looked like her, but I didn't believe them. She had dark hair; mine was blonde. She had brown eyes; mine were blue.

As a teen, I was clearly more avant-garde. I had a Styx album, listened to it on my personal stereo, recorded it onto a cassette, saw them in concert, and bought the T-shirt. She had one eight-track tape that would only play on the clunky console in the living room . . . Engelbert Humperdinck.

The differences were so apparent.

The biggest difference—the one I felt most—was that I was emotional and she was stoic. I wore my emotions on both my sleeves. She never showed her emotional hand in public. In fact, until my father started having memory problems, I had hardly ever seen her cry. My children have seen me produce tears to fill dry creek beds.

I don't mean to imply she wasn't a terrific mother. She was. My mother was a snapshot of the '60s. Had Jacqueline Kennedy known her, she would have used my mother as a poster for the nation. She baked cookies. She made Kool-Aid, which we sometimes froze into ice pops . . . using the molds from Tupperware.

She cooked supper in a yellow kitchen. She sewed badges on my Girl Scout banner. She took my brothers and me to the Richland and Green Hills Libraries on hot days in summer where we sat on cool benches and took hours to run our hands and eyes over the many glistening choices. We could each get eight books with our cards, and sometimes we were so enamored with our selections that we brought them to the supper table.

And she let us.

My mother taught us to love books and stories. She was sensible, even-keeled, and wise . . . a real Rock of Gibraltar.

Me? I prefer beauty to practicality, my moods spiral hopelessly up and down, and while I wish I could claim wisdom, I can't. A boatload of foolishness has been bound up in my heart.

As a mother myself in the 1990s, I was dazed and confused. I pursued advanced degrees and worked full-time while raising children but longed for a writing career. A cloud of guilt followed me everywhere.

One day I wailed to my mother, while crying of course, that work was causing me to be a less-than-stellar mother. It seemed only a matter of time until my daughters would be on *Oprah*, blaming me for something, possibly for everything.

My mother said, "Oh, Leanne. Good mothers are good mothers whether they work or not."

She, the retired first-grade teacher, would know. Her practicality has always swept over my foolishness just like this . . . like a calming west wind.

These days her hair is gray and I'm trying to hang on to blonde. Her eyes are still brown and mine are still blue like my daddy's. And while my mother mostly remains stoic and tries never to cry in public, I continue to be something of an emotional mess.

But we seem to be meeting in the middle.

When that blue-eyed man we both loved was declining first in a hospital, then in a hospice bed, we could often be found sitting side by side watching him, our legs and hands folded in sync, causing many a medical professional to do a double take. On first sight, we are apparently the older and younger versions of the same woman, separated by twenty short years. One doctor's eyes kept rolling back to me until he finally shook his head and muttered, "Remarkable."

I don't mind anymore. I'll claim it. Instead of stroking our differences, I'm drawing nearer to our likeness.

I know now that this woman who held the earth so steady for all of us *can* cry. Not to fill creek beds, like me, but she's more than capable. And I am capable of sucking up my tears. For the first time in my life, I could actually feel them coming and sometimes turn them off. Like an unwelcome storm you close the blinds to. Like flipping a switch.

I realized how much I, too, hate to show strong emotions in front of others. For all my everyday, cry-at-the-drop-of-a-hat tears, I don't want people to see my gut-wrenching, feel-it-from-the-depths-of-my-soul tears.

It used to bother me when it felt like someone was suggesting I was a mirror image of my mother—that a friend like Wendy could make the tour through the house and sunroom, her eyes sweeping over evidences of the things that fill my mother's soul, recognizing how similar they are to the things that fill my own, and declare, "This explains everything about you."

But she's right. And I'm honored that she noticed.

Leanne W. Smith is the author of Leaving Independence, *an inspirational historical fiction novel. She's also a professor of management for Lipscomb University's College of Business in Nashville. Leanne believes that when something calls to you, you should journey toward it. She and her husband have two creative daughters and a son-in-law who make the world a more beautiful place through their art, photography, songwriting, and mandolin playing. Visit her website at www.leannewsmith.com.*

Could Be Worse

BY ALICE SULLIVAN

By fifth grade, I'd decided I wanted to be just like my mother. Sitting cross-legged on the golden-hued shag carpet in the living room, I spent hours flipping through old leather photo albums, learning faces and stories of family and friends. Pictures of my mother always stood out.

At three years old, my mother, Louise, was a chubby-faced ballerina with poorly cut bangs, a tutu, and a wand in an old 3 x 3 black-and-white photo with her older sister. In another picture, she sat with her two sisters and her brother on a couch at Christmas, bright-eyed and excited about the gifts in festive wrapping paper under the tree. She was the spirited high school cheerleader in the blue-and-white uniform, her beautiful auburn hair perfectly accentuated by the cute bob cut popular in the '60s. Another picture was of her and the handsome football player she dated. A few years later, there she was: the homecoming queen. But the pictures I loved most were the two of her sitting on dirt bikes she raced. Her shoulder-length hair fell perfectly over her black leather jacket, and her smile was as crisp as the air must have been that morning on the trail. *Gosh, she is so cool!* I'd think. I wanted to be just like her. Of course, I had no idea what that really meant. No idea what she'd been through.

My parents met in art school and married young. In one of the photos from their wedding day, Mom is in her white dress, holding a bouquet of flowers, hair still in curlers, but lying on the carpet as though she were dead in a coffin. *That should have been a sign*, we would joke decades later. While my brother, sister, and I were still very young, our parents divorced and both of Mom's parents passed away. During the final years of her own mother's battle with cancer, Mom attended college—studying and doing homework after she'd put us to bed. Then she began a long career in radiology, treating cancer patients.

When I was fourteen, Mom made the painful decision to sell the home we'd all lived in together—the gray stone Tudor her parents purchased in the late 1940s—when the upkeep and repairs grew too expensive. She and I had grown apart by then, my teenage moodiness and angst driving a wedge in our already-strained communication. During one argument, my mother, in tears, likely exasperated by my stubborn attitude, looked at me and said, "I don't even know who you are anymore!"

My heart broke. And in that moment, I decided to be nothing like her.

We managed to survive the teenage years, an easier relationship forming gradually with time, trust, and patience. When I went to college not far from home to play soccer and tennis on a dual-sport scholarship, Mom became the official "soccer team mom," bringing water, Gatorade, and sliced oranges to every one of my home games. For the next eight years, she spent countless hours traveling to various sporting events and awards ceremonies as all three of us kids went to and graduated from college. Her weekends were spent helping us study for tests, sewing our friends' ripped clothes, housing students during holidays when they couldn't afford to go home, and often entertaining an entire houseful of rowdy kids who consumed nothing but pizza, nacho cheese, chili, and soft drinks. She was the "cool mom." Our house was the house where everyone was welcome.

Now in the back end of my thirties, Mom and I have a great relationship. People still often comment about how cool my mom is, and I have to agree. Our little family has stuck together through divorce, raging hormones, high school, college, and many other bumps along the way. I attribute most of my siblings' and my success as adults to the woman who sacrificed so much for us to have a better life, often at the expense of her sleep, finances, temporary sanity, and emotions.

These days, Mom spends her weekends gardening and enjoying the occasional shopping trip—the same way many of my own weekends are spent. One Saturday not long ago, I went to her house to visit and pulled out my brand-new silver wallet for show-and-tell. Mom tilted her head back and laughed as she reached into her own purse to show me she had bought the *exact same one* weeks earlier.

"Well, crap!" I said, because this isn't even close to the first time we've purchased the exact same item. There was also the time we each wore the same bright, mood-changing lipstick to meet new neighbors. The woman looked a little surprised as we introduced ourselves, and when we explained we were mother and daughter, she said, eyes wide, "I can see the resemblance!" It wasn't until we walked back to Mom's house and looked at each other that we realized the clear lipstick we'd slathered on an hour earlier (thinking it didn't work because there was no instant color) had now miraculously turned a garish fuchsia. We laughed the entire fifteen minutes it took to scrub it off. "I guess we do look alike!" Mom cackled.

Shoving my silver wallet back into my purse, I faux grumbled, "I'm turning into my mother!" I plopped down on the couch, smiling as Mom smiled back.

"There are worse things," she said, stirring the large pot of chili for that night's family dinner.

The truth is, she's my hero. Her love is unconditional. Her patience and problem-solving skills are off the charts. And she has the uncanny ability to make anyone feel instantly at home. She's still the cool mom—and the best mom. In fact, I still want to be just like her when I grow up.

Alice Sullivan has worked in the book publishing industry since 2001 as a ghostwriter, author, writing coach, speaker, and editor. She's worked on more than one thousand titles, including eleven New York Times *bestsellers. She partners with publishers, agents, and authors to develop books that are both entertaining and memorable. Connect with her at www. alicesullivan.com.*

Small but Mighty

BY DORRIS WALKER

I was born on a cold, snowy Sunday morning in 1956 in a county hospital. There were no antiseptics, no epidural blocks, just a strong, caring woman determined to give me a chance at life. My mother was a prayer warrior, so I imagine that she prayed and prayed through the pain. No cursing, no gnashing of teeth. Just prayer. That was my mother's way.

On the day I was born, my family was being forced to move. All that loading up of box after box, all the sweeping and mopping of floors and the washing of windows and the cooking—that's what put Mom in labor. That's how my siblings tell the story anyhow.

So Momma got to carry her new baby girl into her new home. She cleaned me, fed me, bonded with me, thanked God for me, and fed me again—all while she unpacked the house and then cooked dinner for the family, carrying a newborn in her arms. Did I mention she was still in excruciating pain?

My mom has been a tower of strength as long as I've known her. She was strong in spirit but short in stature. At five-foot-two, she wasn't tall, but she could raise the hair on your head with the powerful words that came from her fast-talking mouth. She and Daddy had five children—six if you count their first son, who died at the tender age of two months. Mom bore that loss like all the rest: with prayer and faith in the Lord.

Her name was Lockey Dee Williams. Then she married my daddy when she was twenty-seven and became an Utley. She was an amazing homemaker. She sewed our clothes, cooked and cleaned from sunup to sundown, all the while singing and praising the Lord. She was faithful to God first, then to her husband and children.

On occasion, when food was scarce, Momma would pretend that she wasn't hungry until everyone else had eaten their fill. While scraping our plates to clean, she'd pick out enough eatable scraps for her own little bowl.

That is the kind of woman my mom was. Compassionate. Resourceful. Humble.

Momma instilled the fear of God and the power of prayer in her children. She believed in God with her whole self. Every meal we ate we said grace over. And we never went to bed without reciting our prayers. Life with Mom was good because I knew she had the faith to move mountains. She'd do anything to take care of me and my four older siblings.

It was Mom who taught me that music is food for the soul. She would hum and sing while doing her chores. When we were sick, she would always comfort us and tell us that God said it's gonna be alright. She had an amazing assurance that God would do just what He said He would do.

My mom would pray daily, sometimes continually. I'd hear her talking to the Lord as she worked, often breaking into song. She carried us to church to be fed the Word of God. She lived poor so that others could have what they needed. When we lost my daddy in a tragic shooting when I was a girl, Momma held the family together. After my father's death, I watched her become the sole provider, the loving mom and the one who dished out disciplinary action well. I watched her grow gardens and flowers and make unbelievable dishes out of nothing.

Years later, when I took to wandering the streets of Nashville, addicted to drugs and selling myself, Momma never lost faith in God's ability to restore me or in me to be restored. I'm just grateful she lived to see the day that I got clean and sober. I'm living proof of her answered prayers. I know this because my loving, kind, sweet, wholesome mom had an amazing assurance that God would do just what He said He would do.

Momma died peacefully in her sleep on a very cold Sunday morning, March 28, 2010. She had been on the earth for ninety-six years. Not all were good, pleasant, and fun years, but as she always said, "It's gonna be alright."

God made me in His image. He allowed my mom to form me in her image and standards. Thank you, Mom, for teaching me how to be a mom and never give up.

I heard about faith from my mom. I watched her faithfully go on her way. She's why I am a faithful daughter—faithful to God, faithful to prayer, faithful to get up when life knocks me down. And though she's gone, I still love her with all my heart, for now and forevermore.

Dorris Walker is director of events for Thistle Farms, an international nonprofit that creates handmade products by women survivors of trafficking, prostitution, and addiction. As a survivor of prostitution herself, Dorris is committed to offering hope to women in the most dire circumstances. A lifelong lover of music, Dorris serves as president of Howard Chapel Senior Choir and secretary of Divine Inspirational Choir. She's also a singer and songwriter. She lives with her husband, James, in White House, Tennessee. She's a proud mother and grandmother and sings with her granddaughter in the youth choir.

The Roads Leading Home

BY MARY WEBER

"All roads eventually lead home. Some just take a few more turns to get there."

Those words stir in my mind as I drive the quiet, winding backstreets into town, past the fog-soaked hills and salted-ocean skyline. Past the cows and cars and wineries. Through the stoplight where I turn and pull in to the hospital.

The roads that lead home . . .

My entire life I've heard my mother talk about such things in her teachings, her books, and even in raising us six kids—of how a person's legacy is a road to lead others home. Those words are now shuffling and reframing their meaning as I step through the sliding-glass doors, past the nurses' stations cloaked in yellow overhead lighting and the smell of tired cafeteria food, and tread the way back to her hospital room.

First floor. Left wing. Bed 2. By the tiny window.

My throat tightens. She's asleep. Looking more fragile than I've ever seen her. I pull the blanket to her shoulders and watch her closed eyelids as she rests on this bed that is not her own, in a thin gown separating her skin from the rest of the world. Much like the too-short, too-breezy curtain that's supposed to separate us from the loud voices on the other side, which are suddenly making it clear, now that I'm here, that they resent sharing this space.

As if this room weren't cold enough already.

A text whispers across my phone's screen. "Did they get it all?"

I blink. I don't know.

"How is she?"

I . . .

Don't know.

I begin to type, then stop and set the screen down, and slip my hand over her cool one as the tears start spilling. This hand that looks so much like my grandfather's once did—strong and firm, papery and frail, with tracks of blue veins racing like highways just under the skin. Full of blood and cells that sometimes congest with a variety of illnesses on their way to the heart. *Beat beat beating* with life and age and the love of something bigger than both of us.

Her chest rises and falls.

My memories rise and fall with it. To the roads that have led me here.

The road I took a bike down at the age of five, only to find it was too steep and the asphalt unforgiving. The resulting crash ground blood and blacktop into my skin, making me scream until my mother's arms reached out to carry me back up the hill to the place where healing could be found.

Like the dirt road my brother and I joy-rode down in Dad's old VW Rabbit, only to skid into a tree that took out the car and almost took us out with it while Dad and Mom were away on their anniversary vacation. They came home grateful we were alive, and Mom promptly reminded us how her nightly prayers included requesting that, whatever any of us kids were up to, we'd always get caught so we could make it right with ourselves, others, and Jesus.

We always did.

Or like the road I drove away on at the age of eighteen after I'd stood in the hall and cussed her out. To which she'd calmly replied that I could treat myself however I wanted, but I couldn't treat her that way.

Or like the 405 freeway I drove all the way down to college a few months later—growing more nervous the farther I got. For weeks I called her every day, thinking maybe I should come back home because I didn't even know what I was doing there. "I love you, but you're staying put," she'd said. "I won't allow you to let yourself down. We'll be here when you're done."

I did. They were.

Just like she was there the morning of my wedding, driving with me along Main Street to get our hair done.

Like she was there fifteen months later as my husband drove us over the giant grade to reach the hospital in time to deliver our first daughter. Mom helped me breathe.

It's the same grade I drove last week when I called her for advice on the same daughter, now much older. "How do I reach her heart and keep it from traveling the paths that terrify me, Mom?"

"Love her. Listen to her and offer boundaries like the lines on the road you're driving. Her path will look different, but no matter how curvy it gets, it'll lead home. Yours did."

Yes. It did.

The memories fade and the tears come faster as I grip my mother's hand tighter in the quiet space between a window and a too-short curtain. As the reality weighs thick in this room that home isn't just a place or a belief system. Home is also here, lying on this bed in front of me. And, oh God, what if the home this illness leads to isn't an earthly one?

Her hand moves, her veins rippling beneath mine with the love and legacy she has crafted to my soul, and that have held my heart more times than I can count during my thirty-four years of traveling life's variety of roads.

Mom's breathing slows. Her eyes open and settle on mine. She smiles. "Hey there," she whispers. "I knew you'd come."

Mary Weber is the multiple award–winning author of the best-selling young adult Storm Siren Trilogy and The Evaporation of Sofi Snow series. An avid high school, middle school, and conference speaker, Mary's passion is helping others find their voice in a world that often feels too loud. When she's not plotting adventures involving tough girls who frequently take over the world, Mary sings '80s hair band songs to her three muggle children and ogles her husband, who looks strikingly like Wolverine. They live in California, which is perfect for the ocean, Comic-Con, and stalking LA bands.

Mary's books have been featured in the Scholastic school book fairs and endorsed by best-selling authors Marissa Meyer, Jay Asher, Wendy Higgins, and Jonathan Maberry. You can also find Mary's fun interviews in the paperback of Marissa Meyer's New York Times *best-selling* Cress *and in Jay Asher's* 13 Reasons Why *movie tie-in edition.*

A Completely Different Life

BY MARJORY WENTWORTH

I am writing this essay at Mepkin Abbey, a Trappist monastery located about forty miles from my home. It is a serene and spiritual place. These are not words you'd use to describe my mother, so I hope this environment will make the writing go a bit easier.

I just read David Sedaris's *New Yorker* essay about his mother, "Why Aren't You Laughing? Reckoning with Addiction." He regrets not confronting his mother about her alcoholism during her lifetime and describes her embarrassing behavior in graphic detail while acknowledging her fierce and abiding love for him, even suggesting that her storytelling abilities are what launched his career as a writer. He is still conflicted about his mother, as am I.

About a year ago, my mother passed away in a hospice center near our home. And I miss her terribly. I lost my father when I was a teenager, so she was my only biological parent for most of my life. My mother was generous to a fault and thoughtful in countless ways. She was a self-taught gourmet cook, and her home looked like it came out of a magazine. She had amazing parties! Charming to a fault, my mother was a social butterfly. It's doubtful that she ever logged on to the Internet, but her life was a precursor to Facebook. She had so many friends, many she had only met a few times yet who were nonetheless people she stayed in touch with through the phone, or through a thoughtful note as holidays approached, or upon family milestones. With my mother, if you friended her once, you were friends for life.

But my mother was also the saddest, most self-destructive person I have ever known. Her mood swings were terrifying, and she was probably bipolar. Despite all her friends, she was often at war with those in more sustained relationships, particularly members of her family. The roots of her problems with addiction ran deep. Born into the middle of a family of eight children and raised in rural Maine, she was raped when she was nine or ten years old. My mother didn't tell anyone about the rape until decades later, and she walked around with that deep wound that never healed.

Like a lot of women in the '50s, she married young. She became a housewife on Boston's North Shore. Her life resembled the lives of women in John Updike's novels; in fact, he and my father were in the same class at Harvard. She thrived in the Waspy world that my father came from. My mother was devoted to her family and she excelled at motherhood, but she was completely dependent on my father financially and psychologically. She also suffered from issues with her back and seemed to be off her feet a lot. When my father was in his early forties, he was diagnosed with leukemia, and despite going to some of the best doctors in the world at Mass General Hospital, he died when he was forty-three. My mother became a widow at the age of thirty-eight. Nothing would ever be right for her again.

She rarely got out of bed for months after Dad passed away, and she attributed the inactivity to her bad back, but there was certainly depression going on there. Once again, she needed help, but either none was available or she didn't know where to find it. Various family members helped with the finances, so my mother never worked in my lifetime. This was the worst possible thing that could have happened, because she remained completely dependent on others until the very end. She was completely heartbroken over the loss of my father, and once my brother and I were off to college, her life seemed meaningless. It's as if she filled her hours with social engagements but she never found any inner peace. I am a poet, and I am deeply religious. My inner life is the biggest part of me, so in very profound ways, we didn't really understand each other.

During my freshman year of college, Mom remarried an Irish-American lawyer named Bob Tully from South Boston, and they moved into a beautiful home where my husband and I later held our wedding reception. The first few years were fun, and we all adjusted. Bob was easygoing and kind, but he was completely the opposite of my father, who was a charming, high-energy, outdoorsy guy with a great intellect. Crazy as it sounds, it's as if my mother was angry at Bob for not being my father. Together they were toxic, and they dealt with it by drinking themselves into a stupor every night. If you forgot and telephoned after 6:00 p.m., she would slur into the phone.

My mother and stepfather fought when they were drunk. Dishes would get broken, and toward the end, he hit her a couple of times. Nasty stuff. I stayed away as much as possible. Moving seven states down the Atlantic seacoast made it easier. I tried talking with my mother about her drinking, but she was in denial and became defensive, and all it seemed to do was make things more stressful. I also tried to get one of her sisters to do an intervention, but we couldn't ever get enough people on board to go through with it. My husband and I should have done it ourselves.

My mother and stepfather burned through all their money and then some, and their marriage ended in a nasty divorce. My brother and his wife lived closer to Mom and helped secure an apartment, but she blew through all the money from the divorce, fell, and needed surgery. Eventually my husband and I took over her care and moved her to South Carolina.

My mother's health was never good, but she used illness to get attention, and you never really knew what was real and what wasn't. She loved being in the hospital and spent as much time there as possible. Maybe there's a name for this; maybe it's a syndrome. If one of her siblings had a triple bypass or a stroke, for example, Mom would become defensive and list her litany of ailments as if it was a competition that she wanted to win.

At some point, she stopped drinking. I'm not sure if all the heart and blood-pressure pills added up to the revelation that she was going to kill herself if she kept up, but she stopped drinking. Unfortunately, she never went to Alcoholics Anonymous or confronted the reason she drank in the first place. Like a lot of alcoholics, she continued to blame everyone else for her problems and she felt sorry for herself. After she fell a few times and had some knee injuries, she became addicted to oxycodone. It's like she switched from alcohol to pills, and of course the opioids lowered her pain threshold. Even the doctors couldn't be sure what was physical and what was mental.

I told my sons once that I've spent my entire adult life trying not to be my mother, and they said that I succeeded. But I've paid a price. I would go back and work less, and spend more time with my sons when they were growing up. More than anything, I wish I could go back and get my mother the help she needed decades ago: a good therapist, rehab, AA, and so on. But I was a kid and then a young adult, trying to figure out my own life. I didn't understand how much pain my mother was in and how much help she needed. I wish I had. We could have had a completely different life . . .

Marjory Wentworth's poems have been nominated for The Pushcart Prize five times. Her books of poetry include Noticing Eden, Despite Gravity, The Endless Repetition of an Ordinary Miracle, *and* New and Selected

Poems. *She is the cowriter with Juan Méndez of* Taking a Stand: The Evolution of Human Rights; *coeditor with Kwame Dawes of* Seeking: Poetry and Prose Inspired by the Art of Jonathan Green; *and the author of the prize-winning children's story* Shackles. *Her most recent collaborations include* We Are Charleston: Tragedy and Triumph at Mother Emanuel *with Herb Frazier and Dr. Bernard Edwards Powers Jr.; and* Out of Wonder: Poems Celebrating Poets *with Kwame Alexander and Chris Colderley.*

Marjory is on the faculty at The Art Institute of Charleston. The cofounder and former president of the Lowcountry Initiative for the Literary Arts, she serves on the editorial board of the University of South Carolina's Palmetto Poetry Series and is the poetry editor for Charleston Currents. *Her work is included in the South Carolina Poetry Archives at Furman University, and she is the poet laureate of South Carolina.*

Unbecoming Mother

BY LAUREN F. WINNER

Like so many of us, it was when I heard myself say what she always said: "I can't ever have anything nice."

That's what she said when some prized possession got broken, when a wineglass snapped at the stem or tomato sauce spilled on the blouse or the cat scratched up the upholstery. It was never said with irony; it was always straight—bleak and despondent, as though everything hinged on that blouse.

I said the same words, aloud to no one, when I broke a small cordial glass, pink with tiny flowers etched into the cup. Even though I still had plenty of nice things; even though I had enough money to replace the cordial glass without noticing a dent in my budget. I also didn't speak with irony.

I look just like her. Like her, I drink too much. Like her, I am prodded by a restless ambition that doesn't know where to land. I am suffused, periodically, by bilious resentment and bitterness—bitterness that makes no sense when you look objectively at the circumstances of my life, but which tells me that the world's decks are stacked against me and everyone else is getting things that I'm not. In this way, I am very like my mother.

I often wonder what she would make of my life. When she died, I hadn't finished school; I didn't own a house; I was about to marry a man I've since divorced; I wasn't ordained; I lived three hours and one state line from the place I live now. I was still all horizon. I wonder what she would make of me now, circumscribed by nothing more dramatic than the passage of time. I visit my mother's grave, but mostly, her death is a relief. When I look at her from afar, I see much to esteem, and I can speak of my mother in terms of rueful admiration if I try. But it is hard to look at her from afar.

I think she watched her life like it was a film, and she felt helpless to change it. In her fifties, she tried to seize control of the reins a bit—she took a few trips abroad and joined a gym and hired a trainer. I, in my twenties, thought those things superficial and stupid. I am forty now. My life often feels like a film, and I am helpless to change it. Last year, I joined a gym and hired a trainer.

Among other shapes, my mother's life had an economic shape. She began life at something close to poverty; she married into a spacious, mid-century ranch house and a country-club membership; and then she divorced into financial fragility—she held on to her middle-class perch, but not to the three-bedroom house or the club.

As for me, I save obsessively for retirement; I save and I save. I read *Money* magazine, and I run retirement projections, and I work an extra job and throw the salary at my fear of being seventy-eight and destitute. This saving is a way of nurturing the idea that providing for myself is the task I most urgently must get right, and this, too, I learned from my mother, who wasn't invested in self-reliance so much as she was devoted to the sense that she had no one else to rely on, that there was no one to take care of her.

Given my commitment to the axiom that I am just like her, writing all these checks to my SEP-IRA is strange. If I am, in fact, my mother, I'll be dead at sixty and should spend the money now.

So the saving is not only an effort to avoid late-in-life privation or ward off my own sense of vulnerability. Every one of the checks I write is also a bid for difference—a bid to outlive her; to have a life that exceeds her; to unbecome her.

Lauren Winner is the author of Girl Meets God: On the Path to a Spiritual Life, Mudhouse Sabbath: An Invitation to a Life of Spiritual Discipline, Still: Notes on a Mid-Faith Crisis, *and* Wearing God: Clothing, Laughter, Fire, and Other Overlooked Ways of Meeting God. *An Episcopal priest and assistant professor of Christian spirituality at Duke Divinity School, Winner is the daughter of a Jewish father and a Southern Baptist*

mother—raised Jewish, then converted to Christianity and baptized into the Anglican Church while pursing a master's of philosophy at Cambridge University. She writes and lectures on Christian practice, the history of Christianity in America, and Jewish-Christian relations.

Lauren has appeared on PBS's Religion & Ethics Newsweekly and served as a commentator on NPR's All Things Considered. She has written for the New York Times Book Review, the Washington Post Book World, Publisher's Weekly, Books and Culture, and Christianity Today, and her essays have been included in several volumes of The Best Christian Writing.

So We're a Little Jumpy Sometimes

BY CHRISTY WRIGHT

I remember coming downstairs one Saturday morning half-asleep, looking for my mom. She was cleaning the bathroom, and she had CMT blaring on the television. The song was "She's in Love with the Boy" by Trisha Yearwood, which is still one of my favorite songs to this day. I was about eight years old, and as I turned the corner by our couch to say hi to her, she turned around and saw me standing there in my baggy sweatpants. She made eye contact with me and then—with a completely delayed reaction—she almost fell over and let out a scream that I am sure terrified the entire neighborhood.

Was my face bloody or was I wearing a terrifying Halloween mask? Nope. Mom was just that jumpy. I looked at her with the same exasperated look I always had when she did this. And she *always* did this. "Mommmm! It's me! I am RIGHT. HERE! I mean, you even saw me! What are you screaming about?"

To say that Mom is "jumpy" is the understatement of the century. And to say that I get annoyed with it is about the same. Still to this day, she screams when she sees me and didn't expect to. And, to my pain and embarrassment, I do the exact same thing. I'll walk downstairs early in the morning, thinking I am alone, and almost fall over when I see my husband standing by the coffee maker in his boxers. I've walked into our bonus room by myself, and when I see my husband sitting in his recliner watching football, I scream and run out, almost tripping down the stairs, simply because I thought he was outside. One time I was sitting in my car in the driveway after just getting home from work, and I was sending an email on my phone. When I looked up to my left and saw Matt standing by my window trying to say something to me, I let out a scream that led to neighbors almost calling the police. I am my mother's daughter.

Mom was a single mom when I was growing up, and I was an only child. We were more like best friends than mother and daughter, and there's no one on this planet who shaped the woman I am today more than her. Mom has so many crazy qualities that she passed down to me. She talks fast, walks fast, and gets way more excited than anything actually warrants. She's jumpy and intense and weird and persistent to a fault. I am all of those things and then some.

But for every crazy quality that Mom passed down to me, she passed some pretty amazing ones as well. She's the most creative person I've ever met. She's hilarious and so much fun to be around. She's resourceful and insanely hardworking. She's generous and loving and selfless and serving. She's the person everyone wants at their party and the person who brings light into a room the moment she walks in. She's also the person who makes you feel like a million bucks when you talk to her because she is always interested in you, and in what you're doing and how you're doing. And when you talk about those things, she really listens. She's also loyal to the ends of the earth, and when everyone has left your side, you always know she's in your corner and would drop everything to do anything for you. She's a fighter and a survivor, a mover and a shaker. She's also really, really smart about people and about life.

"Don't worry about being right, Christy; just worry about being kind," she'd say when I wanted to have the last word in a fight with someone when I was growing up.

"Do what's right," she'd say when I was caught up in teenage girl drama in high school.

"Just because you can do something does not mean that you should," she'd say when I overcommitted myself *again*.

"If they have the nerve to ask you, you have to have the nerve to say no," she'd say when I felt guilted into doing something I didn't want to do.

"You're better than that," she'd say when she saw me getting wrapped up with a guy who was no good or in a situation that wasn't smart.

And every single one of those quotes I still not only remember, but also use to this day when I travel to speak to thousands of people on stages across the country. Mom's wisdom and legacy go with me every-where.

I may scream and run and jump and flail every time my husband walks into the room. And I may walk and talk way too fast. But that's a small price to pay for getting to be like one of the most amazing women I've ever known: my mother.

Christy Wright is the creator of Business Boutique, a certified business coach, and a Ramsey Personality with a passion for equipping women with the knowledge and steps they need to successfully run and grow a business. Since joining Ramsey Solutions in 2009, she has spoken to thousands across the country at women's conferences, national business conferences, Fortune 500 companies, and her own sold-out live events. She is the host of the Business Boutique *podcast and has written a book,* Business Boutique, *released in 2017. You can follow Wright on Twitter and Instagram @ChristyB-Wright and online at christywright.com or facebook.com/OfficialChristyWright.*

Dear Friend,

This book was prayerfully crafted with you, the reader, in mind—every word, every sentence, every page—was thoughtfully written, designed, and packaged to encourage you...right where you are this very moment. At DaySpring, our vision is to see every person experience the life-changing message of God's love. So, as we worked through rough drafts, design changes, edits and details, we prayed for you to deeply experience His unfailing love, indescribable peace, and pure joy. It is our sincere hope that through these Truth-filled pages your heart will be blessed, knowing that God cares about you—your desires and disappointments, your challenges and dreams.

He knows. He cares. He loves you unconditionally.

BLESSINGS!
THE DAYSPRING BOOK TEAM

A Room for the Summer

A Room for the Summer

Adventure, Misadventure, and Seduction in the Mines of the Coeur d'Alene

FRITZ WOLFF

M.McCANN

UNIVERSITY OF OKLAHOMA PRESS : NORMAN

Publication of this book is made possible through the generosity of Edith Kinney Gaylord.

The drawings in this book are by Mary McCann.

Lyrics from the song "Ballad of Baby Doe," by Douglas Moore and John LaTouche, are used by permission. Copyright © 1956 (Renewed) Chappell & Co. All Rights Reserved. Warner Bros. Publications U.S. Inc., Miami FL. 33014. Lyrics from the song "I'm Movin' On," by Hank Snow, are used by permission. Copyright © 1950 (Renewed) Unichappell Music Inc. All Rights Reserved. Warner Bros. Publications U.S. Inc., Miami FL. 33014.

The poem "Promise" is reprinted by permission of the author, Rita Levitz, from *Images and Voices of Lighthouse Country*, copyright © 1997 by Rita Levitz and Leah Willott.

Parts of chapter 19 appeared in a slightly different version in *Mining History Journal* vol. 7, 2000.

Library of Congress Cataloging-in-Publication Data

Wolff, Fritz, 1937–
    A room for the summer : adventure, misadventure, and
    seduction in the mines of the Coeur d'Alene / Fritz Wolff.
        p.   cm.
    ISBN 0-8061-3658-8 (alk. paper)
       1. Wolff, Fritz, 1937– 2. Silver miners—Idaho—Kellogg—
    Biography. I. Title.

HD8039.M732U69 2004
622'.092—dc22
[B]
                                       2004053742

1 2 3 4 5 6 7 8 9 10

To every hardrock miner who ever spit a fuse, and to my grandfather, Anton "Tony" Hauger, who thought any idea I ever had was a good one

The real possibility of the personal essay, which is to catch oneself in the act of being human, . . . means a willingness to surrender for a time our pose of unshakable rectitude, and to admit that we are, despite our best intentions, subject to all manner of doubt and weakness and foolish wanting.

—Tobias Wolff

Contents

Preface

I used to spend a lot of time in meetings—corporate management business that makes up the entire week. Invariably, my mind wandered during the inevitable speeches made by the informed and uninformed, or when the corporation went into a save-the-ship mode. "The sky is falling. Lay everybody off!" some great voice would say, and the room would fill with cigar smoke thick as egg whites. At such times I drifted back to several college summers spent working underground in the Silver Valley's famous Bunker Hill mine. I thought about my old partner, Chris, about the life-saving cook at the boardinghouse, and about the mind-boggling ride down a 6,900-foot inclined shaft. The experience was my boot camp, primary training—that place where we all get started one way or another. I had a lot of growing up to do.

At first, I wrote the story in my mind. The catalyst that got it down on paper was a comment a teenager made a few years ago. "Man, that happened in 1956? That's a long time ago. That's a history kind of thing." It was tough to imagine that transposing oneself from Seattle's affluent View Ridge–Laurelhurst neighborhood to a late

1950s mining camp might qualify as a part of the "western experience" or that at the age of eighteen I had been involved in western history. It didn't seem like history to me at the time.

But those days in the Silver Valley were about to disappear forever. That's reason enough to document the time, to make a contribution to bigger questions such as Where did we all come from? What happened before I got here? What was it like? What did people do for a living?

So after making a silent acknowledgment that I lacked the literary skills of my heroes Norman Maclean and Farley Mowat, I started to write. But I continued to fret. Even if I could tell the story properly, I fretted that historically it didn't rank in the same league as wagons grinding over the Oregon Trail, the shootout at the OK Corral, or Pinkerton agents infiltrating labor unions.

The tough part about writing a memoir, maybe writing anything, is answering the question, Who cares? You know it is going to be asked. Indeed. Who does care? A second question posed by the author Judith Barrington is equally important: "Why do you [the writer] care about this?" One reason we should care is that our culture seems to have a short memory. We forget the last bear market in a matter of days, the last politician with a hand in the public coffer even more quickly. It takes crises like the statistically remote chance of rescuing the nine coal miners at Quecreek in 2002 to focus a temporary spotlight on the underground miner, those hardrock stiffs who enriched corporate coffers with plenty of sweat, supported a family on chump-change wages, destroyed their hearing, sucked silica and coal dust into their lungs, joked their way around broken bones and bad backs, and rescued each other in nightmarish conditions. These people paved the way. They built the country physically, filling the counting rooms of the Guggenheims, Rockefellers, and Mellons. Absent that stash of national wealth, the Dow Jones 30 would not have come of age.

Also, there is an uncanny bond between mining people, largely unspoken, but there nonetheless. I suspect it is an outgrowth of that which comes from the daily sharing of hard, dangerous work. Anyone who has ever fished for crab during a storm in the Gulf of Alaska knows what I'm talking about. The feeling haunts me today, and it haunts a number of my contemporaries. Each June, at the annual meeting of the Mining History Association, the members present papers and hold discussions. At a recent meeting in Tonopah, Nevada, Joe Wagner, a former mine operations manager, presented a well-prepared discourse on the Missouri lead-zinc mines. But the closing slides were not about stopes and tunnels; they were a tribute to the crews who worked underground. Reaching this juncture in the presentation, he turned to a panel moderator and said, "Would you mind reading this for me. I can never finish it without falling apart, but it needs to be said." That's what it's like.

And there's something to be said for the privilege—after drilling, blasting, loading, and timbering—of standing on a piece of the earth where no man has ever stood before. It is a time to contemplate one's insignificance. It is a moment to reflect on the solemn chords of Verdi's Requiem.

Finally, aside from the desire to say a few words about an industry that's almost forgotten, it's interesting to take a look at the world of the 1950s to see how much has changed, and the speed at which change has occurred. It never occurred to me that terms like "hoistman" or "misfire" would disappear from common usage, or that the population of mining engineers and mill men would shrink to such an extent that they barely qualify for a heading in the Yellow Pages. In 1953 there were three television sets in the Silver Valley, a few more by 1956. The town of Wallace sported five or six whorehouses, Kellogg two or three. All are gone.

No one knew what a Honda was. Visa and Mastercard had not been invented. No one had ever heard of a compact disc or a liquid crystal display. *Crash* meant something that happened to an automobile or the stock market, not a hard drive. Two and a half bucks an hour was good money. Maybe the Beatles signify the point at which the rate of change went exponential. We need a milestone of some sort.

Change threw a world of complexity at us. Too many people, too many choices, too much to deal with and seemingly far less time to deal with it, too many problems that we can't seem to find answers for. Think of what happens to your psyche when you get a drop-down box on a computer screen: of the ten possible choices you barely understand what two of them mean. In desperation you select the one that makes the most sense, and an error message pops up: "This program has committed an illegal operation." To yearn for a simpler time is not altogether nostalgia.

Today the Bunker Hill mine is famous because it is one of the Environmental Protection Agency's biggest superfund sites, not because of the 430 million ounces of silver it produced or because it provided a living for thousands of families for more than a century. Today the aerial tramways carry gondolas full of skiers instead of ore-laden buckets descending from airy portals high up the mountain.

I understand now what I could not at the time—that the experience instilled in me a powerful sense of place and a keen appreciation for the impact people have on people. Hardrock miners are a breed apart. Their very survival—every minute of the eight-hour shift—is dependent on what every other worker does or does not do. Like an attack submarine's crew, they are all in the thing together. It matters little whether you are under an ocean or under a mountain.

My last shift at the Bunker Hill mine was in late spring 1960, just before what turned out to be a long, nasty labor strike called by the Mine, Mill and Smelter Workers Union. By that time I had graduated from the New Mexico School of Mines in Socorro (now New Mexico Tech), and it was time to move on. But what I had learned during the experiences of three previous summers in the mine had done a lot for a naive city kid trying to make his way. Because of these experiences, the world seemed a whole lot less threatening. I had stood at a bar in the Brass Rail saloon and drunk whiskey from a shot glass. I had held down a man's job and been paid for it.

Of course, it's a great exaggeration to assume that everyone I met or worked with might qualify to serve as altar boys or to sing in the choir. But my admiration for all of them is unbounded. I pray that I have done them

M. M^{c}CANN©   CONSOLIDATED SILVER MINE

justice in this book—that I have treated them with the
dignity, grace, and respect they earned.

The following story recounts my experience. All scientific facts have been verified, but the conversations, of
course, can be only as good as my memory. No work of
this type can be totally free of errors, but I have striven
to depict the material as accurately as possible.

Acknowledgments

Writing a memoir on events that took place fifty years in the past is like looking at a page of Morse code. It's all dots and dashes with spaces in between. The dots and dashes are what you recall; filling in the blank spots depends on who is available to help out. Others join the team to comment on what works and what doesn't. I thought the writing process would be easy. It isn't. It's hard work.

Former Bunker Hill employees and others appearing in the book gave generously of their time and hospitality. Chris Christopherson spent hours recalling jobs we tackled together underground. Edith Helfer, Chris's aunt, along with her husband, Ed, provided information on his early years. The chapter on the hoistmen could not have been written without the patient help of Virl McCombs, Lee "Curly" Seufert, and Gary Hoffman. The description of the traumatic fire at the Sunshine mine is a very condensed version of one written by Gene Hyde, which appeared in Jerry Dolph's book, *Fire in the Hole* (1994). In the backroom wine department of his store in

Wallace, geologist Norm Radford and I spent an entire afternoon discussing the formation of ore deposits.

Dora and Dee "Tater" Tatham filled in the missing spaces concerning characters I had remembered at Pat's Boarding House. Betty Lou Tatham Arens contacted me in Seattle to share additional information. Bob Hopper, president of the New Bunker Hill Mining Company, took time to give a private tour of the Kellogg tunnel and hoist rooms. Ray Chapman's accurate documentation of Silver Valley mining history was a comfort. June Chapman and Maxine Brewer shared memories of their friendship with Doris Woolf. Jack Morbeck recalled details of growing up in Kellogg during the 1950s. Some of the material in the chapter bearing Orval "Shorty" Drapeau's nickname were stories he told on himself. Ethel Drapeau also pitched in. Joe Gordon contributed information on the mine's infrastructure and personnel.

I drew information on executives who appeared at the Woolf's cocktail party from Robert Ramsey's book, *Men and Mines of Newmont* (1973). Former Minnesota Vikings tight end, John Beasley, explained how the team wound up in Murray and used Chris and Lucille's bar in the hotel as headquarters.

I attribute the enthusiasm I have for this subject to former professors and mentors at New Mexico Tech: Woodrow Latvala, Bill Long, William Bertholf, Anthony Budding, and Gerald Greene. They are behind the scenes on each page. Terry Abraham's staff at the University of Idaho library provided expert help during my research on the Kellogg tunnel.

Toni Reineke, Ph.D., runs a small business called Author's Advantage in a home overlooking Puget Sound.

It is to her that I owe a great thank-you and a generous amount of appreciation. Early on, she said, much like the piano teacher with a student in need of practice, "You have a book here. You must keep writing." At times I could pay her for the edits and formatting, sometimes not. It didn't matter.

The query process with a potential publisher, including various reviews of the manuscript, usually takes five or six months. Charles E. Rankin, editor in chief at the University of Oklahoma Press, kept me informed as the process evolved, answered all my questions, and offered continual encouragement. His courtesy and professionalism was a boost to my spirits. Alice K. Stanton, managing editor, kept me informed on what to expect as the manuscript moved closer to production. I have a new perspective on what it takes to turn a collection of words into a book. And to Sheila Berg, copyeditor, I owe a debt of gratitude for smoothing out the manuscript's rough spots and unraveling the mysterious array of punctuation conventions required for the printed page. If anyone thinks copyediting is an easy job, read *The Chicago Manual of Style*'s fifteen pages devoted to the comma.

Thanks also to my writer's group emerging from the University of Washington's Non-Fiction Writing Program: Rose Mary Gordon, Nancy Reichley, Jim Teeters, Rachel Zimmer, Sarah Gage, Sven Couch, Sheila Kelly, and Debbie Staub.

My kids, Jesse, Anna, and Andrew, listened to exaggerated versions of these stories as youngsters and never complained. Of course, at the time they were a captive audience. I hope they didn't mind. Friends Jan and Raye Murray used up a whole pad of sticky notes correcting typos I had overlooked. And to Mary, a good and kind wife, I offer my gratitude mostly for being who she is and keeping me on track; the fact that she happens to be skilled with brush and pen just adds to the journey.

A Room for the Summer

1

Lux Rooms

I left home on Saturday, June 2, 1956. It's not that you never set foot in the door again—just that it feels like you're only a visitor as time goes on, and home becomes somewhere else. I owned a light blue 1939 Chevrolet coupe with four tires, six spark plugs, a distributor, intake and exhaust valves for six pistons, a water pump, and little else. You didn't have to be a computer technician to fix it.

The long pull up the hairpin curves of Pine Canyon on U.S. Highway 2 north of Wenatchee grew tougher as blankets of heat rolled down from the basalt rimrock, melting the asphalt. As the steel blue Columbia River slipped away in the rearview mirror, I felt the charm and charisma of upper-middle-class life in Seattle receding as well—barbecued steak, extra-dry manhattans, gleaming coral and cream Ford Crown Victorias, luxurious Chrysler Imperials. I chafed a little under the constraints imposed by our first chakra, the one that provides food, shelter, and clothing and protection from the physical world; where we learn what we *should* do and how we *should* behave. But safe or not, there's a time to start making your own mistakes, to roll the dice and see what happens next. At age eighteen my time had arrived, and in the great Anglo-Saxon spirit of doing something—build a memorial, buy stock, get married—whatever it is, my gut told me to find a job in the mountains. I always felt good in the mountains. Any range, just about anywhere, would do. Some, like the North Cascades, were friends of mine.

At my family's version of the leaving-home ceremony, well-meaning parental warnings rang out across the driveway in the View Ridge neighborhood. "Be careful now." "Be sure and write," they said. "Try and find a nice place to stay." "Are you sure you want to do this? The other boys have jobs here in town."

"Yup. Don't worry," I said. "Kellogg isn't the end of the earth. I'll let you know how it goes. I've got to get going now. Bye." So I left, with half a tank of thirty-cent gas and everything I owned stuffed behind the front and only seat.

A job offer tucked into the overhead visor from the Bunker Hill Company kept the accelerator glued to the floor, but truth be told, I hadn't the least idea of where I would stay for the summer and who I would meet, or more than a vague idea of where Kellogg, Idaho, was located. I knew it was in the Bitterroot Mountains. I was obsessed by the idea that the Old West lay out there in isolated towns, where the lace-booted mining engineer held court and made decisions that affected men's lives and filled corporate coffers. Drill and blast, drive tunnel, eat smoke, pump water, cuss, spit, and chew. Drink whiskey, draw maps, cut brush, use a transit, and spot diamond drill holes. Look at every outcrop. "Go to the mountains and learn their secrets." John Muir said it all.

The letter minced few words. On crisp bond paper emblazoned with the company's logo, it said, "Your job will be a miner's helper at $2.37 per hour. We appreciate your interest in our company and hope you enjoy your employment and stay in Kellogg. Report to the hiring office on June 4 for further instructions." Walt Scott, the hourly personnel manager, signed it.

As I broke over the last curve in the canyon, fields of winter wheat the color of thousand-dollar bills stretched before me one hundred fifty miles to the eastern horizon and Spokane. Here and there a patch showed golden signs of ripening. The Chevy's six-volt filament-tube radio with cracked plastic knobs snapped back to life on Wenatchee's only radio station, KPQ. Hank Snow's big western tune "I'm Moving On" played across the airwaves. Sure, I might have been flatass broke, but there's nothing like up-tempo traveling music to put you in new-shoe spirits.

> That big eight-wheeler rollin' down the track,
> means your true lovin' daddy ain't comin' back.
> I'm moving on, I'll soon be gone.
> You were flyin' too high for my little old sky.
> I'm movin' on.

Hank made a lot of vocals in the 1950s that put him on the charts, but he could pick a pretty fair solo break on the guitar too—straight and clean and crisp.

I listened real close because I planned to pick my own version of that solo by the end of the summer on a plywood

Stella guitar I had purchased at Sears for twelve bucks. It came with a Mel Bay instruction book. The encouraging cover read, "Simple to learn. Amazing results. Fast." What it didn't say was that if the steel strings are a quarter inch above the fret board, your fingers will bleed and ache just trying for a C-major chord. Humility arrives quickly enough when you first pick up a guitar.

I had joined the Book of the Month Club and brought along two high-minded volumes: Churchill's *Triumph and Tragedy* and *The Silver Chalice* by Thomas Costain. The books lent an air of respectability and intellectualism to an undertaking that probably lacked both. Besides, they were the introductory freebies.

In a few hours Mica Peak and the forested hills surrounding Spokane took shape. After shifting gears in a seemingly endless succession of pre-freeway stoplights downtown, I passed through Coeur d'Alene and struggled up the long grade leading to the summit of Fourth of July pass. Chevrolets were built in Michigan, which is flat. It always seemed to me that the engineers at GM had never seen a mountain highway or realized what the tiny radiators did when those of us who happen to live in the West drove on one. We didn't just drive along, however. We performed engine management, sweeping the instrument cluster every thirty seconds for signs of trouble. Fortunately, there were real gauges with needles that told how hot the engine was in degrees Fahrenheit, and when the gas gauge read empty you were out of gas. As I approached the 3,079-foot summit, the temperature gauge inchwormed toward 190 and then 200. Soon the pungent odor of hot antifreeze seeped through the firewall—a harbinger of things to come. I pulled off on the shoulder as the physics of boiling water overtook the plans of a mere mortal like me, assuming everything would work out on the downgrade on the other side. But steam hissed out of the radiator cap and deep-seated, distant rumblings emanated from under the hood. That engine and I had done time together, serving shade-tree mechanic apprenticeship as all high school lads did in the 1950s. I knew every wrist pin, every valve guide, every bearing shim. It deserved to be treated with deference and understanding. I decided to call it a day.

How do you wind up on a distant mountain pass, far from hearth and home, with a boiling radiator? In my case it started with an idea about how to make a living, taking root by virtue of water and fertilizer, luck, and predestination. My high school chums, Jim, Ted, and Phil, and I spent precious little time discussing what we intended to do the rest of our lives. Someone probably said, "I'm going to medical school," or "I'm going to run a hotel." No one said, "I'm going to be a major in the U.S. Army." These were the two choices available: go to college or join the army. Not wanting to offend the military with a bad attitude, I chose college along with the others.

I remember a guy with glasses as thick as Coke-bottle bottoms going on at some length about banking and economics, supply and demand, and all that stuff. What I understood about those subjects was that my body *demanded* contact with the opposite sex, of which there appeared to be almost no *supply*. Intrinsically, I suppose I understood the concept. But who else besides the Federal

Reserve Board chairman cared about supply and demand? I clung to the idea that a career lay out there in the unknown that made you want to get up in the morning and go to work.

Serendipity intervened on my behalf, as it does sometimes when you and God are on the same wavelength. It came in the form of a family friend, Robert I. Bennett, six years my senior. Bob had attended the Montana School of Mines in Butte after a tour in the navy. In the process of driving a fish-ladder tunnel near Granite Falls, Washington, Bob learned of an old copper prospect, the Bonanza Queen. In 1955 the price of copper went sky high. But the Queen was no easy touch; she lay like an osprey nest perched high on the almost vertical north slopes of Long Mountain, near the ghost town of Monte Cristo, Washington.

One day Bob phoned. Would I like to go along and help bring down some pipe fittings from a tunnel blasted in a cliff six hundred feet above the road? I said, "Sure, you bet," and spent the evening greasing my black leather boots and stuffing a Trapper Nelson pack with rain slicker, lunch, and canteen. Before there was high-tech outdoor gear, there was low-tech, and the Trapper met all the qualifications: a canvas sack hung on a couple of one-by-two-inch slats. A generation of hikers knows that the narrow straps cut into your shoulders like tourniquets when the pack was loaded with canned peaches and Dinty Moore beef stew and other staples. They were heavy, but they fed us long before the existence of freeze-dried turkey tetrazzini or dehydrated Swiss steak.

We left Seattle before sunrise, rattling along the sinuous road hugging the South Fork of the Stillaguamish River.

We drank hot coffee from a thermos. Bob entertained with a string of back-to-back mining tales and spit black globs of Copenhagen chew into a soup can at predictable intervals.

"When I was in school, we drove a drift from the Mountain Con over underneath the old Orphan Girl mine to get at a bunch of high-grade ore. God, it was hot. One of the stopes was on fire." And he pointed out the way the highway curves were laid out on the Everett and Monte Cristo railroad-grade tangents.

By the time we crossed a log bridge spanning Deer Creek and had the red Ford pickup parked next to the Queen's dump, it was close to 9:30 A.M. The skies were clear. Steam rose from the brush as it does in the summer when the night dew surrenders to the sun. Bob pointed his arm in the air about eighty degrees from horizontal. "It's up there." A terse understatement if ever there was one. Nothing to do but throw the packs on and start up, first skirting the towering cliff bands and then using roots and saplings for handholds to gain elevation. There is something in us, on occasion, that thrives on adversity; looking back on a few Cascade bushwhacks, I have to say that hours of breaststroking through spiky devil's club, nettles, and slide alder is punishment going downhill. Going *uphill*, the experience is borderline masochistic. Still, we persisted. Bob summed it all up very nicely while mopping up a stream of sweat soaking his hickory shirt. "Christ, partner, the fecundity of the foliage is just overwhelming!"

Finally, at a rocky promontory on the side opposite the tunnel entrance we stopped the ascent, put on hard hats, and climbed down a snow-filled avalanche chute toward the opening in a cliff. As far as I was concerned, this was about as good as it gets. I was scared spitless. The distance between my boots and the red pickup was mostly air. Fortunately, we had a rope tied to a convenient cedar. Inside the entrance a chill breeze struck us head-on. Our lights flashed around the walls, lighting up strips of high-grade copper ore glistening saffron in the damp quiet.

"Isn't that just a beautiful sight?" Bob asked. I had to agree. It was beautiful. It represented wealth but wealth a long way from a bank deposit. A late 1890s hand-cranked pneumatic drill stood upright in an opening. It looked like the miners of '98 had left in a hurry, saying, "She's deep enough for me," when a flood on the South Fork washed out the watergrade rail line for the third and last time. I grabbed as much ore as I could carry for souvenir purposes, and we headed back up the rope and down the mountain.

On the return to Seattle we drank beer and swore. Bob told more stories, bigger ones than on the way up. By the time I walked through the door at home I knew what I wanted to do. To spend a day in a mine, out in the woods, seemed to me about as much fun as anyone could have. I was hooked on the concept. The hot, dirty, sweaty part of the job would be acquired soon enough, changing the meaning of "fun," but for the time being, my experience had been a defining moment.

This new perspective caused a family uproar of no small proportion. My father, a consulting civil engineer, held distinctly patrician beliefs, the fundamental one being that people of good breeding and intelligence work with their heads, not their hands and backs. In a word, white-collar jobs.

The trip to the Bonanza Queen changed everything. In the spring of my sophomore year at Whitman College, I applied for admission to the New Mexico School of Mines, in far-off Socorro ("help" in Spanish). At the same time, I sent a letter to the Bunker Hill Company rustling a job, any job, at their huge operation in Idaho.

I brokered the news on both decisions to my father by letter; an uneasy silence followed. I wanted his approval, but I knew this was not going to be a quick sale.

At home on spring break, we had a Well-how's-it-going-son? discussion in the living room. Dad sat back in his easy chair, and I perched on the fireplace hearth.

"I got your letter. So what's the draw to this mining idea? What do you want to do that for?" he asked.

"Well, just because." My answer lacked detail.

Never one to give up at the first sign of resistance, he said, "I know you and Bob are good friends and had a lot of fun up there in the mountains, but that doesn't mean you want to devote your life to it."

I took umbrage to this bit of fatherly logic because I was looking for encouragement, not a critique. I knew my decision was steeped in instinct and intuition, and I was blowing in the wind. On the other hand, I *knew*.

I fired back a testy "Maybe, maybe not," with all the bass timbre my voice could muster. "It's a recognized engineering degree like yours."

Not a bad answer, I thought. He looked surprised and scratched his forehead thoughtfully. Things were changing fast between my father and me at that point—like St. Paul's revelation on the road to Damascus.

"Well, I think you should look at some other options. There's electrical engineering, chemical—lots of new plastics being developed. You could study law, medicine, all professional fields. Just make sure you feel you're doing the right thing."

I wasn't sure what to say in reply. It seemed like the ball was in my court. If I had possessed ample prescience at the time, my reply would have been, Joseph Campbell is going to write *The Power of Myth* thirty years from now, in which he will state: "If you follow your bliss, you put yourself on a kind of track that has been there all the while, waiting for you, and the life you ought to be living is the one you are living."

Instead, I replied, "I'll think about it, but I've already sent my applications in."

"OK. I hope it works out for you."

Whether it was the right thing to do for the wrong reason or the wrong thing to do for the right reason didn't matter. I was gone.

Stalled out on a mountain pass with a hot engine a few months later, and only five hours from home, I had a problem of another kind to solve. The sun and the radiator temperature appeared to be going down at about the same rate. Just before it got totally dark I decided to bivouac with the available resources: a worn-out sleeping bag and a small tarp.

"You wanna be in the outdoors, you're *in* the outdoors," I said out loud, and felt foolish since obviously there was no one within earshot. I stuck a flashlight in my mouth to light the way along the crest of a stony ridge and set off through the underbrush clutching a green, canvas-clad sleeping bag to my chest. The bag, stuffed with a stringy substance called kapok, kept you reasonably comfortable down to about fifty-five degrees and weighed nine pounds. It would not sell well today. I stumbled around, cussing the rough terrain and things I couldn't see in the dark.

I spread the tarp on an area with only small lumps; they looked softer than some of the bigger ones. I crawled in the sack with all my clothes on, knowing it was going to be a long night, and lay on my back looking up through the bitterbrush and pine canopy. A sliver of moon rose over the mountains to the east. My comfortable room and soft bed with clean sheets in Seattle seemed a lot farther away than a mere three hundred miles of blacktop. Then I began to wonder how and where I would find a place to stay. It struck me that I didn't know a single person in the Silver Valley, or where to begin the search.

I wondered about working underground, whether I could cut the mustard. Would the rest of the crew accept me? Would it be a tough town with drunken fights and crimes of passion? My thoughts strayed to a girlfriend I had left behind. Today this adventure reminds me of what you find out about the stock market *after* you start investing. The revelations are astounding, as is the cost of the education. Black bears and other things come out of the woods at night. The difference between what you know and what you don't know is what causes anxiety. I couldn't remember if black bears attacked humans straight out like old silvertip, *Ursus horribilis*. I figured if they do, I won't need to worry long, and if they don't, I won't have to worry either. I drifted off to sleep listening to the sounds of the great outdoors doing what it does at night.

By six o'clock the next morning I lay in a state of near-hypothermia; my hips and shoulders felt as if they had been beaten on by neighborhood kids wielding ball peen hammers. But the sun came up as promised, immediately liberating that spirit-warming alpine perfume from high-country firs.

In the mid-fifties if you left a car on the shoulder of a major highway, not only was the car still there the next day, but all the parts, including hubcaps, were intact as well. After the briefest of morning hygiene, I drove down through the serpentine curves until in only a few miles the highway struck across a vast wetland-plain fed from backwaters on the Coeur d'Alene River.

Something incongruous, out of whack, appeared in the picture before me. The South Fork, like all rivers in Idaho, was supposed to be crystal clear and light blue. Instead it was the color of white mice, muddy and opaque even in the sunlight. Glacial sediments, I thought. Second thought: Impossible, no glaciers.

I watched the river carefully as I made my way toward Kellogg, disheartened that it never changed color. I stopped at one of the bridges and crawled underneath an abutment for a closer look. No signs of algae or weeds appeared on the submerged rocks or cutbank, just a thin coating of floury mud. This was my introduction to lead water, a mixture of mountain stream, metalliferous mine water and mill tailings, and sewage from upstream communities stretching to the Continental Divide, fifteen or twenty miles away.

Undeterred, I advanced through a gentle green countryside of rolling hills that gave way to increasingly mountainous terrain. I drove past the settlement of Kingston, then Pinehurst, and as I rounded a sweeping curve the three-hundred-foot smokestack of Bunker Hill's lead smelter lay before me with its sulfurous plume streaming out toward Montana.

The smelter's slag pile, an immense black dune fifty feet high and three football fields wide, loomed ahead of me for more than a mile on Jackass Flats. Folklore has it that Noah Kellogg's mule discovered the Bunker Hill vein while Kellogg took a nap.

A cluster of houses and the Last Chance tavern stood close by on the right, identified by a small sign, Smelterville. Amusing name, I thought. It could have been Smelterburg, or Smelterdelphia, but "ville" certainly works. Farther in the distance mill buildings and tailing dams perched on the valley edge next to residential neighborhoods. The earth looked like it had been turned inside out, sanded, and repainted, which in many respects it had been.

Near the smelter, the steep, dusty slopes were barren of vegetation and soil. I thought of the Spanish word *quemado*, meaning "scorched." If you include the inescapable pungency of sulfur dioxide, the atmosphere also represented eighty years of mining culture and unimaginable events, some better known and some better forgotten. A lot had gone on here, and a lot was still going on. Headframes standing like sentinels over vertical shafts, tunnels, and dumps were scattered around all the slopes to the south; roads benched into the sides for exploration drilling and erosion control spiraled up to the timberline far above the valley floor. I thought it was the grandest thing. It took a while to soak in.

This first impression of Kellogg wasn't exactly threatening, but it wasn't exactly nurturing either. Wallace, another mining town, lay a few miles farther up-valley, so I decided to continue on and see what it had to offer. The mountainsides took on a deeper verdant hue with each passing mile away from the smelter. A stand of second-growth Douglas fir and white pine took over the landscape, interspersed with more tunnels and waste rock dumps half-hidden in the undergrowth, like the Consolidated Silver Mine and Mill. There must be some tall tales buried in those weathered timbers and shot rock, I reasoned. What had gone on—riches, success, and glory, or double dealing, treachery, lawsuits, and heartbreak? Blood and sweat soaked into the drifts and shafts? Kept promises or broken ones? I made a covenant with my spirit to haunt every one I could get to before the summer was over, dope it out, try to figure what was left behind and why.

Wallace housed a railroad, a highway, a residential section, and a neoclassic downtown that seemed to step out of a well-attended 1930s. Storefronts sported polished brass kickplates and doorknobs. Glossy dark green paint trimmed huge plate glass windows. High-grade silver ore adorned the entrance to stock brokerages like that of the Pennaluna Company. Red brick buildings bore the names of local entrepreneurs and politicians—the H. J. Rossi building, the Arment—complete with terra-cotta fascias. A confusing array of creeks and rivers made their way through town, crowding the residents into a triangular space about four city blocks per side. Ninemile and Canyon Creeks flowed in from mountain valleys to the north, and Placer Creek roared through a concrete channel draining the Bad Tom Mountain country to the south. These tributaries joined the Coeur d'Alene River flowing from east to west right through town.

At 10:00 A.M. that Sunday, downtown Wallace was virtually deserted except for a busload of fellow pilgrims stretching their legs at the Greyhound bus terminal. The snowpack runoff had peaked a few weeks before my arrival, but I remember the background music all this water made, trying to get downhill as fast as possible, reorganizing the streambed, breaking the quiet, and sounding strange but good to my citified eardrums. I stopped for a few minutes in the warm sunlight, awed by the manner in which the mountains seemed to hold the town like a pair of darkly inviting bookends. The transition from town to mountain took place in the distance of maybe three steps from one to the other. It seemed you could start prospecting over the fence from someone's backyard if the mood happened to strike. Now this idea captivated my attention for a moment, but, captivated or not, I was in for a surprising turn of events.

I drove around town for a few minutes hoping to find a room-for-rent sign staked out in front of an elegantly whitewashed, turn-of-the-century mansion. As I negotiated a U-turn on Sixth Street, only a stone's throw from the South Fork, I spotted a two-story frame building with maroon siding and white trim at 212½ Sixth Street. A sign, Lux Rooms, hung over the corner with a white arrow underneath pointing to an entrance on the north side. I knocked on that door thinking, this looks perfect, right on the river. I hope they have a vacancy. I'll decorate my room with crossed snowshoes and fishing gear. I'll play the guitar and send pictures of my new digs to friends back home. Dad will be impressed with what a savvy youngster he turned out.

At first no one answered. A discouraging half minute went by. I turned around to leave. As I did so, a fiftyish-looking woman unlocked the door. She wore a floral print bathrobe and fuzzy pink slippers. She looked disturbed but not all the way to angry.

Before I could say anything, she said, "Sorry, Sonny, we're not open."

I didn't care much for the "Sonny" handle, and her comment struck me as odd, begging the question, Open for what?

I stammered back, "I've got a job at the Bunker Hill mine. I need a room for the summer. I saw the sign out front. Any vacancies?"

She said, "You what?"

We stood and looked at each other in what might be called a moment of absolute miscommunication. We were a long way apart.

Then two more women, much younger but also in robes, poked their heads around the doorway. "What's going on? Don't he know we're not open yet?"

Ignoring them for the moment, floral print and pink fuzzies turned to me and said, "All we have here, my friend, is girls. And by the looks of you, I doubt you could afford a half hour here, let alone a whole summer!"

She paused. "You should try Pat's Boarding House in Kellogg. They're more in the line of what you're looking for."

At this point in the dialogue, it sunk in that "Rooms" preceded by "Lux" in this town meant something considerably different from "Rooms" as in "Rooms for Rent." So in essence what I had just done was attempt to rent a room in a whorehouse; and it was Sunday, the day of rest.

Damn, I thought. I am now stuck in the greenhorn's nightmare in less time than it takes to tell about it. I need to rethink. This is all new. No need to tell anyone about this. Who would ever know?

I cleared my throat. "Yes ma'am," I said. "I see. Yes, of course." I took a deep breath. "Sorry to have been a bother."

"No bother at all," she said with a smile that belied knowledge of the way the world worked and I had yet to figure out.

One of madam's minions, a blond, said, "Come back when you have more time. No, come back when you get paid!" All present laughed and gave joyous applause.

Except me. I strode back to my only touchstone, a worn-out Chevy, with a dignified cadence that disguised my embarrassment. I prayed for the engine to start. Ignition on. Clutch in. Touch the accelerator on the first couple of turns. I pulled away from the parking lot at about the same speed as an advancing glacier.

Driving back to Kellogg, the thought occurred to me that I might have attained a kind of celebrity status. The madam might say during a crew meeting or a quiet moment, "Remember the kid who showed up on Sunday morning and wanted a room for the whole summer? I mean, sweet Jesus, the whole summer!"

2

$2.37

The town of Kellogg straddles both sides of the Coeur d'Alene River, each with its peculiar mixture of residences and businesses. The original residential section and a block-long stretch of bars and shops, known locally as downtown, lies to the south against the slopes of Wardner Peak. Intuition led me to search there first for Pat's Boarding House. Men, for the most part, seem to have an intrinsic faith in their ability to find things on their own. It's a trait whose hard-learned lessons often lead to humility. Dead reckoning is like asking directions to the airport in a place like Malta. The gas station attendant answers in Maltese and points down the road. You nod your head in feigned understanding and mutter something like, "Got it." A hundred yards later you're lost. It's a great process, and you get to see a lot of country that way.

On that June day in 1956 I approached Kellogg for the second time, turning off U.S. Highway 10 at the Roxy Theater, showing *The Conquerer* starring John Wayne and Susan Hayward. Uphill past the post office a resilient assemblage of maples and oaks stood proudly beside the dozen or so streets, having miraculously survived years of attack from sulfuric acid smelter fumes and tough winters. The greenery lent an air of quiet, genteel respectability to this part of town, which appeared to have been hooked by gravity and pulled downhill from the site of the original Bunker Hill strike at Wardner, a hamlet perched a thousand feet higher in Milo Gulch. The streets ran at weird angles to one another, because when God made the gulch, he forgot to lay it out in rectangles. The topography slants.

I expected to see cookie-cutter company housing but didn't. Each home displayed the kind of individuality arrived at after three owners, thirty years, and five, tight-budget remodelings. The eleven o'clock Sunday sermons had come to a solemn close, and respectable gatherings of the faithful filed out chapel doors, standing around, chatting in their Sunday best. The Catholic congregation, as I recall, displayed a statistically significant number of redheads, maybe 40 percent.

A drugstore occupied one corner of the intersection joining Main and McKinley Streets. Beneath it lay the Korner Klub tavern. On the opposite side a sign advertised Vern Sass Jewelers, which came off the tongue a little different from the way it read. I turned down McKinley Street, counting twenty-two drinking resorts in one block, open for business, Sunday or not. Outwardly, the impression was one of muted prosperity. I remember thinking, Kind of hard to make this place shine.

I stopped midstreet and asked a chap exiting the Rio Club Hotel directions to Pat's.

"Oh, Poffenroth's place? Go down there opposite the YMCA building and hang a left. It's up the alley and around the corner. Can't miss it."

I found a two-story building about the size of a small-town dime store chiseled into the slope just where he had indicated. It was a concrete box painted eye-rest green. Evenly spaced single-hung windows ran across the sides and front of both floors. Descriptors like *strong* or *functional* might have worked, but it was a structure overlooked for inclusion in *Architectural Digest*. On balance, it appeared to look more like a boardinghouse than the Lux Rooms, and I had begun to acquire some judgment on the subject.

I parked and peered into a front window. Four or five masonite-topped rectangular tables occupied most of the room, which was obviously a mess hall. A sea of waxed and polished, nine-inch-square, green-and-white tile adorned the floor. Things looked shipshape and businesslike. As I stood there like Don Quixote before the windmills, a nearby exhaust fan shot a draft of apple pie into the alley.

I sensed that my fortunes were about to gain some altitude, so I pushed the door open a few feet.

"Anybody home?" A voice from a distant recess answered, "Yup, just a minute." A strong, pleasant woman in her early to mid-forties rounded the corner, wiping her hands on a flour-dusted apron.

"Name's Dora. I'm the cook. What can I do fer ya'?"

At this point in the odyssey I worked hard at not surrendering to a growing sense of desperation on how this was all going to turn out—not unlike the question Clark must have asked Lewis every morning: "Where we gonna' camp tonight Merriwether?" "Damfino!"

I cleared my throat. "Well, I've got a job at the Bunker Hill, and I'm trying to find a place to stay for the summer."

"You're welcome to stay here if ya want to. It runs three bucks a day—room and board. We have one room left, number thirteen just at the top of the stairs there, if you want to look it over."

"Be right back."

I tore up the stairs two at a time and entered number thirteen thinking, This has to work. I'll make it work. The eight-by-eight-foot room looked out over the tar-papered roofs of bars and stores. I slid the window open a notch. The breeze carried an odd mix of cigar and smelter smoke, stale beer, pepperoni, and Precambrian slate. But redemption: the room had a view—"territorial" in the parlance of real estate agents—looking out to the north at the Bitterroot Mountains and the Coeur d'Alene National Forest. The room was stuffed with an iron frame bed, a straightback chair in one corner and a cheap, three-drawer dresser. The dresser stood so close to the front of the bed I couldn't open it more than four inches. No bullet holes and no kicked-in plasterboard from bodies ricocheting down the hall toward the common bathroom. I went back and told Dora, "Sure, you bet. That'll work just fine. What do I need to do?"

"We need to know who ya are and where yer a-workin'. Aside from that the guys come and go as they please. Our regulars are a fairly quiet bunch and we don't seem to have a whole lot of trouble with drinkin' and hell raisin' from them. But with them young tramp miners—that's another story." She paused a moment, sizing me up with an experienced eye.

"You've never been in a mining camp before, have you?"

"Nope."

"Ol' Uncle Bunker's a pretty good mine. The bosses and such are pretty good. Not like at some mines I could name. Anyway, as for here, you'll find the food good because I do it all, breakfast and supper. Guys make their own dang lunches from that table over there."

"What about the money? Do you need a deposit?"

"No, not if you've for sure got a job with Bunker Hill. We have a payroll deduction plan worked out with the company. But you'll have to talk to Mrs. Sims tomorrow. She's the actual boss here. You can move your stuff in now if ya want." She turned away as if to tend the pies getting hot, then turned back again.

"You need to know the schedule. Breakfast starts at 5:30 A.M. and runs up to noon in case you're on swing shift. Supper is from 4:00 to 6:30 in the evening. Steak night is Thursday. We generally serve fish on Fridays. You're kind of skinny. Want a sandwich? Help yourself. We'll be serving supper in a while."

I took an immediate liking to this gracious woman, the kind of person who restores your faith in humanity. Friend Bennett's last words of advice before I left Seattle rang true: "Get in solid with the cook. In camp, the cook is the main thing." My Robert W. Service–inspired image of a cabin on the river with crisscrossed snowshoes evaporated. I needed succor and comfort, and a place to call my own even if it wasn't. As the day wore on I felt less embarrassed by my encounter at the Lux Rooms. Providence had shown down brightly upon me, for the madam had steered me in the right direction after all. Well, what the hell, a start is a start, I thought. Make your own damn luck.

I ventured downstairs to the mess hall after unloading and stowing my sparse possessions. I picked a vacant spot at one of the tables starting at one minute past four o'clock to fill up with my new peer group. On occasions like these, you size up the competition in a hurry. It was a disparate collection of age and ethnicity. They looked a whole lot bigger and tougher than I was. All I could see from one end of the table to the other were hairy paws the size of cantaloupes and forearms the size of fence posts. One guy wore a sweaty full-length union suit, Police-brand braces, and a pair of black wool pants. He was a quiet fellow. I imagined it was because he only had one tooth.

Food arrived in quick succession, piled high on thick putty-colored crockery with a green band on the rim: boiled carrots, lumpy mashed potatoes, and a platter of well-done roast beef. Some bowls emptied before making the circuit around the table. It didn't matter. Others appeared from somewhere. There seemed to be no convention about how much was too much.

Conversation was minimal to nonexistent for the first ten minutes. The idea was eating. Every so often someone started a mining story about heavy ground or sinking shaft in a subterranean downpour. No one mentioned women. In between the clatter of silverware and thirty miners eating dinner, it was mostly "Pass the butter" or "Here with the bread."

I kept my mouth shut and ears open, listening for a protocol if there was one—a sign of what worked and what didn't. In retrospect, I think it came down to everyone minding their own business and a preoccupation with the thought if they weren't stuck clear the hell out here in no-man's land trying to eke out a buck, they'd be with family back in Oklahoma or Colorado. Most were bachelors, or near-bachelors, or tramp miners on the move. Some may have been camping at the boarding-house until they could bring a wife and kids to Kellogg. In those days a job was a job. You did what you had to do. There was nothing on men's minds so much as pay-day. A few, judging by the way they mined, must have been sheepherders or truck drivers, but I came to that judgment later on, wiser and more experienced after a whole month on the job.

At that first dinner I realized that if I had any doubts about what I was doing, it was too late; the train had left the station and I was on a fast freight bound somewhere. The question my father had asked at the outset of this odyssey crossed my mind: "What do you want to do that for?" My reply was only what you might call a good esti-mate at the time. If asked at dinner that night my answer would have been, "Because it feels just fine. This will be my new gang if I survive the experience. I'll worry about whether it was a good idea or not some other time. In fact, I don't *care* if it was a good idea or not."

A mean-looking hombre with a big scar over his right eye asked a man across the table: "Wasn't you pulling shifts at the Mountain Con in Butte last winter?"

"Yeah. Talk about misery. Stopes so hot you think yer in hell one minute, and by the end of the shift soaking wet. Five minutes later you're freezing your ass on top, and it's forty-two below zero on that god-forsaken hill. I come out of there and my diggers froze solid between the shaft and the dry house. Had to get a bar and set me loose or I would've died on the spot. Never seen such a country."

Another fragment of conversation floated by: "Hell, if it weren't for bad manners, I wouldn't have no manners a'tall."

Eventually, the guy with the scar picked me out. I tried to look small.

"You just come in, kid?"

"Yup."

"Where you workin'?"

"Bunker Hill. I'll find out what the deal is tomorrow."

"Been here before?

"Nope. First time."

"Go to college, do you?"

"Yup."

"If I were you, kid, I'd keep going to school. You quit going and you'll be chasin' these mining camps one after the other forever—just like me and all these other stiffs. Ya never get nowhere 'less you're lucky enough to find a good woman and settle down in one place. You got the right idea."

"Sure thing."

"Stay out of the bars late Friday and Saturday nights. Leastways, out in Pinehurst. Finns can be tough, ya know. Keep your head down and you'll do all right."

"Thanks. Appreciate the talk."

The next day I made my way to the hiring office, just a block away in the old red brick YMCA building. A crowd of job seekers lined the steps leading up to the office. Thinking that I was probably already on the fast track with my letterhead offer, I slipped past them and placed it surreptitiously on the secretary's desk. She motioned me into Mr. Scott's office without saying anything. I drew some hostile looks from guys I hoped I might not see again.

After doing the payroll paperwork to ensure the government wouldn't collapse without my contribution, Mr. Scott said the main thing to do next was to get over to the clinic and pass the physical. If that went okay, I was to report to the mine office at 6:30 A.M. the next day.

"You know where the mine is. When you get there, ask the foreman—probably Paul Sloan or Jim Cantrell—for instructions. You need to be dressed and ready to go when the man-train pulls out at seven o'clock. If you miss it, it's a difficult business to get back on track. No pun intended. You'll need a hard hat and hard-toe boots, which you can buy at the office and have deducted from your paycheck. We supply headlamps and all the tools you need. You'll be a miner's helper, so your pay is $2.37 per hour. Oh, I forgot. Student or not, you must join the Mine, Mill and Smelter Workers Union. Dues are five bucks a month."

"Why do I have to join the union?"

"You don't have a choice. It's a closed shop, and our contract stipulates that all workers must join the union, period."

"What do I get for my union dues then?"

"They represent you every three years in bargaining with the company for more money and benefits. If you go out on strike, sometimes the union will pay a family for a box of groceries once a week."

"You mean no cash?"

"No cash."

It occurred to me that there must be a whole lot of dough going somewhere else if the union could only ante up a few beans and potatoes for a striking miner. I harbored grave doubts that the union would consider me a family. Crap on the union, I thought. I've got to make enough money to survive. I wonder if I'd have to go on strike even if I didn't want to?

He saw my quizzical expression and said, "You would go out like everyone else, because that's the way it is. And you won't want to scab on the labor bosses and go through a picket line. Don't ask me why, you just won't. But don't worry about it. The contract isn't up until December of 1959."

I said, "Okay, union dues it is then," picked up my papers, and headed over to the clinic where I was examined by a Dr. Staley. I think Doc Staley was a pretty good M.D. He treated a lot of guys with cracked heads and broken bones over the years. But the preemployment physical amounted to little more than being able to fog a mirror, as the saying goes, and be free of hernias. I passed, and spent the rest of the day getting ready.

I had one problem: I had purchased a shiny aluminum lunch pail with a lousy tan thermos and red plastic cup inside. It looked too new, like a neon sign advertising the just arrived greenhorn. And not being smart enough to realize that even old hands bought new buckets from time to time, I took it up the mountain behind my room and dunked it in a mud puddle and scratched it up. Pretty soon it looked like a new bucket, artificially aged.

As the evening came to a close, I took the twelve-dollar guitar out of the three-dollar case and tuned it according to the Mel Bay instruction book. My fingertips hurt so bad after that experience that, with a newfound respect for those who could actually play, I put it away. I ran a process check on my Westclox wind-up alarm with the radium dial to ensure it would go off at 5:30 A.M. But I needn't have worried. I lay abed all night with that brand of anxiety you cook up before a big corporate pitch, or before a predawn flight from an airport twenty miles and two traffic jams away.

Dora had the grill fired up when I came down to the kitchen.

"How's it going? What would you like?"

"How about two eggs and hash browns?"

"Sure. Looks like yer goin' to work today. Don't let some of those dingbats get you down. They'll be after a new guy with all kinds of tricks—send you after a sky-hook. Here's yer eggs."

I grabbed a bowl of clingstone peaches in heavy syrup to help convince my stomach to squaff down two thousand calories before the sun came up. City kids aren't supposed to be up at that hour. I knew what I had to do. I ate. At the lunch-assembly table I laminated the first sandwich in a series, ultimately consuming, as my future boss, Jim Perkins, put it, "enough peanut butter to lubricate the wheels of progress for forty years."

As I drove to work that morning, streaks of sunlight shot down from the ridgeline four thousand feet above my left shoulder. Cool mountain air hanging in the low spots mingled with the sweet odor of reagents from the enormous flotation mill across the street. And the mine getting ready to go to work made its own special noise: transformers hummed, wheels squeaked high-pitched against the subdued murmur of loading and unloading and muted conversations. I left my car in the tiny parking lot below the office and joined the file of men heading up a long flight of wooden steps to the dry house, or Dry, where everyone changed from street clothes to work clothes. You won't hear the term "work clothes" in a mining camp; they're your "diggers." Armed with my bucket and diggers and my heart stuck somewhere around my tonsils, I marched across the crushed rock and rail tracks in the mine yard to the office. I was going to work, but this was a whole lot different from going to work at Ted Murphy's Service Station.

A bunch of snoose-chewing shift bosses stood around on the building's covered porch as I approached. They had to be bosses because they stood hunched over as if their backs hurt and tucked the thumbs of both hands under their armpits, or hooked them under suspenders or jacket lapels. All bosses do this. It gives them something to do with their hands, and rendered an air of machismo to the discussion. I asked one of the bosses where the new hires reported.

"Paul Sloan is the foreman what makes the assignments. He's at that desk over there."

"Morning. You're Wolff, I see. Physical's OK. Worked underground before?"

"Well, yeah, but not like this. That is, not a full-time job or anything."

"You're in engineering school—mining?"

"Yessir."

"Good. I'm going to partner you up with Chris Christopherson—he's one of our top hands. I want you to pay close attention to what he says and does. You understand?

The men get careless and next thing you know they're either in the hospital or pushin' up daisies. There is no such thing as a small accident underground."

"Yessir."

"You need to get a hook in the Dry. You know where that is? And change out of your street clothes. Make it a point to memorize the number on your basket. You'll use the same one every day. Get your hard hat and boots, and check out a lamp from the lamp room over there and be on the man-train no later than five to seven."

"How will I recognize Chris?" I asked, because the hundred or so miners gathered around the man-train all looked the same to me in a polyglot sort of way. Rock dust and drill oil stained every ragged jacket and pair of blackened pants, although the hard hats provided some differentiation. Some were plain aluminum. Most were a deep maroon-colored fiberglass, sitting on the owners' heads in various horizontal and vertical angles. Most were Coeur d'Alene–style hats with the rim all around to keep water from running down your neck. Others were Butte-style hats with a bill in front and no rim.

"See those two guys standing next to the last car? The tall drink-of-water in the bib overalls is Bill Lathrop. He's relief shiftin' for Art Russell this week. Chris is the shorter fella next to him. He's on Bill's crew. I think Chris is square-settin' in the Okie stope—down in the May country. You'll get off on the big haulage level at 19 and ride over to the May Raise and go down to 20 or 21."

I had no idea what that meant, but I snapped up the lingo like a hungry dog. Sure, you bet—my new job was in the "May country." Wherever this country might be I knew it must be something; at least a big enough part of the mine to be called a *country*. Well, I thought for a punk kid like myself, this is a pretty lofty-sounding assignment. The Oakie stope in the bottom of the Bunker Hill mine might be just pretty damned hot stuff in the mining world. If I put that on a résumé sometime no one would have any idea of what it meant.

Time was tight, so I made a mental note of who Chris was, gathered up my gear, and dashed over to the Dry where my clothes hook and basket, suspended from the ceiling on the end of a ten-foot chain, turned out, if I remember correctly, to be number sixty-three. I changed into the Filson whipcord timber-cruising pants and Pendleton shirt my father had given me—both 100 percent wool. He said they were just the thing for working-men to wear, and he was right because it was a good outfit for timber cruising. But, I drew some curious looks at the time. It took a week before I understood what the problem was. One of the fringe benefits we enjoyed was a free company laundry set up to wash diggers. They used lye soap and water from the plant boiler. There wasn't much left of my outfit when it returned it. The maroon Pendleton shirt turned orange and had short sleeves. The forest green Filson pants were brown with cuffs up above the ankle, and I had to leave the top three buttons of the fly open to make a thirty-two-inch waist.

Others suited up in throwaway T-shirts, grimy jackets, and blue jeans with cuffs unceremoniously sawed off just above the ankle to keep from getting snagged. Somehow I managed to get out the door of the Dry with the lamp and battery attached to my brand-new light belt. The hard hat went on top, and, thus attired, I straggled across the yard like the Tin Man in *The Wizard of Oz*. I found Chris and Bill.

"Mr. Sloan said I was supposed to start out helping you today."

"Yah, they told me I was going to have a new partner. This here's Bill. He's the shifter."

"Hello, Bill."

"Yanh," Bill replied. Not exactly a long-winded fellow.

Chris and I shook hands. Or I should say, we shook my hand and his calluses. I pushed his arm slightly in the process. It did not move back, sideways, or forward; it reminded me of pushing a building. Same with Bill, a lanky chap rolling a worn-out toothpick from one corner of his mouth to the other. My name didn't seem particularly important just then, so I was content to remain known as "partner."

Chris's age was a tough call, probably late forties. He stood about five feet six inches, and his shoulders bent forward in the manner of someone who had spent a lot of time working hard in small places. Sometimes you notice something about a person that either sets you at ease or sets you on edge. Usually it's the eyes. In Chris's case, I sensed that what you saw was what you got—no bluster, no hidden agenda. I also had a sense that this was a guy who was a true craftsman. He had probably already broken in a number of beginners like me, and he seemed content to start on yet another one with a sense of humor. I knew intuitively that I had lucked out.

I had spent enough time around my Norwegian relatives to recognize "Norsk" when I heard it. Chris's accent was either Minnesota or North Dakota—not much Wisconsin in it. When he said "partner" it was hyphenated: *part-ner*.

A glance at the circular clock above the tracks at the mine office showed 6:59 A.M. Among those mustered out the willing and not-so-willing clambered onboard for the trip to the end of the tunnel, where underground hoists lowered crews more than a mile down inclined shafts on a 1⅜-inch-diameter wire rope.

"Time to go," Chris said. "You stay next to me, but keep your head inside the car and your hands off the rim or you'll lose 'em."

The man-train consisted of ten cars about twelve feet long fabricated from thin steel plate in utilitarian, miner-like fashion, meeting only the requirements of form, fit, and function. Each car had enough room for sixteen men loaded into four tiny compartments. A curved crown kept water and rockfalls off the occupants in transit. A heavy electric locomotive, the "motor," provided power. I found that getting into the compartment was more of a struggle than it first appeared. To do it with grace required a person to simultaneously duck, twist, turn, and sit. Hard hats, lamps, batteries, lunch buckets, boots, and bodies had to arrive at the same place at the same time. If you got the sequence wrong just about anything stuck, and you had to start over.

Inside, two wooden benches faced each other separated by a spare fourteen inches. This meant your knees wound up about two inches from the opposite bench—or two inches from the other fellow's private parts, depending on how the opposing knees were situated. Chris noted my hesitation and said, "If we don't have any sudden stops you can go between-knees. It's easiest though to put both knees to one side. You go the other way. There, you got it."

After everyone was aboard, "Big Bill" Lathrop looked up and down both sides of the train, ensuring the all-clear. "Let 'er go!" he hollered in a sonorous baritone to the motorman up ahead. The cars jerked forward one by one as the loose couplings caught hold. We growled out of the yard noisily, steel on steel, and slid under the tunnel's portal into a narrow world of darkness.

3

Oakie Stope

A s we entered the tunnel in total darkness, I thought all the men would have their lamps clipped into their hard-hat brackets because that's what miners are supposed to look like. But almost no one did. Like the other guy in our compartment, Chris wrapped the cord from his battery pack up under one armpit and around the back of the neck so the lamp drooped down on his chest. This looked like the thing to do, so I followed suit. It took about a pound of weight off your neck, and let you have the lamp on without shining it directly in someone's eyes, a sure sign that you had never spent a day underground. The cords swung back and forth like pendulums as we rocked along the bumpy track splices. The effect was surreal, a yellow and black kaleidoscope flickering on and off, reflected light bouncing around the compartment and off the wall rock and timbers as they flashed by. Conversation was impossible above the noise, but in reality there was not a great deal that needed to be said at this point in the shift; everyone seemed content with their own thoughts. At some points the track and the wheels disagreed on the fit—making noises like those poor marriages make.

I mused that the narrow-gauge railway we rode on ought to have it's own name, like the Dry House and Southern. It didn't take long to understand why Chris had cautioned me to keep my hands inside. Every so often the tunnel took a slight change in direction, and the car cleared the drift timbers by only a few inches. A torrent of water roared downgrade toward the portal in a foot-deep trench next to the tracks. The water came from pumps deep within the mine, but some rained down to the tunnel level from sixty-year-old workings hundreds of feet above us.

At 7:08 we hit a section of passing tracks where the tunnel intersected the Osburn fault, full of soft claylike gouge and water. I learned that when the tunnel crew had blasted their way through this section in February 1899, the ground caved and ran into the tunnel from far above the timbers. A few seconds later we passed through a mechanically operated air door used to control ventilation, the same one that "Air Door Pete" wiped out with the front of his locomotive when he forgot to yank the opener cord on the fly. I suspect his family didn't call him Air Door but everyone else did.

At 7:15 we slowed down and stopped, 10,800 feet from the portal. The crew disembarked at this junction, the mine's central nervous system. It housed huge ore-storage bins carved out of solid rock, chutes for loading cars, double tracks, and a thirteen-thousand-volt transformer station providing power for three hoists perched above steeply dipping inclined shafts. A maze of narrow openings led off in mysterious directions to these installations.

Chris grabbed my arm, motioning me to follow as the crew funneled into a drift by twos and threes toward the station platform for Number One shaft. Fifty pairs of boots sucked each step from a layer of soft, iron-stained mud. The metallic jingle of lunch bucket handles and stiff diggers accompanied the squish and suck. It's a kind of music; everyone going in the same direction for the same purpose. It's a reassuring sound, easier to grasp than terms like "downsizing" and "restructuring," or a day filled with back-to-back meetings where the guy who talks the loudest and longest always wins.

The shaft station was a room about the size of a two-car garage, with curved steel panels bolted to the arched ceiling. A couple of incandescent lights hanging from twisted wire cast a dim beer-hall glow around the room. A waist-high railing surrounded the dark opening in the floor where the shaft disappeared into the earth at a fifty-degree angle.

As we arrived, the wire rope pulling the skip we were to make our descent in snaked up the shaft, humming with the work it was doing. It threw foul-smelling cable lube up in the air as it disappeared into the rope raise leading to the hoist room, behind us and hidden from sight. This went on for several minutes while the crew stood around chewing and spitting. I asked Chris what was happening.

"Skip's empty. Hoistman's making a clear-the-shaft run. If there's a wreck, better it have nothin' in it than us in it."

The crew bunched up into small groups depending on who was going where. Twenty-one levels lay below, and ore came from a dozen or more vein systems. Paul Sloan's crew gathered in one area; Art Russell's in another; Bill

Lathrop's bunch was destined for 21. "Red" Morgan shifted on Level 23. Everyone knew where to go.

Looking back, I must have been an odd sight standing there in a dry-cleaned shirt and wool pants, new hard hat and boots, having no premonition of the work that lay ahead. The old hands counted on the day bringing much the same thing as the previous day, and the one before that, taking small comfort in a routine that had produced no rockfalls, blasts gone wrong, or fires with their strangling poisonous smoke filling every opening. No one wasted any motion. A long day lay ahead.

Chris and the others exchanged a few words of greeting.

"Morning, Stogey."

"Yup."

"Dum Dum."

"Hey, Chris."

"This here's Jack Tyree, that's Hunky Joe. They work in the same stope. This here's Grapefruit." Turning in my direction, Chris said, "This here's my new partner."

It appeared that I wouldn't have a name except "partner," and that having a real name was less important than having a nickname. They would call me what they wanted to when the time came.

"Hello," I said.

"Howdy."

"Yup."

"You can't have no more fun for the money. You'll love it here."

The morning's journey locked me in a state of acute anxiety, of living in the moment, as taught by Tao Te Ching and other Oriental philosophers. But fear creeps in despite our best efforts, upsetting the moment, putting forward things to be fearful about whether we believe them or not—like claustrophobia. I wondered what would happen to my sense of equilibrium, of OK-ness, when I landed in the Oakie stope five thousand feet below where I now stood. I was already almost the same distance below the top of Wardner Peak, so what difference would another mile make? I was warm and dry and had lots of company. The experiment was about to begin.

"Where's this Oakie stope, anyway?" I asked Chris.

"Close to Spokane, I guess. Take a half hour yet. Get off on 19, go over to the raise in the May country, then down to 21. Lot of countries in this mine anymore. Too many to keep track of."

The wire rope speeding up the incline changed pitch and slowed down. In a few seconds the skip rumbled slowly into sight from below, stopping precisely at the lip as the skip tender gave one quick pull on a bell lanyard, the hoistman's signal for "stop."

The wooden skip resembled a pickle boat about twenty-five feet long and three feet wide. It held twenty-two men stacked one above the other in eleven rows of two seats each. It had no seat belts. The sides reached shoulder level to a man sitting down, with a comforting but probably useless handrail on top.

When our crew's turn came to load up, I stepped gingerly onto the bottom row and climbed to the top bench. Gingerly, though the thick steel cable holding the skip had a tensile strength of three hundred thousand pounds. Still, it pays to be mindful.

I sat down on a rough plank next to Chris. The miners following us jumped aboard with the suave insouciance one might display at a square dance instead of dangling, as we were, thousands of feet from the bottom. I peered over the side for a brief look toward the journey's next phase. The view was what you might see from one end of a New York sewer tunnel—black with the exception of a very slight glow every few hundred feet that marked the locations of mine levels. The shrinking perspective ate up everything until the blips of light disappeared and it was just plain black.

At that point a certain fear crept in, the kind you experience when contemplating expired medicine. You're uncertain what is going to happen, and only one of the possible choices is good. Turn back while there's time, a voice inside shouted. Nah, can't. Not now. You'd be a sissy. Well, at least you'd be a *live* sissy. The voice continued. Suppose the power goes out midway and the bridle jerks out of the skip. Suppose the cable clamps slip. Suppose the hoist wire is corroded somewhere and nobody knows it. Suppose the skip jumps the tracks.

I knew that this round trip had taken place for more than fifty years. The process, whatever it was, must work. No one else seemed the least bit concerned. And next to us sat an identical shaft compartment with a wire rope extending to oblivion. Whatever was attached to its bitter end would provide a counterbalance to the load we imposed, one skip descending and one skip rising. And next to it, in a space called the manway, a wooden ladder rested on the rocky sill. It provided a theoretical means of escape should all else fail. Obviously, walking out— actually, climbing out—was an option.

As the skip continued loading, I glanced up at the clearance between our position and the overhead shaft timbers. It looked like twenty inches, thirty at the most. Maybe miners were shorter when they sunk the shaft in 1902. Chris caught me peering over the side. He took out a pinch of Copenhagen chew and tucked it behind his lower lip. "There's a big spring at the bottom. If the hoist-man forgets us, we just bounce up and down for a while."

"You must be kiddin' me."

"Yah, maybe so."

"Keep your head down. And don't ever stand up or try to get out until the skip tender or the shift boss stops the skip. That's because the hoistman can't see us. All he knows is where we're supposed to be, and he won't move until he hears the bell."

"Got it."

The last man stepped on the skip and we poised for a moment ready for the descent. Ding. Ding. Ding. Ding. Ding. Four bells plus one, destination Level 19.

I held my breath for the first seconds as we slipped off into the darkness, free-falling a few feet, then accelerating to a steady speed of about one thousand feet per minute, or twelve miles per hour. The bellowing, windy descent down the 55° incline sounded like a freight train crossing a bridge as we sped past the timbers. I snatched a look at my Timex's second hand thinking we'd be at Level 19 in about half a minute. But we kept on going. Two minutes went by. Every second we left the world of cheeseburgers and cashmere sweaters farther behind, speeding toward a nether region where, to quote Will Durant, "Life takes place by geologic consent, subject to change at any moment." An invisible force slowly put the brakes on after four and a half of the longest minutes that ever existed.

In a room far above, a hoistman watched like a hawk as the Nordberg's twenty-foot-diameter drum slowly unwound one final wrap of the cable until the marker and dots lined up for "19." We stopped one inch from the station lip, bouncing ever so slightly at the end of our very long umbilical cord.

We walked a few yards from the station to a miniature flatcar and climbed up on benches facing each other. Someone said, "Let 'er go!" one more time, and we struck off to the west in the direction of the May Raise. ("Raise" seems an odd name for an opening that you descend into. It's called that because it's carved out of rock from an opening below it—in the case of the May, from Level 23—and in essence raised up. The difference between a shaft and a raise is impossible to discern by looking at them. It's necessary to know the construction history. When they're completed, it doesn't make any difference anyway; they both go up and down.)

The climate changed. Beads of sweat trickled down my forehead and neck as we rolled along in subtropical heat. Chris quickly stripped to his army surplus T-shirt. I sat there wondering how long I could survive in my Pendleton shirt.

"Jesus, how hot is it down here?" I asked.

"About ninety-four in the shade. Humidity's about ninety-four too. You don't need a shirt like that down here. Sometimes I don't wear nothin' above the waist."

At the May Raise, we descended six hundred feet more to Level 21. The skip tender announced, "Sea level, everyone out."

We struck off down the drift for several minutes in darkness illuminated only by our headlamps. It didn't take long to acquire the miner's habit of pointing your head in the direction you wished to see. I still do that in darkness, fifty years later, but of course it's nonsense without a headlamp. We entered an opening that suddenly appeared in the wall to our left and climbed down a ten-foot ladder to the floor of the stope, our home away from home for the next three months.

"Here we are," Chris remarked.

"Nice place."

It was 8:00 A.M.; we had been in transit almost a full hour. So this was what the union's old battle cry for portal-to-portal pay was about. Travel two hours, work six, and get paid for eight, as opposed to two hours of travel on your own time and then eight hours of paid work.

"Ever see a square-set stope before?"

"Can't say I have."

A virtual forest of posts and overhead beams stood before us, extending about forty feet in either direction right up to freshly exposed faces of high-grade silver ore, infused with veins of massive lead and zinc sulfides (argentiferous galena and sphalerite) accented by patches of snowy white quartz and calcite.

Square-set timbering is a technique for mining massive ore bodies in heavy, caving ground. It is a court of last resort because of the expense—not only the amount of timber required but also the immense logistics problem of getting it to the point of use. From above, a square-set stope resembles a 3-D checkerboard whose squares are five feet on a side and eight feet high. A day's work is to excavate a red square and timber it, repeating the process the next day on a black square. To minimize the danger of shifting sets occasioned by opening up too much ground, waste rock is brought in to backfill mined-out areas. Viewed from the side, each set contains a vertical post at each corner. The posts are tied together across the top and bottom with timber caps and sills. The top of the set is "lagged" shut with three-by-ten-inch rough-cut boards laid up in log cabin fashion to keep the back from caving in. Each set resembles a box about the size of a hotel elevator, providing a safe place for drilling blastholes to make the next round of advance.

Since the Scandinavian work ethic runs strong in our family, my first thought was to find out every detail of the work ahead in order not to make mistakes or cause delays. So I asked a lot of anxious questions. Chris sat down and poured a cup of coffee. "Now partner, just take it easy. Yer gettin' all worked up here. We'll take it one thing at a time. Yesterday I shot the round you see over there where there's no timber. We'll take a peek here in a minute and see what it looks like."

Chris took a long steel bar and chipped away at loose material hanging overhead, while I wrestled two-foot-diameter, seven-foot-high posts and ten-by-twelve-inch caps and sills over to the work area. The timbers had been fabricated from Douglas fir in the mine's own sawmill. The posts, which were peeled and cut to length, weighed about two hundred pounds. They had lain in a ditch full of water for several weeks, leaving them slick with goo. It's hard enough to handle something that heavy, but not being able to hang on to the bastards sort of grated on your psyche—about the same experience as getting your arms around a two-hundred-pound halibut.

We excavated enough floor to get the sills in place, then set the posts upright, making sure they were in line and level with the previous square-set. The eight-by-twelve caps fit into notches on top of the posts. My job was to trim them to just the right length if they didn't fit, which was often. We grunted the caps into place on top, blocking everything in with wedges. After that we stepped back under cover of a previous set and had a meeting because the area over the new set was still just bare ground. And that's where the danger lay.

"This is when we have to be together. When we get this here bulkhead up tight against the back we'll be all right. What I want you to do is get laggin' and wedges handy and pass them up to me as fast as I get them in place. We got a whole mountain to hold up. We got to move fast."

Chris moved out into the middle of the set, standing on a temporary platform. I handed three-by-ten-inch rough-cut lagging up to him, and he laid them across the caps on opposite sides, alternating layers log-cabin style until after two feet or so the bulkhead started making contact with the overhead rock. Chris hollered directions down—"Here wit' a three-foot," "That one's too wide, find another one," and so on. Later, "Here with the ax and a wedge." Sweat flew off Chris's brow as he drove the wedges home. At the first few blows the wedges emitted a dull thud, then began to ring as they took weight.

Good enough was never good enough for Chris. He made sure everything fit together before we hoisted big timber up into the air. All the joints were square and true; if they weren't and something caused them to shoulder an eccentric load, the entire stope could fold up like dominoes on a countertop.

But a rockfall starting over our heads when he got through wouldn't have gone an eighth of an inch. Chris hit the posts with an ax when he came down off the platform to see if they sounded proper. He smiled. "Tight."

"This here's called a jackleg drill," Chris volunteered after lunch. "Someday I'll show you how to run it, but right now all I want you to do is stand up at the face and hold the drill bit steady when it starts turning. After that, I'll drill and you keep the air and water hoses straight and the line-oiler filled."

When we were ready, Chris carefully extended the drill steel up to the face and cracked the drill's throttle open very slightly. I stood four feet away holding the octagonal steel with my bare hands. He nodded his head up and down momentarily to signal "Let's go." Then, after a few turns of the bit, he flipped the throttle wide open. High-pressure water used to wash the cuttings sprayed all over the place when it hit the rock face, and fog spewed from the drill's exhaust port accompanied by an explosive racket resembling what you might hear standing behind a Boeing 747 at takeoff power. I couldn't see what I was doing; conscious thought was out of the question. I shouted at Chris, "Is that it, for God's sake! What you want?" He nodded through the noise and spray. Our headlamps blinded each other in the process. The bit began to hammer and twist its way into the rock inch by inch. The drill water coming back out of the hole turned black when it cut veins of high-grade ore.

After lunch we continued drilling until half-past one. Like John Henry, the "steel drivin' man," the time had arrived to stuff twenty-one holes with dynamite.

We left the stope for a time and climbed back up to the powder magazine tucked to one side of the drift behind a steel door. Chris picked up a case of DuPont Gelex 2 dynamite. I wrapped the eight-foot fuses and blasting caps around my neck, carrying them with as much care and respect as one might attach to half a pound of mercury fulminate.

I watched as Chris loaded two holes. He slid the primer stick containing the cap and fuse in first, then rammed home another five sticks with a wood tamping stick. Wood produces no sparks. Wood is good. Then he said, "Here, you try it for a while. This'll be your first lesson on how to be a miner. I like to push the powder in there 'til it stops and then lean on it hard enough to crush it. Get 'er good and tight in there." Which I did, gaining confidence and noting with some relief that the potential energy we crammed into each hole behaved exactly as it should have.

"Keep the fuse tight when you slide the powder in. Don't crimp it."

Chris stepped back at two o'clock to look things over. "I think we're ready." He bunched the fuses in little groups of five or six, explaining why the sequence was important. "When the round fires, it has to start with the center cut. Those holes create a space for the ones on the side to break into. They're called the trimmers. Then backholes up above go off, and the last ones are the lifters on the bottom that are supposed to throw the muck pile up and out."

"How're you going to light everything at once?"

"You'll see. First we have to make a spitter. Here's how you do it. Need a cheap knife like this one, because you can get 'em sharp as a razor."

Chris made about ten angled cuts in a piece of fuse at two-inch intervals. Each cut went only as far as the powder train and no farther. "Got to keep the fire moving or it won't work. Careful not to cut all the way through. OK, here we go."

"Fire in the hole!"

He lit the end where the cuts began. As the fuse burned, a yellow flame shot out of each cut for several seconds, long enough to light four or five fuses in the right sequence. Chris folded the burned portion underneath his hand to expose the next cut as the fire burned down the spitter and tried to keep the hot liquid tar dripping off the fuse wrapping from scalding his fingers. I kept my lamp on the fuses so Chris could see through the cloud of smoke filling our surroundings with acrid fumes. Chris neither blinked nor hurried. If there's such a thing as absolute concentration, the ancient practice of lighting a round with a spitter demands it. You cannot stop, and you cannot forget what you are doing or have done. Once begun, there is no turning back. If only half the fuses are lit and the others abandoned for some reason, the swing shift will confront a perilous heap of broken rock, dynamite, and primers—probably leaving it for you to unravel the next morning.

Black fuse is supposed to burn at the advertised rate of forty-five seconds per foot. I calculated that one of our allotted six minutes had been used up by the time fire spit from each fuse. Finally, Chris said, "That's it—let's go." The trick in leaving a burning fuse round is to give the appearance of not being in the least bit of a hurry. I would say our exits were dignified but not lethargic. Once we entered the haulage drift above the stope we were safe.

Everyone blasts at the same time. Shots sounding like muffled depth charges detonated about this time, above and below us and on every side. Then a louder group went off. Whamp, whamp, whamp—about five sets of rapid explosions.

"Those our shots, partner?" I asked.

"I think so. Sounds about right. Pretty good today. Pretty good."

I hit the sack early that night, a solid hour before the sun went down. I lay on my back staring at the ceiling, trying not to move or laugh. I hurt everywhere. Lactic acid invaded my body, stultifying every muscle, every ligament and tendon. Whatever the pain, I knew I'd lived through a day I'd never forget. I hoped Chris thought I was a good enough partner. I was scared most of the time but not too scared. I'd learned a lot of stuff I hadn't known the previous day. It was a start. It all made a tremendous amount of sense to me. It didn't seem like work. I had paid attention and made $18.96.

4

Up

I spent an inordinate amount of time looking for mineral specimens during my first month underground. The thrill of seeing the vein's new face every morning proved irresistible. Way above us in the Cherry Raise, the early miners had discovered spider web–like wire silver the size of garbage can lids. I fancied we would have similar luck, but we didn't. Undeterred, I kept looking. I had to creep out beneath the unprotected overhang and wash the blasting residue off with drill water. Chris took note of this obsession but suffered in silence. One morning he said, "Partner, you'll never see a rock falling *up*, but you'll see them falling *down*. Dat's why I look up all the time when we're away from the timber."

It reminds me of a scene from *Butch Cassidy and the Sundance Kid*. Butch and the kid had been hired to ensure that the payroll for the Apex Mine made it from La Paz, up the mountain to the mine. On the way down *without* the payroll, the two pseudoguards looked around nervously, anticipating an ambush at a narrow point in the trail. The mine boss, Percy Garrett, turned in the saddle and said, "Morons! I have morons on my team! The bandidos will not rob us on the way down, because we do not have the money. When we have the money, on the way back up, that is when they will try to rob us." So the lesson for the day became, look up until we get the timber in, then continue looking up.

The idea, of course, was to stay alive by barring down chunks or slabs of rock loosened and fractured by the previous day's blasting. "Never do anything till you bar down, partner," Chris said. He passed his lamp's little beam of light fastidiously around the brand-new local geology, inspecting every shadow or crack like a dentist looking for the tooth that needs a root canal. He poked and pried suspect areas with an octagonal steel scaling bar about six feet long, not only to jar loose material down to the floor, but also to see how the bigger ones *sounded*. These bars weigh only about ten pounds, but it doesn't take long with it cantilevered in front of you before the lower-back muscles surrender in a painful spasm. Sometimes shattered quartz fell out, sounding like someone had thrown a set of dishes out a two-story window. If you poked a suspicious area that looked solid but sounded like balsa wood, you knew it was loose. When that occurred, Chris said, "There. I thought so." He had a sixth sense for those widow makers. Maybe he smelled them, I was never sure. He just seemed to know.

Blocks the size of small cars had been known to fall out of the back where the quartzite's natural bedding planes dipped toward a new opening. Chris told me that one fell fifteen feet from the station ceiling on Level 23 and killed a man.

I usually stood on Chris's right side when we barred down, sometimes with a bar of my own. I tried to evaluate the same features he did, making a judgment call separating good ground from bad, attempting to figure out

what Chris was thinking. It wasn't that he didn't communicate. Just that a lot of what might pass for actual
talk sounded more like monosyllabic musing—"bad, OK,
loose, punky, mmmm."

After a few weeks of tutoring, I began barring down
every other day. Chris supervised while I poked and wig-
gled the bar until my arms felt as heavy as the lead we
were mining.

I learned two things. First, barring down was no time
to be in a hurry. Second, by the time you observe something falling on you, it's too late. We assume with a hefty
dose of arrogance that our reflexes will save us, that there
is always enough time to move out of the way. It doesn't
work no matter what we think. The same instant you
say, "That's falling," it hits you.

You had to be quick to jerk the bar from the path of
loose stuff once it started toward the floor. If the rock
shower landed on the bar it might catapult you or the
bar somewhere unpleasant, or send a sine wave of vibration up through your ligaments that you might remember
weeks later. My biggest problem was not technique but
attitude, trying to do too much at one time. "Yesus, yesus!"
Chris exclaimed time and again. "You've got a hold of
the whole mountain. Here, let me show you. Just go up
like I'm doing and wiggle that part out. Then move over
and do that one there. Pretty soon you've got it all.
There, see what I mean?" He was right.

Events unpredictable and unforeseen happen underground. The force of gravity is to blame. I recall a noise
like a freight train hitting a bridge during our lunch nap-

time. BANG! It shook every timber in the stope. We both hit the floor at full attention, ready to flee.

"Holy shit! What was that?" I said, reaching frantically for my hard hat, getting it on backward, fumbling for the light switch.

"Don't know. It was big. We better go see."

We were still in one piece. How long that condition would continue was a matter of conjecture. I took comfort in the realization that whatever had happened had quit happening. We looked at posts and bulkheads nearby, thinking one had given way. Everything appeared normal, but about forty feet away in an old part of the stope wood splinters the size of baseball bats lay all over the floor. We approached the scene of destruction with measured steps. A chunk of solid galena the size of a spare tire, weighing 475 pounds per cubic foot, had slid out of the vein, fallen not more than three feet, and gone straight through a solid ten-by-twelve-inch timber like it had never even been there.

"There's a lesson for you, partner. Hard to believe anything that small could do so much damage. You scared?"

I lied. "Nah. How about you?"

"Was. Still am, maybe."

5

Old Bill Bradley

Once in a great while you cross trails with someone whose voice, appearance, personality, or other characteristic leaves an imprint on your soul. The person might be a former coworker, lover, or teacher, like Miss Mead, who was a knockout even by the standards of a fat third-grader with a crew cut. A fellow resident of the boardinghouse, Bill Bradley, sticks in my memory like contact cement. There are reasons for this.

The reason everyone called him "Old" Bill remains a mystery. But in a way the description fit. He seemed old. Maybe it was because he had only one tooth left in his mouth, a front canine incisor, as my dentist explained to me during a root canal. You can assume that most people would go out and get a set of false ones when handed a deal like one tooth. But Bill wasn't having any of that. He was a keep-your-own-counsel kind of fellow who came and went quietlike, taking up but a small fraction of the earth's resources.

Bill ate a lot of soup and mashed potatoes. I noticed he occasionally took a stab at carrots and peas or canned corn with a singular concentration not practiced by those fortunate enough to have a full set of teeth. The Thursday-night steaks we all looked forward to presented a problem of Brobdingnagian proportions. No one, however, could peel an orange faster or better than Bill when he got started with that backhoe tooth—living proof that not all handicaps subtract. He held the fruit in one hand and rotated it like a lathe chisel against the tooth, which produced a canal in the rind at just the right depth. First latitudes and longitudes and then a diagonal or two thrown in for good measure. Darwin would have been pleased.

In sepia photographs of workmen taken in the late 1800s, logging crews stand proudly next to their twelve-foot crosscut saws leaning against huge Douglas firs, and railroad crews pose in front of tunnel portals blasted through the Rocky Mountains. These are the men who made E. H. Harriman, president of Union Pacific Railroad, and George Weyerhaeuser, the lumber king, rich. The faces in those photos haunt me. They stare straight at the camera. They look sweaty and tired and gaunt. They probably are. Their clothes are soiled. They are somber characters, absent smiles. If one could truly warp time, I think Old Bill Bradley might have stepped unnoticed into those photos from a distance of seventy years.

Bill had thick, coal-black eyebrows that hung like hedgerows over deep-set eyes with a five-mile stare. A stark white forehead, not unlike that exhibited by all working stiffs who wear hard hats, transitioned like a tide flat to thinning gray hair. Two or three days of beard stubble completed the picture. No one seemed to know his real age. He might have been forty, and he might have been seventy.

He wore the same outfit all the time: wool longjohns (top two buttons open at the neck for ventilation) and no shirt; braces with brass clamps and light green elastic risers holding up black trousers cut off at the cuff. The union-suit underwear exuded a sweaty aroma extending outward like Doppler radar, two weeks away from the last washing and a week away from the next. They were as yellow as old newspapers.

Old Bill might have been hirsute, long of tooth, and short on dress code, but he made a contribution. A mining camp is supposed to look like that. Take Bill out of the picture and something is missing. He was an icon, a classic—underestimated and probably misunderstood but above all a decent fellow.

I often ran into him when we fixed our lunches in the morning, and sometimes we sat at the same table at dinner. One evening I asked him how things were going.

"O-O-O-kay," he stammered, fighting for the "kay."

We talked for a few minutes. He had been in the navy and had worked at Bunker Hill "almost forever." I asked him if he had any family. He said, "Yup. Missus lives down there to southern Idaho." The rest of the sentence drifted off into some far-off corner of consciousness. "Got a daughter too. Yup." That glimmer of another life or the weather is about as complicated as our conversations ever became. Over time I guess we became friends, but it took a while because a guy with one tooth is at something of a disadvantage when it comes to discourse. We stuck to the basics.

One afternoon after work I grabbed a leftover cookie from the lunch table and headed up to my room, thinking I'd settle down to a quiet read of *Triumph and Tragedy*.

When I closed the door and started down the written page, filled with what seemed like most of Churchill's many-thousand-word vocabulary, an unreal sound arose from somewhere down the hall. It seemed to fill up the whole space, like a grade school trombonist practicing lip slurs. I hollered down the stairs, "What's that noise, Dora? Something wrong up here?"

"That's Bill. He's snoring. He's on graveyard this week."

One day I asked her husband, Dee "Tater" Tatham, what Bill did at the mine.

He said, "Old Bill Bradley? Bill's what we call the Bunker Hill mucking machine. That's all he ever does— muck track. Yup, that's all he ever does—muck track. If the motorman don't bring him a car to put the muck in, he'll run right on down the track and catch him and make him bring him a car back."

Mucking track is a nobler calling than it sounds. Ore pulled out of production stopes is soaking wet after it passes through loading chutes. The miniature railcars hauling it to the shaft tend to leak, and the chutes leak. Ultimately, the tracks fill up with fine-grained material to a point where the wheel flanges fail to engage the rails, causing a train rolling along with twenty tons of ore to derail and slam against the timber drift sets. The train isn't moving fast when this happens, but there's more than one motorman in the world with a set of broken legs from a derail on a dirty track.

This is the stuff Bill attacked with ceaseless devotion. All day, Bill slid his square-point shovel along the ties picking muck off the floor, flipping it with dexterity into his car, which he pushed along by hand. It's dark and lonely work, but someone has to do it, the saying goes. No one knows what Bill thought about down there by himself, but it's a setting where great philosophical thoughts are born. I wish I knew what he had come up with.

Before I left at the end of that first summer, I stopped to thank Dora for keeping me fed. As we chatted, Bill happened by my car. We shook hands. I said, "Well, Bill, good luck. Maybe see you next year if I come back."

"Ya, g'luck Woof. Maybe nex' year."

Then we laughed. Two travelers from different watersheds; we shared a few meals, talked the talk, made a few sandwiches side by side.

♟ ♟ ♟ ♟ 6

The Bunker Hill Mine

Gold is a fine thing
For those who admire it.
....
But I am a child
Of the moon, and silver
Is the metal of the moon.
Secret-smiler, wrapped in wonder
Floating in her cloudy magic,
'Tis the moon that mints her silver
In the deeps of darkened earth. . . .

Ballad of Baby Doe, 1956

When you think about the thousands of tiny dumps and ratholes that dot the American West, it's easy to come up with the perspective that the whole epoch of hardrock mining was a boom-and-bust cycle of small operations—high-grade veins a few feet thick, empty hotels and cabins left behind. This picture is actually quite accurate. The gigantic copper deposits at Butte, San Manuel, and Jerome are exceptions. The deep mining at Cripple Creek, Leadville, and Telluride are others. But the lead-zinc-silver veins in the Coeur d'Alene mining district stand out in any crowd of big deals. The Sunshine was down a long way when they quit mining in 2002. Hecla's Lucky Friday mine is at least 6,100 feet deep, the Star-Morning shaft about 7,900 feet. But the Bunker Hill was the granddaddy of them all, at least in terms of "big."

Trying to describe the 135 miles of drifts, shafts, stopes, and other development that took place at the Bunker Hill is a task not unlike explaining the driving habits of taxicabs in Namibia. But it's possible. Visualize standing on the shoulder of Interstate 5 facing south toward the Silver Bowl ski lift above Kellogg. If you hold your right hand up at eye level, palm facing away, with your thumb and index finger extending straight up, your other fingers curled, and your elbow slanting off toward Spokane, you get an approximation of the manner in which the rich ore bodies of the mine were situated. The valley between your thumb and index finger represents Milo Gulch, the site of Noah Kellogg's discovery. The elevation there is about 3,600 feet above sea level. The thumb is the Sullivan side of the original Bunker Hill and Sullivan Mining and Concentrating Company veins. The index finger represents the southwestern high-grade veins worked from 1886 to 1905. Right above the middle finger knuckle is where the Kellogg Tunnel was driven. It lies at an elevation of 2,400 feet and runs two miles into the center of the mountain. The last three fingers folded into your palm represent the paucity of ore found at the end of the tunnel (Level 9)—only a smell, really. But the last level mined, number 31, 1,400 feet below sea level and two miles to the west of the Kellogg Tunnel underneath the former zinc plant, lies near your representational elbow.

If you ask a Kellogg native to describe the Bunker Hill in one sentence, he or she will say: "Two miles in, a mile down, and two miles toward Spokane." Thirty-one horizontal levels were driven two hundred feet apart vertically. These were haulage ways to transport ore from the production stopes to the hoisting shafts. Shaft #1 was sunk in 1904 to develop what appeared to be an enormous ore body, the March. It ran from tunnel level to Level 23 and later became the ventilation system's exhaust shaft. Shaft #2, also called the White, ran from tunnel level to Level 25. It became the air intake shaft. Shaft #3 was also sunk from tunnel level but several thousand feet to the west. The Service Raise ran from Level 23 to Level 31.

A geologic cross section of the mine gives the impression of an incredible jumble of rock units thrust against, beside, over, and under each other by faults both large and small. Color coding helps only a little to comprehend this nightmarish assemblage of hardrock geology. The most productive veins were called Link veins because of their connection to the Cate fault, which runs northwest to southeast through the entire mine, top to bottom. The country rock is Precambrian—about 1.8 billion years old. The Revett and St. Regis formations accounted for most of the productive ore bodies. They are part of a 21,000-foot section known as the Belt Supergroup. The rocks were deposited in a shallow near-shore depression long before life began on this planet.

So one might ask, how, when, and where did the ore come from? Every investigative geologist or engineer who ever worked in the district—they number in the hundreds—has asked the same thing. Most of the early theorists held that it was a hydrothermal process, by which ascending aqueous solutions of hot nitric-hydrofluoric acids invaded latter-day faults and cooled and solidified as ore-bearing sulfides. There is a great deal to be said for this notion since these corrosive solutions will dissolve almost any substance known to humankind, including glass. But the solutions themselves had to come from somewhere. Deep undersea "smoker"? Probably not. A cooling granitic magma volatilizing and spewing off metal-laden sulfides in the process? Maybe. Some veins fit that model, but some even locally close to the granite intrusives do not.

In the 1980s some geologists suggested that the lead-silver minerals were always there, deposited syngenetically at the same time as the original muddy sand and reorganized at a later time by a very powerful mechanism that concentrated the material into the veins eventually mined. It's difficult to visualize pea-sized blebs of galena, sphalerite, and tetrahedrite groping their way through cemented siliceous quartzite toward some distant opening wherein they assembled and agreed to become ore. But I'll leave that argument to the experts, for fifty years later I am still a student.

Clearly, movement along the huge faults in the district had to take place before any "plumbing" was available to concentrate ore. And the Revett and St. Regis formations host the largest ore bodies because they have the highest compressive strength—which translates into openings that stay open, or at least partially open, after the faulting has taken place. Highly acidic aqueous solutions at 700 degrees Fahrenheit could transport sulfide minerals into fault zones, or leach minerals from the surrounding strata. Temperatures generated by even low-grade metamorphism could have accomplished the same thing as island arcs collided with and compressed coastal margins.

Who's right? I'll venture out on a limb and say everyone—to some degree. Why? Because supporting evidence can be found for each concept somewhere, at some depth, at any mine in the Coeur d'Alene district. So it's something like being right about the stock market. In July all your stocks are up. You've made all the right moves, and you're a genius. When October rolls around a few weeks later, you're losing your shirt and wondering what went wrong. Being right is time dependent. If there are three or four possible explanations for what has been found across the entire twenty miles of mineralization, then that poses a difficult situation for anyone trying to make a one-size-fits-all explanation. If those few mechanisms were at work simultaneously (a profound possibility), then the level of complexity increases exponentially. Time, temperature, and pressure are the only driving forces available. Unfortunately, the mechanisms can't be duplicated in a laboratory. It's humbling work. The more we find out, the more questions we have. What we see today in and on the ground is the net result of two billion years of folding, faulting, shifting tectonic plates, island arc docking, shearing, vapor pressure, valence, violence, pH, magma, solidification, precipitation. If all mining theorists were honest, we might admit, "To tell the truth, it kind of bankrupts your imagination."

A tantalizing question to consider is whether "Has every deposit in the Silver Valley been discovered." My answer is, not by a long shot. One of the reasons it's possible to venture that opinion is because so much ore has been discovered by accident and serendipity, by driving development work with no thought of hitting a well-reasoned "geologic target," as was the case when the shifter reported to the mine superintendent, "Oh, by the way, we cut a six-foot vein of wire silver on that last drift shot."

The Bunker Hill was still in ore when Gulf Resources shut down the mine in 1981. At a depth of six thousand feet, the entrance to rock-burst ground, residual stresses relieve themselves explosively and without warning. There is no place to run or hide. The drift and stope walls implode instantaneously, slamming shut on anyone or anything in the way. So conditions were changing rapidly at that depth, and it might have been a whole new ball game. But at the end there was mineral.

7

Sanitary Pete

We seem to be creatures of habit, taking comfort in routine and ritual. Although the clientele at the boardinghouse constantly revolved, I sat at the same chair, at the same time, at the same table, no matter what. So did the other regulars. It came to a point where someone might say in a virtually empty room, "You can't sit there. That's Bill's place."

One chap, with whom I had only a nodding acquaintance, came down the stairs every afternoon for dinner wearing a sport coat, tie, and slacks. His shoes shone brightly. I placed his age at about fifty years plus or minus. He worked somewhere in the mine. He chain-smoked Lucky Strike cigarettes and packed a paperback novel around for company. He rarely said a word to anyone.

No one else on the premises even owned a tie, let alone a sport coat. For some reason, he polished his silverware with a napkin every night before the food was served, blowing on the pieces and rubbing them with a weird dedication as if he were taking them to an auction.

I didn't pay an awful lot of attention to this fellow until I ran into him one early Saturday morning in the washroom. Usually we were alone since everyone else was busy nursing hangovers. When someone spends three or four minutes scrubbing washbasins that were cleaned every day by the staff, it gets your attention. He acted as if *E. coli* bacteria had the place under siege. After the Ajax cleanser application, he ran near-boiling water in the bowl until clouds of steam rose up and fogged the mirror. With the surface sterilized, he laid toiletries out on a clean towel like a surgeon preparing for a heart transplant. The first item was a razor, placed deliberately on a specific spot, followed by a toothbrush and hairbrush, face up.

This elaborate process took a long time, longer than a person would want to spend to get the morning's ablutions out of the way. I hung around in the shower, fascinated by the monastic ritual. I looked forward to the following Saturday just to make sure my imagination wasn't running away with itself. It wasn't.

Finally, my curiosity got the best of me. "Say Dora, who is the guy who wears the sport coat and smokes Luckies all the time? In the washroom he carries on like he's in a hospital or something. He wore slippers in the shower."

"That's 'Sanitary Pete,'" she replied. "His real name is Pete Krieger. He's been like that all along. Boarded here for several years now. Nice fellow, but odd. I seen him double wrap his sandwiches in the morning. He used to let us do the linen and bedding in his room, but for a long time now we have to put it in there, and he makes the bed up himself."

I kept an eye out for Sanitary after that. We got to the point where we exchanged hellos in the washroom. He *was* odd, but for a guy who worked underground and wore slippers in the shower, when Sanitary Pete came down the stairs in a sport coat, he *looked* sharp.

A long time went by when no one saw much of Sanitary Pete. I'd show up for dinner and jawbone with the guys, but Pete's chair was empty. No coat and tie at the end of his table. It was like the absence made him more there than when he was there.

One night I woke up out of a sound sleep. I thought I had heard a gunshot. But all was quiet. I tossed it off as something I had dreamed. But in the morning all was not well with the world. An ambulance and police car occupied most of the alley, and some of my fellow boarders were circled around on the pavement. Dora stood in the doorway wiping her hands slowly on the white apron she always wore.

"What the heck's going on?" I asked.

Someone said, "Ol' Sanitary shot himself—shot himself in the head up in the washroom."

"What?" I said. "How can that be?" not wanting to believe the spoken words.

"Yup, he had bone marrow cancer. That's why he quit workin' and we didn't see him around no more. Cigarette ashes and butts in his room two inches deep on the floor. Never seen the likes of it. Couldn't take it. Can't say I blame him."

In a few minutes the stretcher bearing what was left of Sanitary Pete Krieger wrapped in bloody sheets came down the stairs. The rest of his brains were splattered on the walls of the washroom where I had watched him prepare his unique approach to the world. They slid the gurney through the open doors of the ambulance. Then the doors slammed shut behind him.

"Funeral home."

Jesus, he was one of us, I said to myself, still in disbelief, avoiding the thought that anyone I knew could die; my first inkling of how quickly things change, of how vulnerable we are. Here lay a guy whom no one knew very well, with few if any friends. Who did he leave behind?

Someone said, "You're born alone and you die alone, and you're lucky if there's someone there in between to help you through."

Dammit all, ol' Sanitary Pete's dead. Dammit all anyway, I thought. Who will take his place? Now who's going to dress for dinner?

8

A Tea

"Oh, Mrs. Corney, what a prospect this opens! What a opportunity for a jining of hearts and house-keepings!"

Charles Dickens, *Oliver Twist*

Mail takes on a new meaning when you're out on your own. That's especially true if you haven't arrived at the point in acquiring things where you get ads and bills—"send us your money!" If you think nobody cares about you, try skipping a car payment. So I checked my box at the post office on a regular basis, finding it continually empty. I didn't even qualify for junk mail, which had barely entered the realm of corporate advertising at the time. But nothing stays the same forever; one afternoon a note-sized envelope showed up, addressed in fine cursive handwriting. A Kellogg postmark added to the mystery since (a) I wasn't in trouble and (b) I didn't know anyone who might send me a handwritten note.

I tore it open. "You are invited to our annual College Student Tea," it read, courtesy of a "Mrs. Don (Edy) Morbeck." I thought, A tea? Hot damn!

The tea was scheduled for the following Saturday afternoon, "1:00 to 3:00 P.M. at the Morbeck residence, 119 East Market Street." I had never been to a real tea before and figured there was nothing to lose. All things considered, the mention of students suggested at least a fifty-fifty chance of meeting girls. This sound reasoning tipped the scales in favor of attending. There I had stood, wondering if Kellogg had any culture, and in a single lightning stroke fortune served me up an invitation to a gathering that had to be refined, with people of high stature.

The catchpenny clothes I owned at this time did not qualify as a wardrobe. But I had a pair of suntans and a navy blue Lord Jeff cardigan. I tried the sweater on over a red Hawaiian-print shirt. The colors seemed to conflict, but the *texture* was good. Penny loafers and white sweat socks added, I hoped, a casual touch. It would have to do, cool by 1950s standards.

The week wore on, and finally the big moment arrived. The Morbecks lived in a modest but impeccably maintained residence in a quiet, tree-lined neighborhood. I rang the doorbell.

"Hi, I'm Edy Morbeck. You must be Fritz, the college student from Seattle. I can say that because the other guests are all from town. We're ever so glad to see you. Do come in and make yourself comfortable."

"Sure. Thanks for the invitation."

The living room was lavishly stocked with food and soft drinks placed on polished, expensive-looking mahogany furniture. Unfortunately, my arrival was more or less announced as an introduction to the group, at a time when I prayed for a measure of anonymity. Mrs. Morbeck took off some of the edge by saying, "You don't have to remember all our names. We only have to remember yours, so relax and have a bite to eat." A clutch of older women sat or stood at strategic locations around the room, keeping the conversation going—matrons, patrons, or sponsors, I guessed. About half a dozen college students busied themselves eating and making an attempt at polite conversation. With a practiced eye, I sized up the talent in about fifteen seconds. It looked like a dry run, but snap judgments can get you in trouble.

Sometimes a newcomer's best strategy for survival in a room full of people who know each other is eat, listen, and watch. Which is what I did. The conversation drifted around the room. The women knew each other well. They represented, at a minimum, the Who's Who of Silver Valley society. I recognized some of the last names on their name tags: Mrs. Whitesel and Mrs. Staley, both married to doctors at the hospital; Maxine Brewer, wife of the drugstore owner. And I knew Edy Morbeck's husband owned Linfor Lumber. After ten minutes of reasonable attention on my part, I spied a diminutive but very attractive girl off in one corner who appeared to be blending into a glass-fronted china cabinet. She looked bored. She looked accessible. I moved over a few feet for a chat.

She said, "God, I hate these things. But my mom said I had to go."

"Yes. I know what you mean. It reminds me of dance lessons at the Women's University Club in Seattle. I can't figure out why I was invited but decided to come anyway. The food is good. What are we supposed to be doing?"

"Just be polite and talk about college things."

We talked about college things for a while, but my heart wasn't in it. My heart was in lust. Concentration was out of the question. She wore a saffron-colored blouse, on the verge of see-through, and a light blue skirt. Lovely complexion. Engaging smile. Things went okay for a few minutes. Then she figured it out.

"Do you know my boyfriend, Vince? He works in the mine too. He lettered in football, baseball, and basketball all four years of high school."

"Can't say I do. Must be a good athlete, huh?"

This is the point in a hustle conversation called "No chance. Never." I visualized this Vince at six-feet three inches, two hundred pounds, bench pressing a pickup truck. Probably had a last name like Calabretta or Cabrini. I imagined the confrontation before it ever took place: "Name's Vince. Stay away from my girl." "Sure thing, Vince. No need to candy coat it like that."

At this point, sensing a changed atmosphere in our dialogue, a smallish woman in her late fifties with salt-and-pepper hair approached me from across the room.

"I'm Doris Woolf with two *O*'s and you're Mr. Wolff with two *F*'s. Now then, Wallace and I are part of the Idaho delegation going to the GOP. convention in San Francisco next month. We need someone to take care of the house and feed our dog while we're gone. Would you be interested in the job? Why don't you think about it for a day or two and let me know."

I recognized the name and the different spelling because her husband, Wallace, was vice president and general manager of the entire Bunker Hill Company. My shift boss's boss's boss's boss. Take care of the VP's house and dog for a month? I said, "I don't need to think about it very long. Sure, you bet."

"Good. You're decisive. I like that in a person. Here's what I suggest. When you get off work Monday, drive around to our back entrance and we'll talk about how we'll do business. The address is 906 McKinley, right next to the company office. Our dog is a big German shepherd. His name is Rex. He looks intimidating, but he's a softie."

"Yes, ma'am, I'll be there."

It was the only job I ever got without an interview—or perhaps just coming to the tea was the interview. But that's the way things work in a small town. They know most of what there is to know about you before you even say anything. I scarfed down a few open-faced tuna sandwiches with sliced cucumber, thanked saffron-blouse for the conversation, and paid my respects to Mrs. Morbeck. Then I left. Providence had smiled on me in grand manner. Life was good.

Finding 906 McKinley Street was easy, as I passed it every morning on the way to the mine, unable to imagine who lived there. Grandiose and stately, it was constructed on an old river terrace about thirty feet above the valley floor from deep maroon clinker brick with white-trimmed shuttered windows on the first story, dormers and white siding on the second. A wrought-iron fence faced the front walk. A tall, thick, brick wall with shade trees nestled inside enclosed the backyard. The place wasn't pretentious, but it had grace. Understated elegance, if one were to describe it in two words. I parked

on the street and walked around to the kitchen entrance.

All ninety pounds of Rex sat on the doormat. He let out a short "woof," meaning, "Is this guy friend or foe?" Doris opened the door and introduced dog and man. This apparently settled the matter. The keen brown eyes looked up at me, seeming to say, "Any friend of mom's is a friend of mine." He sniffed and filed my scent in the olfactory database that all dogs keep on hand. They sort people out better than most people can. I envy their skill. I got down on one knee, scratched the big fellow behind the ears. "Good dog. Good dog." He gave me a wet lick. His tongue felt like 60-grit sandpaper. I sensed we were going to be okay.

Doris gave me a quick tour of the first floor. The carpet was thicker than anything in my experience; it felt like I was walking in sand. The brush strokes on the painted woodwork were laid along the grain and perfectly tapered—a sign of good brushes and expensive paint. I noticed that because I had painted a lot of woodwork. It gives one a certain satisfaction to know enough about something to critique someone else's work, if only a paint job.

She said, "Now I think it will work out just right if you take the small bedroom downstairs next to the recreation room. You can enter by the back door and come and go as you please." A stairway leading down from the kitchen opened into a recreation room with fireplace. A bathroom and laundry lay right across the hallway from a small bedroom tucked away in one corner. We walked around. "This should do pretty well for you. You can keep all your stuff in the closet and dresser there. What do you think?"

"This'll work swell. Just right. Yes, ma'am."

"Now we need to be clear about how we're going to operate."

"Yes ma'am."

"I don't think we'll have any problems, but it's good to get things straight at the outset, you agree?"

"Yes ma'am."

"When we're gone, just make sure the house is locked all the time you're not here, and keep Rex's food and water going. You can take him with you on prospecting hikes in the backcountry if you want, or wherever you go. He loves to be out in the woods."

"You'll have friends in town and so on, but you'll have to do your entertaining and hanging around outside the house. You understand why. I expect you to take care of your own laundry and keep the room picked up. Aside from that just make yourself at home. It's too much of a complication to think about meals with us, so I want you to keep taking them at the boardinghouse. I think it will work OK if you want to use the refrigerator for Cokes and fruit, that kind of stuff.

"When we return from the convention, Wallace and I will spend our evenings alone, so we'll listen for you to come in and so on, but you needn't worry about where we are."

I asked, "What about my room at Pat's?"

"You might as well stay here with us the rest of the summer. That'll help you save a few bucks for next year. You can park your car in our driveway next to my Volkswagen convertible. In fact, why don't you move your stuff over from the boardinghouse this week? That way you can get into the routine before we leave."

I told Dora at Pat's Boarding House about my good fortune. She cocked an eye at me and said, "So, you're already a-movin' on up in society, huh? You done all right for yerself."

"Ah, it's no big deal. They're awfully nice people. It'll be a chance to save a few bucks."

"Better keep quiet about it at the mine. If the hands was to find out you're a-livin' with the boss of the whole dang company, they'll give you a bad time over it."

I took Dora's advice to heart. But there are times even when you keep your mouth shut when you are called upon by your fellow man. A few weeks later, as I got out of my car in back of the house, Jack Tyree, the other miner sharing the stope with Chris and me, caught sight of me leaving the car. "Hey you, youngster!" he shouted across the lawn, loud enough to reach Spokane. No place to hide. My cover blown, I knew I was sunk.

"Jack, how the hell are ya?"

"What you doin' here walkin' in the vice president's place like you owned it?"

"Yeah, yeah, I know. Just house sitting for a couple of weeks. Feed the dog. That kind of thing."

"Well, I'm thinking I gotta start treatin' you with more respect. You ain't spying on us old hands are ya?"

"Jack, if I was spying on old hands I'd be dead meat by now."

"OK, kid, I ain't going to say nothing. You tell Chris where you're staying though. Here he has his wife, Lucille, as president of the Lutheran church, and now this development with you bunkin' with the company head shed. We'll all be famous."

So I moved into the Big House on the hill.

9
Darkness

After lunch Chris always took a few minutes to look over the morning's work, contemplate the work to come, and estimate the final act. I think he had a great talent for this subterranean seminar, shining his lamp around, making sure everything was caught up properly—that what he thought made the place safe was still safe.

During one of these monologues, his headlamp went out in midsentence. It flickered on briefly, then off. This happened once in a great while underground. The instinct of shade-tree mechanics is to tap, twist the knob, shake it. He did. But nothing changed.

"Done for," he said. "We'll have to get by wit' yours to finish drilling. Can't get another one now. Can you think for both of us? If you turn your head away I won't be able to see anything. Try and keep it pointed so we can both see something."

"No, no, I can do it. Sure, you bet," I volunteered. But I had no idea if we were in a tight spot or just innocent bystanders in a story about to unfold with no particular outcome in sight. What I did know was that we had to blast and be out of there in less than two hours. Leaving right then was an alternative course of action, but that meant explanations to unsympathetic bosses wanting to hear only the sounds of rock breaking.

Chris made the decision to go for it. "Well, partner, we'd better get started."

At first we zigged and zagged out of step with one another, making corrections and overcorrections. As time went on we got better, driven by a sense of urgency growing thicker, increasingly demanding as the afternoon progressed. A mythical spirit stood in the back of the stope pointing a long bony finger at us. "Make haste slowly, for you two are pushing the envelope."

When the time came to fetch the powder and fuses, I had to leave Chris sitting on a timber in the dark. "Just don't forget where I am, OK?"

"I'll be back."

His eyes lit up like diamonds when I returned a few minutes later. "All I can say is I'm glad you didn't get lost up there. Kinda lonesome down here, partner."

We both grabbed tamping poles and crammed primers and powder down the holes with a touch like a velvet hammer, six sticks in every hole. We finished at 1:45 P.M.— way ahead of schedule. I pulled the hoses and jackleg back out of the way of the blast and cleared our exit path out of the stope. We wanted nothing in the way to trip over or slow us down.

I bunched the fuses together while Chris lit them and ensured each one smoked before going on to the next. Smoke billowed upward around us, swirling in the inky atmosphere, clouding our vision as if to challenge what we were up to or hold us back. The black tape wrapping the fuses sizzled, melted, and dripped on the floor as the fire stream burned back a foot or more.

Finally, all was as it should be.

"Let's go."

As we started out, I shouted in Chris's ear, "You go first, I'll come out behind you!" Why I shouted across a distance of two feet in otherwise complete silence remains a mystery. Chris was already on his way and three steps in front of me.

At the top of the stope ladder, we emerged into the haulage drift. Here we were away from any real danger below, one light or two, and headed single file down the center of the track toward the shaft a quarter mile away.

At each step along the passageway, I found myself squinting more often in the unlit drift, searching for detail in the ties and rails in front of us on the muddy floor. It felt as if someone were holding a piece of cheesecloth in front of my eyes. Chris slowed down too. The farther we walked, the harder it became. Long before we reached the shaft landing's illumination, he turned around and looked up at *my* lamp.

"Partner, your light looks like a bumblebee stuck in a black cat's ass."

"Nah, it must be the smoke and stuff. My eyes are sore."

"No. You take a look." I took my headlamp down and the bulb barely glowed. His description was perfect.

It doesn't take long to decide a course of action at times like that. We looked at each other. He said, "Better get a move on," at the same time I said, "We better move it." We took off as fast as two men can wearing diggers stiff with mud clear to the crotch, hard-toed rubber boots one size too large, and hard hats and carrying dinner pails and defunct battery packs. A guy in a Spandex-Nike-air-soled jogging outfit looks different and sounds different. We bucked and clattered along like a runaway stagecoach.

In a few hundred yards we ran out of light and breath at the same time. We stopped dead in our tracks. It was very dark. In fact, there is no darkness anywhere like the silent, isolated, black void we found ourselves in. "Stretch out thine hand toward heaven, that there may be darkness over the land . . . even darkness which may be felt." Exodus 10:21.

"Holy shit, partner! What now?" I asked incredulously. Every sense groped for some sign of normality. All perception changed. I reached out to steady myself on a drift timber, unnoticed and unimportant in previous passages. But now it was a reassuring landmark. Everything that used to be there was still there. One thing I knew for sure was that my feet were on the floor and the floor was "down." I smelled our combined sweat, listened with renewed interest to the sound of our heavy breathing. It seemed like my eyes were wide open, but I was unsure. Maybe they were closed; the same degree of darkness everywhere.

"Damn and thunder!" Chris exclaimed. "How far we got to go to the shaft? It's got lights."

"Four or five minutes yet," I said. "But it's at the end of the big curve we go around."

Side drifts went off in different directions to abandoned workings, and my disaster-prone imagination cooked up a picture of how lost we'd be by the time the shift bosses started counting noses and got it all figured out.

I couldn't see the expression on Chris's face, but I could imagine it. After a few seconds, he said, "This ain't what ya call good luck. I been tru it one other time when I was by myself. Best get down low so we don't fall over. How many other drifts do we go by when we come in here?" he asked.

"Two, I think. One angles off sharp left. Another goes to the right. And then there's the powder magazine. That's all I remember."

"That seems right. We're still facing the same way we were when we stopped?"

"I know I am, and you were in front of me anyway. How can we keep from wandering down one of those blind drifts? Nobody works back there."

Chris thought a moment. "We'll have to crawl as best we can, but keep your hands on the rails. When we get to a switch, we can tell which way it's open and follow the lead rail. They should all be open going to the shaft."

He went first. I placed my lunch bucket beneath my left hand as a tinny, short crutch on which to lean and my right hand on the rusty, wet rail—now feeling oddly cold in the ninety-four-degree heat. We set off in an ele-phantine trunk-to-tail entourage. Our knees searched instinctively, and painfully, for rock-free landing spots on each tie. Sometimes we got out of lockstep and I jammed my hard hat into his backside.

"Look where yer going!"

"If I could look, I would. Nothing personal."

It took a while to figure out the lead of each switch as we came to it, but the plan to use the switches as naviga-tion aids worked flawlessly as we felt our way through.

The odyssey reminded me of tasks in which we try to forget what is really going on, tasks that (a) cause mental and physical punishment and (b) seem to have no end, like spreading six tons of crushed gravel or paddling twenty miles upriver upwind. But the urge to escape being held hostage by the darkness, to have light once more, provided lots of incentive to keep going even after our hands cramped and our knees begged for relief.

Foot by foot, maybe ten minutes went by before we looked up and saw timber and wet sidewalls glistening in reflected light from the shaft. We stood up slowly, stiff and awkward. "Nothin' to it, partner." We strode fearlessly into the station as if nothing had happened.

The rest of the crew, waiting for us, wondered where we had been. One of them said, "You guys look like you been in a swamp or something."

Chris smiled. "Nothin' special. Another day another dollar—a million days, a million dollars."

10

Dora Tatham

It took me several weeks to understand anything of substance about our boarding house cook. Dora cooked early breakfast, each one a short order. She was there when I came to dinner, and she must have been on duty at noon. It was the same story on weekends. She took care of my stomach, and she always had a kind word. Every guy who came to eat had a wisecrack of some kind. Dora had one right back. As time went on I noticed she arrived in the predawn morning and didn't leave until after dinner, around seven o'clock. Today the dot.comers would say, "She works 15-7."

In an idle moment one afternoon I asked her if she had any kids.

"I reckon. Six to be exact. Mary, Marjorie, Dora Dee, Betty Lou, Irene, and Ralph."

"I never see your husband around much. Where is he?"

"Been up in Greenland all summer on an air force job. He's the only one that knows anything about blasting. He works in the Bunker Hill mine when he gets home."

"I don't see how you have time to raise a family and do all this cooking."

"Me neither. But the girls are very good. They miss me when I'm a working all the time, and Dee being gone to make some money. But they carry the load. I worry sometimes. They got too much responsibility. You grow up too fast and miss being a kid."

Dora had no equal when it came to cooking eggs. An over-easy was over easy. A sunnyside-up was perfect. She cracked two at a time with one hand and managed to keep shell chips out of the scrambles and French toast. She served short order breakfasts to seventy-five miners—30 dozen eggs a day—and it wasn't over until the swing shift ate breakfast at noon. Then it was time to bake 24 pies at a clatter, peel 20 or 30 pounds of potatoes, and fry in the neighborhood of 200 pork chops. It makes you wonder. How can anyone do that for twenty years and avoid counseling?

I was intrigued by what seemed to be a regular sorority in the Tatham household. One daughter came over occasionally to help serve tables and bake cookies. Betty Lou was gorgeous. She had smooth tanned skin, not a blemish, and a figure so grand as to make grown men weep. In her deep-set eyes I detected a hint of sorrow and loneliness in my calf-moon rapture. Some nights I couldn't even go to sleep thinking about such beauty. And here she was baking cookies twenty feet from where I sat at dinner.

Finally, I asked Dora if Betty Lou had a boyfriend. "No," she said, "I don't think so."

"Do you think I could ask her out?"

"You can. I'll see what she says."

So we got acquainted. As a predate warmup I offered to take Betty Lou out to Pinehurst to visit Orval Goff's farm, maybe take a horseback ride. But my car wouldn't start when the time came. Damn, what an impression this'll make, I thought. Dora came to the rescue. "You guys take my car. It's OK. Whatever you do, though, don't let Betty Lou drive. That's all she talks about. Driving the dang car."

"No, no, Mrs. Tatham. You can count on me."

So we went out to Pinehurst, talked to Orval, rode a horse, and climbed back into the car for the drive back to Kellogg. The car, as I recall, was a '52 Chevy four-door sedan. Maybe a Plymouth.

Betty Lou said, "Can I drive?"

"Oh, sure." Quicker than you can say "flaky," I abandoned my promise to Dora in a vainglorious attempt to grease my way into her daughter's heart.

With this stamp of approval and confidence from a veteran of the highway, we swapped places in the front seat. The best part of that maneuver was when we had to get real close. I don't think she noticed. She started the car in gear with the clutch out. It leaped forward about four feet and stopped.

"Better put it in neutral."

"Oh, I forgot."

We backed out of the driveway onto a gravel road with the accelerator floored—and into a mailbox. Betty Lou hit the brakes before we got very far into it, but the taillight lens was splintered.

"God. Now your mother will have me hung and quartered."

"Geez. I feel bad. What will you tell her?"

"That I didn't see the mailbox when I backed out of the driveway. You weren't driving remember?"

The experience kind of put a damper on the romantic aspects of the situation right away. But a few nights later Betty Lou and I hit the bright lights of Kellogg. We went to a movie called *The Court Jester* starring Danny Kaye.

Afterward, we drove around town. About the time I thought of stopping to try and buy a six-pack of beer, she offered me a piece of Double Bubble gum and blew a fantastic balloon right out of those delicious lips. The lovesick brain said to me, What's going on here? Out loud, I said, "Say, I was wondering what grade you are in school."

"Oh, ninth grade. I'm fourteen."

Fourteen going on twenty-four. What a mess. Here I was a college sophomore, fraternity man to boot, squiring around a girl-woman in advanced junior high school. The date was not my finest hour. Nor was it Betty Lou's, I'm sure. I took her home soon after the epiphany. The porch light shone brightly as we walked up to the front door—which I studied in some detail (it had a frosted-glass elliptical insert) because I didn't know what to say.

"Thanks."

"Thank you."

11

A Thing Called a Picaroon

Sometimes the previous day's blast left an interesting hole in the ground. Interesting or not, we sprayed drill water over the face each morning to get beyond the blasting dust and find out where loose material might be hanging. This activity quieted down the powder fumes, which, if they were bad, gave you a migraine-sized headache in about twenty seconds. When Chris got through barring down, my job was to go into the opening and make sure the posts would fit and the caps came in level with the previous set. I was supposed to bring the seven-foot posts over to the new work area, but at first I couldn't even move them. Jack Tyree working nearby, took pity on my struggles. "Hell's fire, son, you can't carry them buggers. You can only skid 'em across the floor there. Use that picaroon and drag 'em." That helped, because they were soaking wet and slick.

Together we wrestled each post into the two corners in front. It reminded me of two men trying to waltz in three-quarter time with a greased pig. Every few seconds you felt like you had the thing under control, then you would lift with your face red and your guts straining and nothing would happen. Then you waited a bit and tried again. Sooner or later the thing moved in the right direction and stood where it needed to be.

You will not find picaroons in a hardware catalog. They were designed to stick timber and hang onto it. Probably a tool that died out with the industry. It looked something like a long-handled geologist's pick with a nasty little curl on the pointed end that stuck into timber and held on like a piranha. It's an odd name for a tool: according to the dictionary, a picaroon is a pirate. It fits.

I recall a particular morning when I had pulled, rolled, tugged, pushed, and sworn one of those piss-ditch posts about two hundred feet, finally wrestling it downhill close to where we needed it. For some reason I can't figure out, because he would normally be on the floor with me, Chris stood on a cap above and behind me at about the level of my hard hat. Our idea was for him to lift the monster up to the next level; we may have been catching up the shoring on two sets instead of one. But even with Chris pulling with his arms and me pushing from below, we couldn't move it more than a few inches. He said, "Here, let me try with the picaroon. Hold on—I'll stab it from up here." I moved my head a few inches to one side to give him a clear shot. Down came the picaroon. Something went wrong. It ricocheted off the round post and whistled right past my left temple. It knocked off my hard hat and stuck two inches into the sill so close to my ear I could tell how cold it was.

"Yesus Christ!" Chris catapulted off the timber, landing on the rock at my feet, and grabbed me by the shoulders. "Are you all right, partner? It bounced off. I got off balance.

I should have aimed higher. Ohhhh, yi yi yi. Dat was too close. Too close."

"No, no. I'm OK. I just need a drink and to change my shorts."

12

Lunch

The meaning of lunch, and what it amounts to, seems to have changed a great deal. If you're just an average bloke spending a few leisure hours on the Seattle waterfront with or without your main squeeze, it can be a glass of Chardonnay and a smoked-salmon sandwich on sun-drenched Pier 71. Or you may be a drywall contractor on your way from one shoot-and-scoot job to another. In that case lunch will be a Big Mac or double taco washed down by seventy-eight ounces of sugar water, caffeine (the coffee people had to do something with it), and artificial flavoring called a Big Gulp. It will be eaten in the front seat of a four-wheel-drive, one-ton Ford truck, sitting in gridlock on the freeway. To the indentured servants of corporate America, lunch is in the company cafeteria, which offers a seafood bar, a Mexican bar, a Chinese bar, and fifteen salads plus focaccia. If you sell real estate, you don't have time for lunch. Since no fast-food chain serves peanut butter and jam, I suspect they have been supplanted as the mainstay of the working person's lunch. Chris and I ate a lot of peanut butter. We talked about its quality, and we knew good from bad.

Lunch underground has always been more than just an excuse to eat. It was a sacred time to reflect and plan and recover from the noise and the stifling, mind-numbing heat. It was a time to rest from lifting and pulling the trappings of hardrock mining, which invariably were heavy. And from another perspective it was a *privilege*, shared by a handful of people, to sit in our tiny sanctuary on a piece of three-inch lagging in the middle of what had been a Precambrian sea. No phones, no e-mail, no media, nothing besides our conversation and a leak from the compressed air line hissing softly a few feet away. No one had ever sat where we sat.

In the glow of the one headlamp we left on for illumination, we simply ate, letting accumulations of sweat drop from nose and earlobe. Chris's fine Scandinavian locks stuck together like wet goose down, creating a one-inch mat all around his head where his hard hat had rested.

On a good day I might have had pressed liverwurst and mayo slammed between two pieces of white bread; Snyder's brand, if I remember correctly. The kind of bread that not only feels like library paste when it sticks to the roof of your mouth, but tasted like it. We ate with deliberation—not fast but with a sense of urgency because the ritualized schedule called for a nap at exactly twenty past the hour. We were polite, too; said things like "thank you" and "please" and used paper napkins.

Very occasionally and with great reticence, Chris talked about his family and how he came to be a miner. But I had to drag it out of him.

"In the early days, my folks had a place in North Dakota. I was born about 1910, I think. We had a big family. I mostly helped on the farm, which was why I quit school in about the third grade. But I learnt how to read. Mother was a Dane and my father was Norwegian. Never want to hit a Norskie on the foot ya know—might kill him."

"So they were from the old country," I said. "Ate herring and lefsa, liked to stare out at the sea, knew all about bad weather."

"Yah, blizzards was good, and cold weather.

"In about 1929, at the start of the depression, my brother Edward and I got jobs shoveling in a coal mine near Valley City. We was just eighteen or so, but we got eleven cents a ton for it—loading coal at the face into little hand-trammed cars. Just shovel all day. Not a lot of money, but then hardly anyone had any money or even a job. We were pretty good at it. Between us we probably made a dollar a day. We were on our knees all the time because them coal seams was only four feet high. Couldn't even stand up. Wore out a lot of pants."

"So how did you happen to wind up in Idaho?"

"The folks moved out to Sandpoint in 1936. I worked in the sawmills on the green-chain. Then I got to sharpen saws. Never have had any trouble finding work—always plenty of work if you want it."

"So you got started mining more or less by accident?"

"The accident was I got hungry. Then a friend of mine and I decided to get drunk one Friday night, and somehow we wound up there on the North Fork in Murray. Seemed like a pretty good place to stay. Real quiet. I got a job in the Carlisle-Amazon mine and then sometimes I'd spend the summers in the woods, winters in the mine. Then I ran into Lucille. We got married on Halloween night when I was thirty-eight or -nine. We moved to Pine-hurst when I got this here job at Bunker."

I don't know how it got started, but some piece of mis-placed testosterone got stuck in a guy's tongue one day and overnight all wives became "my old lady," or "the missus." But Chris was different. Lucille was either "the President," or "Mrs. Christopherson," or "Cile." I have a hunch she ran the show in their household and that Chris was proud of her, loved every minute of it. She taught Sunday school, became president of the Lutheran League and of the Board of Deacons at their little church in Pinehurst.

Every so often Jack Tyree stopped by to share lunch and tell a few jokes. I couldn't remember one for more than a few minutes, which didn't add a great deal to the discussions held in the dark. But Chris always managed to pick one up over the weekend. His favorite was the one about the blond gorilla:

Seems a couple of anthropologists were wandering around Africa, and they found this blond female gorilla. After a long study period, they came to the conclusion that this animal was the last individual of a rare species. They decided if the species was to be saved, a man of Scandinavian descent would have to father the off-spring. Well, they looked at a lot of medical records and found a good match with one particular bachelor from Trondheim. They said, "Lars Larsen, we need you for a very important experiment. There is a blond gorilla that needs a mate, and if you will do it with her, we can save the species from extinction."

So Lars says, "Let me t'ink about it. This is no t'ing to rush right into."

In a few days, Lars got in touch with the scientists. "I t'ought and t'ought about this here problem, and I t'ink I told myself to go ahead and do it. But only on three conditions. First, I'll only do it once. Second, there'll be no huggin' and kissin'. And third, all the kids gotta be raised Lutheran."

Chris told it so well that if he hadn't told it for a while I'd ask him to do it over again.

That was how a lot of it went. Lunch was a time when we got to know each other. And every day at 11:20 when the conversation ended, we lay back and took a nap, waking up within thirty seconds of a precise ten minutes.

13

"My Name Is Judy"

There's an old adage that if you set enough bear traps, someday you're going to catch a bear. And if the truth be known, eighteen-year-old men have a trap set all the time whether they know it or not. I think it's especially bad on Saturday nights and Sunday mornings—couples times, family times. You aren't alone, and, depending on how much you happen to love the human race, you may not even be lonely, but it still feels like you're by yourself.

In any event, I remember one Saturday evening when the conversation inside my head reached an intolerable level of chaos. I went out to see what was happening. Entertainment can come cheap in a mining camp when you mix payday and five or six hours of socialization with various forms of grain alcohol. What would it be? When would it start?

It started slow and low-key. I watched a fast-pitch softball game between two rival factions. It may have been the Finns and the Swedes. I don't think they really hated each other, or maybe they did just for the length of the ball game, but it sounded like it. The pitchers were very serious. The ball sizzled into the catcher's mitt after an elaborate, full-circle, underhand windup and release. The sun went down, the lights went on, and the game came to an end about nine o'clock. Players, wives, and kids, in-laws and outlaws, loaded blankets and jackets and beer in their family pickups and went home.

I sat in the empty high school stadium until the exodus ended. Then I crossed the street and walked uphill toward the Brass Rail Saloon. Its open door exhausted an indelicate aroma of old beer, cigarette smoke, and peanuts. Hank Williams's twangy voice blasted out of a jukebox. "Your cheatin' heart will tell on you." The place had atmosphere, and there being no signs of civil insurrection or riot, I made up my mind to step across the threshold and see what was going on. I could buy a drink just like the bigger boys.

The Brass Rail Saloon was laid out like a right triangle. The street came to an end at about thirty degrees on one corner, and the sidewalk in front formed the hypotenuse. The atmosphere inside was thick, raw, and foggy. The bar stood straight ahead, backed up by a plate-glass mirror. Some slow-moving couples groped around on a dance floor big enough to hold about six people if they were real good friends. I strode purposefully across the wood floor like I knew what I was doing and perched western-style on an upholstered barstool, one foot on the brass rail, the other glued to the floor for support. The guy next to me ordered a Beam and branch from the bartender. "Make it two," I chimed in, having no idea what I'd just ordered. My neighbor laid a buck down on the counter. I did too.

I kept my gaze focused on the back bar for a few minutes, sipping the Jim Beam whiskey with branch water like it was double-malt scotch. The crowd in the room was mostly day's pay miners and millworkers and their wives. But my gaze stopped cold on a striking blond woman about my age, give or take a few years. She sat facing my general direction at a table in the shadows with four or five other people. She held a drink in her hand—maybe a rum and Coke. Too dark to tell for sure. The conversation appeared to be rounding out, and she stood up. Instinct told me that the mirage was about to disappear over the horizon in the next few seconds. She wore a white blouse tucked real tight into a belted pair of tan slacks. The blouse stuck out in front like it was badly overstarched, bending in only one direction. But there was more to it than that.

My internal dialogue ran on like a broken tape on remote control. "Oh, oh, oh, oh, hold on now, hold on. Whoever you are, don't leave. Don't leave."

Desperation took over, forcing me to think of what a guy was supposed to do. Why wasn't I better prepared for this moment? The real question was, Is there anything to be done at all? Statistically, my chances of impressing this one were about the same as kicking a seventy-yard field goal. But lust has a way of ignoring situational statistics. I decided to try. What was the line John Wayne always used? "Wahah there barkeep, like to buy a drink for the little sister over there."

Would it work? A long shot, but my brain and gonads were engaged in a lightning-strike dialogue involving unrealized potential. "Say there," I said to the bartender, "I'd like to buy that gal over there a drink. The blond.

Whatever she wants." He said, "Sure thing," and took a drink over to her.

Standing there tall as possible and hanging onto the molding with both hands, I managed a mindless smile when the bartender leaned his head in my direction as the source. The girl smiled back, picked up the drink, and walked toward me.

My guts shook like a sewing machine in a voltage spike—earthquake country. That part of the human cortex that manufactures speech went suddenly numb. I'd started something I didn't know how to finish, and I couldn't remember the next line.

She said, "Gee, thanks. Who are you?"

"Fritz. That is, that's my first name. And, uh, you are?"

"My name is Judy."

"Nice to meet you. I guess I'm just working here at the mine this summer—going to school in New Mexico. Actually I don't have to guess since I know that's what I'm doing," I said.

She laughed.

Damn, things were going along well. I tried to sneak a glance at her breasts while we were chatting without appearing too obvious but didn't get away with it. She knew, and didn't mind.

"Oh, well, that's nice. Me too. That is to say, I'm sort of between terms—a psych major at UCLA."

"All right, good deal. Great school," I said. "What brings you to Kellogg?" I asked, sensing the start of a long relationship. A fool's confidence crept through my blood-brain barrier.

She grabbed her drink and looked thoughtfully up at the ceiling for a few seconds before replying.

"Well, as a matter of fact, I guess I'm a hooker. During the summer I work in the, the houses, you know."

"Oh, uh huh!"

At first I wasn't exactly sure what she said. I was *almost* sure, but it's not something you want to be only partly right about. For the second time in as many minutes I was absolutely sure that I had no idea what to say next.

Fortunately, she had more social graces than I did at the moment; she knew her reply would have an impact.

"I know it's an odd thing to say. But it's not such a bad job. I make tons of money. When I go back to L.A., I live like royalty the whole year. I pay cash for everything."

"OK. Sure, you bet. I was thinking you might want to go up to Bumblebee on the North Fork for a picnic or a hike or something. I suppose that's difficult."

I think she came close to falling apart at the picnic idea.

"Impossible, but its nice of you to ask. No one ever asked me to go on a picnic before. Never! Number one, we can't go out with anyone when we're working, and number two, I have a boyfriend in California. Number three, I'm flying out of Spokane tonight. So maybe some other time, huh?"

My heart hit the floor, along with a considerable slice of ego. But lust lingered in the conversation's twilight seconds. I knew I was toast, but admitting it proved hard work. Saying farewell to that ebullient femininity was all I could muster. "Some other time would be fine," I said with funereal solemnity and the certain knowledge there would never be another time.

"Well, I've got to make tracks to Spokealoo. Good luck at school. See ya."

"Yeah, same to you. See ya."

The bartender did what all bartenders are supposed to do. "Don't take it so hard, son. She's a heartbreaker. When you get to be my age, you won't worry about stuff like that."

"Yeah, I suppose so. The trouble is, I'm not your age."

"Hell's fire, son, you did good. She liked you. I tell ya, don't worry about it. You'll eat your guts out. There's more'n one woman in the world looks that good."

He washed a few glasses and shined them with a towel. We both thought about the psych major from UCLA for a few moments. Finally, he said, "Looks ain't everything. She probably can't even cook. What you want is one 't likes to cook and'll keep you warm on a cold night in the mountains."

I said I'd think about that.

14

Nicknames

Gorilla Mike was a Russian. He stood about six feet nine, weighed three hundred pounds. At a time when all any of us normal mortals could do was drag one seven-foot post down the drift, Gorilla Mike took one under each arm and walked off. At the start of every shift he stuffed a whole package of Beech Nut chewing tobacco in one cheek and half a sack of Red Man in the other. He called the tobacco stuffing process the "hard way" and the "easy way."

When Curly Seufert first hired on at Bunker Hill he was Gorilla Mike's helper. In those days a miner's helper was called a pimp. Curly went back to Nebraska around 1950 to meet his in-laws for the first time, folks who'd never seen an underground mine, let alone heard any of the lingo. His wife's father asked him what he did for a living out there in Idaho. "Oh well," he said, "I'm pimpin' for Gorilla Mike down on Level 23." Curly told me he had to clarify matters in a hurry after that.

Posthole Gene worked on the surface. No one knows what his real name was aside from Eugene something. Suffice it to say "Posthole" wasn't on his paycheck. One of his jobs was to build a fence around a sump or other dangerous opening on the surface. The job required fifty or more postholes. In the morning the foreman said, "Now we don't want anyone falling in these holes, so cover 'em up when you go home this afternoon." So Gene worked all day digging holes. After they were all dug—it was tough work—he thought of the boss's warning. So he not only covered them up, he grabbed a shovel and filled them. That way no one could get hurt. The boss came the next morning. "What the hell did you do that for? How are we supposed to get a fence post in the goddam holes you dug when they're all filled up? I'm gonna call you Posthole Gene from now on."

One of the guys on our crew was called Dum-Dum. I asked Chris how he got stuck with that nickname. Chris told me he helped on timber repair. One day they had to hoist a wet twelve-by-sixteen-inch drift timber on top of posts standing eight feet apart on opposite sides of the drift. He volunteered to pick one end up and lift it into place. Gritting his teeth and straining, the timber didn't move up, down, or sideways. Dum-Dum said, "That's pretty tough on that end. I'm going to try and lift the other end." Shaking his head in disbelief, the lead man said, "Ya know, you're not only dumb, you're dumb-dumb!"

A motorman named Ray got in an argument with a guy named Ray Beile about where a woman went to the bathroom. Ray Beile said, "It comes out from the same place as a man enters a woman. Down there."

Ray the motorman said, "No, they don't pee that way. They can't."

"Well, gosh, they do."

They bet ten dollars. Next day Ray the motorman said, "Here, Ray Bronze, here's your ten dollars. You're right. I checked it out."

"OK, we're going to call you Peehole from now on." And that's the way it was.

There were others: Crowbar, Quiverlip, Sixteen Penny Shorty, Buckshot, Crown Prince, Google-Eye Slim, Vaseline, Mighty Mouse, and Slippers. IBM, Pickles, and Plushbottom made the list too.

The nicknames and the christening stories stuck like contact cement. No one asked about Gordon Flanders or George Henry. Instead it was, "Haven't seen Cue Ball for a while. Where's he at?" "He's workin' with Hi Guy up on 19."

15

Doris and Wallace

If you had met Doris Woolf in the summer of 1956, the odds are you wouldn't have said, "That woman should run for president of the United States." It would be conceivable if the meeting occurred today, fifty years later. We haven't changed much, but we've changed a little. She could have made it. She was that kind of timber. Behind that diminutive woman's sparkling eyes lay a combination of toughness and intelligence that would have served us well.

It's dangerous to put words in someone's mouth, especially if they're no longer here to defend themselves. But I will venture an imaginative guess to provide a glimpse of the person I remember.

Doris cajoled and jawboned every mining company CEO who came to town, and some were pretty high rollers. She finagled them for donations to local charities. She remembered their kids' names and asked things like, "Your dog was sick last year when you were here. How is he doing?" One also sensed that she wanted to steer the conversation in a meaningful direction, that there was some purpose besides ordinary socializing. She knew a litany of the good-old-boy backroom jokes that still provide a source of camaraderie and comfort to corporate America's leaders.

As my candidate for president, I hear her drawing a line in the sand when the smoke cleared and the posturing, politicking, and egocentricity came to an end: "So this is what I heard you say for the last two hours. You agreed with me on three points. Now, did you mean it or not? Will you stand behind what you said? I want some commitment. If we don't have a deal, we'll start over tomorrow morning and keep going until we have one."

She stood an inch or two over five feet. Short gray hair encircled a not quite angelic face, resembling the Mamie Eisenhower cut minus the bangs. Her voice might take on a bite when discussing big-picture issues like human tyranny and oppression; spirited but never mean-spirited; purposeful but never self-righteous. The word *sparkplug* comes to mind. A person who got things going, a source of ignition. All who knew her would agree that she was a character; in my opinion, a woman of great character. I think she occupied a space way ahead of her time.

Sometimes she came to the end of a long stream-of-consciousness dissertation and laughed at carrying on. "Oh well, that's just my opinion." We often had on-the-fly conversations in the kitchen as I went to and from the mine. From them I learned that Doris didn't give a hoot about where a person came from or the particular social status and educational credentials someone might pack around. Friends were friends. Look them straight in the eye, treat them with dignity and respect. Everyone was on the same playing field. She said what was on her mind whether she should have or not. So people around her needed to appreciate this quality and take things as forthright as they were given or stand aside, often bewildered.

She was a charter member of the Fancy Ladies Bridge Club, one of whose bylaws governing play required members to wear a hat at the table. She packed everything for a three-month trip to Europe in one suitcase, including a brown baked potato costume she wore at trade gatherings promoting an Idaho product other than silver. She loved to take trips. "Let's go to Missoula today," she would say to her friend Maxine Brewer. They took a spur-of-the-moment trip to Seattle on a Greyhound bus full of military men. By the time the bus hit Ritzville, forty minutes south of Spokane, she had them all singing barbershop quartet songs and "Onward Christian Soldiers."

Because of her reputation for being a shaper of opinion, the John Birch Society sought her out as a potential member. But their right-wing dogma was anathema to her way of thinking. She told them, "No thanks. Please spare yourself the trouble."

Working underground leaves you sucked dry, dehydrated beyond imagination. It's tough to restore the balance. Water helps but doesn't do the trick. Cold beer helps quite a bit. But one afternoon I spied three lonely Sunkist navel oranges sitting in the refrigerator. I downed them all. Maybe I was afraid of getting scurvy. Kitchen privileges or not, I knew I had overstepped the bounds of our agreement. Doris noticed the missing fruit. All she said to me the next day was, "Did you know oranges cost twenty-three cents a pound?"

"No, but I do now."

I've never met a person as dedicated to answering a question that might come up in conversation—not just any answer but a good one, based on data. It's a rare quality. No one has time anymore. Once she invited me to dinner at their family cabin on Rose Lake, a side arm of the Coeur d'Alene River. As we drove along U.S. Highway 10, now Interstate 90, the conversation turned to politics. I asked, "How did the electoral college get started anyway?"

"You know, I'm not positive. I think it had something to do with the fact that information took a long time to get from one place to another. And of course they didn't have voting machines. Let me think about it."

Three weeks went by. Doris was deep in thought, pulling weeds from a flower bed as I parked my car and started toward the house. She looked up at my approach.

"It was an issue of trust—that is, a lack of trust."

"What was?" I asked, puzzled.

"When we went to the lake, you wondered about the electoral college. I went to the library and found something on it. In the time of Washington and then Adams, the Federalists didn't trust the Republicans, and the Republicans didn't trust the Federalists. So this intermediate body of electors was formed and charged with the responsibility to represent, therefore vote, the will of the people in their state. In other words, chicanery in politics is nothing new. Something else, though. I never thought of this before, but information—whether it was news or votes—didn't travel any faster than a horse could run between point A and point B. Interesting, huh?"

Initially, I had no idea what Wallace Woolf was like, only that as VP–general manager, he was in charge of all the company's Kellogg operations. In the purview of any eighteen-year-old, that was great plenty. I needn't have worried.

I met him for the first time a few days after I moved into the basement digs. For all of Doris's effervescent qualities, Wallace was surprisingly reserved and soft-spoken. That's not to say cold or standoffish. It may have been only my perception, but I felt his thick shock of graying hair and finely trimmed mustache, coupled with pressed and trim blue-gray business suits, created an air of distinction, of formality, an inherent sense of decency; someone who paid attention to details. But by day's end, with rolled-up shirtsleeves and suit coat slung over the shoulder, he resembled anyone else coming home from a long day. I think he probably didn't mind being the next thing to president of the Bunker Hill Company, but I sensed that his real career love lay in the quiet back rooms of the metallurgical laboratories up the road.

When we first talked he wanted to know what college I attended and what I was studying. He wanted to know whom I worked for in the mine and where. He asked, "How is morale underground? What do the guys talk about? How do they feel?"

One afternoon he took me around the head office and introduced me to the staff: Austin Park, chief engineer; Roger McConnel, chief geologist; Al Lenz, diamond drill boss; Bob Muhs, ventilation engineer; E. B. "Ted" Olds, superintendent; even the secretaries. Doris called him "Wally" in private, and office management called him "Wallace," but I felt more comfortable addressing him as Mr. Woolf. He was *the* boss, and I was raised to respect people in high positions. Besides, to use a more informal greeting would presuppose a familiarity that I had not earned solely as a result of camping out in their basement bedroom for a few months. He seemed completely unaffected by his standing in the company, concerned only about making the best decisions and looking out for the entire crew's welfare.

One day I overheard Lee "Curly" Seufert, hoistman in the Service Raise, describe a conversation with Mr. Woolf. The fact that a day's pay union miner had the ear of the company's vice president tells you something about the sense of community that existed at that time. From what I could learn, Curly wanted to take his son to the Boy Scout jamboree in Valley Forge, Pennsylvania, but was afraid he'd lose too much pay for time off the job.

"So, I told Mr. Woolf at the weekly Scout meeting that Jerry Furnish kept my time, and I think he'll dock me if I go to the jamboree since I was out of vacation. Know what he said? He said, 'No, you go right ahead and go. Enjoy the trip with your family. I'll stop by the office and take care of your time card. Don't give it another thought.' And you know, he took care of it just like he said."

Wallace Woolf came out of the University of Utah School of Mines with an advanced degree in mineral dressing, the science of concentrating minerals after they're mined. When he went to work for the Bunker Hill Company in 1918, one of the principal problems in treating the ores of the district was the amount of zinc minerals mixed in with the lead-silver ore. Either one by itself could be concentrated fairly quickly. But the combination usually meant that one or the other metal wound up in the tailings, usually the sphalerite-containing zinc fraction.

In conjunction with a consulting chemist, U. L. Taiton, Wallace developed a wet-chemical process that electrolytically deposited 99.999 percent pure zinc on special anodes. The metal was then cast and poured into various shapes for use by industry. It was a major breakthrough. He engineered and supervised construction of the zinc plant housing the new process and spent all of the 1930s and 1940s managing the plant.

Wallace was a long-standing member of the North Idaho Chamber of Commerce. In November 1958 he was asked to give a keynote address at the annual meeting. This was a time when the domestic lead-zinc industry was on its lips. Pork-barrel legislators had seen fit to subsidize sugar growers with federal tax money, built refrigerated warehouses to store tons of butter, paid farmers not to grow wheat, but somehow left the miners to fend for themselves in a market inundated and price dominated by offshore producers. Wallace introduced his topic as a wake-up call to lobby for government support:

> It seems we have no friends in high places. This story says it all.
>
> Some time ago in a small isolated Idaho mining town, funeral services were being held for one of the local citizens. In the absence of a regularly ordained minister, a volunteer was holding forth and doing his best. He read from the book of prayer and spoke a few words of eulogy. Feeling that the proceeding up to this point had been uninspiring, he asked those present: "Does anyone want to say a few words for the departed?"
>
> Now the deceased, although prominent in the community, had not been well liked. No one volunteered.

At the end of an awkward silence, a stranger in the group arose and said: "If no one wants to talk about the deceased, I'd like to say a few words about California."

Had I been asked to talk about the lead and zinc industry of North Idaho a short time ago after Congress adjourned, I might have suggested some other subject, even California. And the analogy can be drawn even closer for it appeared that the domestic industry was indeed sick unto death, and it too appeared to have no friends.

Someone at the meeting suggested turning the mines into farms. "Dear Senator, we have a silver farm out in Idaho. We're broke. Can you help?"

16

Jackleg

I don't know what nicknames the jackleg drill may have acquired over the years, but in recollecting my first attempt to use one I am reminded of something Mark Twain wrote: "The person who has had a bull by the tail once has learned sixty or seventy times as much as a person who hasn't." The jackleg is one of those machines that takes you where it wants to go, and you, the operator, must relinquish thoughts of total control. One must treat it with respect, use gentleness and understanding, and take plenty of time in the process. That having been said, the point is that if you get in an argument with one, you'll lose.

The concept is simple. A basic air hammer, similar to a pavement breaker, is attached to a telescoping cylinder, or leg, about four feet long via a hinge at the hammer's balance point. So the leg, which has a prong on the bottom that keeps the whole thing from slipping when you crowd the bit, can swivel up or down but not side to side. By carefully opening the valve controlling the leg, the operator can raise or lower the hammer and apply pressure to the drill steel at the same time. It is a rate-sensitive process, and that's where the trouble comes in. You can't let the drill steel get too high or too low as the bit advances because the steel will stick, nor do you want to try to drill the hole too quickly because the same thing will happen.

The operator has to position the leg in such a manner that it centers the hammer and steel with the hole to be drilled and simultaneously apply some forward pressure to the bit. The leg, then, is always at some angle to the floor. Regulating the throttle setting on the hammer, extending the leg, and keeping the bit unstuck makes patting your head in one direction and rubbing your belly in another look like a cakewalk.

Though it takes a lot of getting used to, and some never get it, the jackleg is an ingenious device for the purpose it was intended. It allows the miner to drill holes from ankle level to three feet above his head without a lot of fuss and bother and set-up. But, to borrow a line from Meridith Wilson's *Music Man*, "you have to know the territory."

At the start of my third summer with Chris, June 1959, he said, "I'm tired of doing all the drilling. Why don't you give it a try?"

The drill lay twenty feet back in the stope, propped up against a post. I walked over and grabbed it by the hammer's handle. I gave it a forceful jerk off the floor as if I owned it. This motion only succeeded in tipping the hammer into the mud face down, cracking the leg's air valve open and extending the inner cylinder out across the floor. The entire machine then stretched out ten feet instead of six, but I hadn't let go or given up. I lurched back to a laughing Chris with the thing more or less in tow. It felt akin to sliding a couple of fifty-pound nail cartons to a new location, one in the left hand, one in the right, and me in the middle.

"Turn the leg off."

"OK. OK."

"Now collapse it."

"OK."

"Tilt 'er back on the foot and balance the hammer so I can get the steel chucked."

"OK."

"You look tired, partner. We haven't started drilling yet."

"I know. Let's keep going. I feel fine." My back hurt and sweat dripped off my nose.

"Now just balance 'er on the face with the steel out there like you seen me do."

"It looked easier when you were drilling."

"That's what everyone says the first time. Don't fight it now. Let the leg work for you. Take your time. Get the bit up there where you want to start the cut, and then just crack the throttle a little with your left hand and add a *little* pressure with your right hand on the valve. That's about the right angle on the leg. OK. Ready now, here we go."

So I opened the throttle on the round's first hole and started drilling. Initial success led to the Anglo-Saxon desire for more production. I got in a hurry—eager to show how a young buck like me could burn holes in rock faster than anyone. What happened next is what happens when you rush a golf swing: instant, humbling disaster. The steel stopped turning. The drill motor sounded like a popcorn popper. The bit stuck hard in the hole.

Chris didn't say much.

JACKLEG / M. M^CCANN ©

"Sometimes the bit sticks when you start to crowd it too fast."

For twenty minutes we beat on the steel with an ax, then hung on it with a three-foot pipe wrench with all our weight. It refused to yield. We were running short of time. We had to finish drilling in the next half hour or we were sunk for loading and blasting, and the shift boss would be pissed. I felt terrible for having done so well and then so poorly at my debut. It had happened to others, but small consolation. Finally we beat and twisted with the drill sputtering away and the leg pushing upward and outward until all of a sudden it broke loose.

"Boy, that's a lot of work," I said.

"Yah. What you need to do is listen to the ring of the steel as it advances. When it quits sounding chunky and starts to ring, that means yer close to getting stuck. Gotta' listen."

For a long time after that, I traded drilling duties with Chris. He welcomed the rest and I the challenge. He taught me to think where the hole would end up, six feet out in the vein, and the importance of heading the steel in the right direction at the very beginning. He improved my technique for balancing the drill and using its weight and heft to my advantage instead of attempting to manhandle it like it was a king-size mattress. And I listened real hard without earplugs—so well, in fact, that today when the piccolo player stands up for the solo passage in "Stars and Stripes Forever," I know she's playing because I can see her fingers moving on the keys. But that's all I know.

17

Always Faithful

"Will you walk into my parlour?" said a spider to a fly:
"Tis the prettiest little parlour that ever you did spy."

—Mary Howitt, "The Spider and the Fly," 1834

Towering, blue-black cumulonimbus clouds pile up on the Silver Valley's skyline in summer afternoons when the atmospheric conditions are right. Around nine o'clock in the evening, the air starts crackling like the rattle of musketry, and flickers of lightning spike the darkness. Thunder caroms off the exposed cliffs and rolls down the gulches. You're not merely a spectator in the fireworks. You become part of the system, tasting the chaos, hearing it, smelling the ozone. I stood on the Woolfs' back porch during one such storm, watching and thinking, change is in the air. A river of darkness hung over my head, darker than the clouds flying by. I had never slept with a woman, and I was almost twenty-one. Close doesn't count. Talking it over doesn't count. Doing it counts.

Rex sat on his haunches by my side. I said, "What do you think, Rex? This can't go on for seemingly goddam ever. Right? I mean it's not fair. Right?" He yawned and licked his jowls with his eleven-inch tongue and lay down. I looked into his eyes, seeking compassion and understanding, and I knew he understood.

It was a problem—a problem big enough to warrant a word of its own in *Webster's* dictionary: *concupiscence*. It is a word not widely used anymore. My lack of success wasn't due to a lack of interest. I loved girls. I loved all of them but some more than others. Genetics created the drive. I just showed up waiting for my chance. I harbored a deep sense of deprivation, felt singled out, had become a touch neurotic about the whole business. Doing "it" with a serious girlfriend or two over the years had been prayed over and deliberated. Still the target remained elusive.

There were reasons. First, the inherited Judeo-Christian legacy that nice girls don't do it before they get married held some of us in an iron grip mentally. We boys were considered nasty by default, unworthy for inclusion in *nice*. I cry out that perhaps we were callow and morally corrupt but not all the way to nasty. The girls were corrupt too but sneaky about letting it be known. So they could defend their nicety, while our only choice was to suffer in silence and put up with the charade. But we knew. We knew it took two people to consummate the act and we were alert and we were ready.

In comfortable urban sanctuaries like Laurelhurst, it was not common knowledge who was doing it, with whom, or if anyone was doing it. We had suspicions, though. One of our school chums, Jim, regularly swiped the keys to his father's Chris-Craft cabin cruiser. He and his girlfriend drifted for long hours a thousand feet from shore in the middle of Lake Washington. The cruiser looked abandoned because no shapes were ever visible above the catwalk. They were probably doing it. He didn't say much, but he smiled a lot. The rest of us were at something of a disadvantage, having no getaway and suffering the relentless distrusting scrutiny of the girl's parents. On the outside, though, it was all bluster and bravado. "Sure, I do it all the time. No sweat."

Fear was ever present, of course. We all wanted to do it, but no one wanted a baby. No one. Fear worked better at reducing the birthrate than any daughterly protection scheme parents might have thought up. I maintain that sex lives for singles only took off after the development of birth control pills. Our technology amounted to condoms, if you had the courage to buy one, and Saran Wrap. *Some* high school girl in Seattle must have gotten pregnant in 1955, but who was it? Girls in our class didn't suddenly disappear from school and go off to her "aunt's place in Spokane." Oh, I forgot about diaphragms, available only with a doctor's prescription, for God's sake. "Mom, can you get me an appointment with Dr. Mulhausen for a diaphragm? I want to have intercourse with Billie Sands." "Oh sure, Sally. That's a very responsible choice you've made." No way. Licensed druggists sold condoms from behind the counter at the corner drugstore. They did not appear on a rack next to the Halloween candy at Safeway. "Get your older brother to buy 'em for you," the guys said. But if you didn't have an older brother, how were you supposed to get one?

I did make a "condom summit attempt" one day near my neighborhood. I was coached by elder statesmen (college freshmen) on how to act and what to say. Finally, after giving my bellwether purchase enough preplanning to pull off a Brinks robbery, I strode into Kelly's pharmacy near my home with all the chutzpah I could muster.

The assault disintegrated in about five seconds. I couldn't see who was behind the prescription counter. *Mr.* Kelly was supposed to be there. But he must have gone home for a late lunch, because who should come around from behind the pharmacy wall but *Mrs.* Kelly. A nice lady. I knew I was sunk when she said, "Hi there, what can I help you with?"

"Those dickheads!" I cursed under my breath. They never told me about this. I tried not to let my knees buckle, but I know my cheeks glowed and sweat appeared. In the face of unbearable danger I stammered, "I need a pack of, a pair of rubber gloves." I bought a pair of rubber gloves, and they were nice ones too.

But three years later, on that stormy night in Idaho, I decided that a life of virtue had become irrelevant. The time had come to work the problem. For five bucks, I could get the job done free of the guilt-ridden perceptions flying around in my brain. Taking care of business with a professional answered the who with? question. The next was, where?

Where was a tough one, compounded by the knowledge that a virtual cornucopia of establishments lay within easy reach. So I put out some feelers as we waited for the skip at the end of the shift. The conventional wisdom, delivered with a heavy dose of the crew's good-old-boy wisdom— "Hey, we've been there before"—directed me to Wallace to visit the Lux Rooms (I knew where they were!), the Oasis, or the Arment. Someone else said, "Oh, they run a pretty nice establishment right here in town—down on Summer's

Flats at the foot of Hill Street next to the Miner's Club Tavern. It's not fancy. The U. and I." I never found out whether the literal translation was "You and I" or something else. I thought it a clever handle for a whorehouse and better than "You and Me," which might have been grammatically incorrect.

Eventually, a calm silence fell over the valley as the thunderstorm blew into Montana. Gentle rain dripped from the eaves; the air felt warm and smelled sweet. "It's now or never, Rex. The attack is on. You stay home and guard the house."

I slid behind the wheel of my car, clear of mind, intent, focused like a pilot shooting a fog-bound final approach to a short runway. At that moment no other thought invaded the conscious. But before I started the engine I sat for a moment, attempting to visualize the scene as it might unravel. It will be warm inside, with the lights turned low. There will be a bar over in one corner and customers sitting around having drinks. A half-dozen girls will be flirting with the guys, making themselves available and drinking soda pop. (I knew they weren't allowed to drink on the job.) There will be jokes going around and laughter. Some girl, maybe two or three, will come up to me and start a conversation. We'll have time to get acquainted—exchange first names. The girls will be dressed in gowns and that kind of thing. High class.

Sure, you bet. It'll be just like that, I told myself. I had a momentary sense of panic. What if it isn't? Our thought systems don't allow for chaos theory to take over. Even if it's a place we've been before with people we know, no engagement ever turns out the way we think it will. Logic doesn't help either. It's a long way from integral calculus to the local whorehouse.

More poignant questions arose. Do you kiss a whore? Damn if I know. Why kiss a woman you don't even know? What if you get scared and the equipment doesn't work? What do they do? Do you run out of time or something? Does a neon sign flash Couldn't Do It as you walk out? I tried to psych myself up. What's the worst thing that can happen? I asked. Not much. It will cost five bucks to find out—two hours' pay in the mine. The opening chords of *Thus Spake Zarathustra* leaped forward, a befitting entrance. "Satan, I rebuke thee! No. Satan, I beseech thee! Lead me on."

I drove around the corner and down Hill Street toward the railroad tracks. By now it was ten o'clock and the Miner's Club was closed. A lonely neon sign advertising Olympia beer blazed in one window. I reasoned the U. and I. must be the wood-frame building next door. A light shone from second-story windows. Otherwise the place looked deserted. My heart sank.

I had learned these establishments always had two stair-ways, usually covered for safety and convenience during snowstorms. The entrance stairs appeared to be on the east side of the building where I stood. The exit stairs looked like they ran down the northwest corner. This duality was a refinement whose purpose was to protect the identity of politicians, sports stars, city councilmen, and other dignitaries who might recognize one another in these surroundings and be at a loss for the proper thing to say. "Hi Larry, how's it going? Been out of town long?"

A small sign, just an arrow pointing upstairs, coaxed me along. I took my time walking up, plenty apprehensive in the pitch-dark unfamiliar surroundings. I paused at the top of the stairway because it wasn't clear whether you were supposed to knock or just walk in. I tried the knob. The door opened inward. As I stepped wide-eyed over the threshold, the scene before me instantly dissolved the picture my imagination had cooked up just ten minutes before.

The room looked like a large living room. Light green paint covered the walls. A lone ceiling fixture in the center of the room cast a sterile glow on a collection of overstuffed davenports and chairs. So much for the seductive lighting and atmosphere. Aside from the furniture, the room was empty, devoid of women in gowns and robes. Definitely no customers having a quiet drink. No bar, and no madam either. I wondered where exactly I had wound up. It occurred to me I might be in a no-man's land between a booze parlor and an illegal card game. Dispirited and bewildered, I just stood there in disbelief that no one was home for my coming-out party.

I walked across the room and stood in front of a window looking out over the street below. Wet gravel pavement reflected the glow from a distant streetlight. A minute or so went by as I contemplated what if anything to do. Then a voice on the other side of the room said, "Hi there. Can I help?"

I knew before I turned around that only one voice was involved; there was no "we." The moment of truth had arrived. I turned around and was pleasantly surprised. A woman appeared, half-hidden in a doorway, wearing an odd lime green outfit that reminded me of a prom dress cut off at the thigh. It had a tight midriff, with some taffeta stuck around the fringes. She was an attractive woman without going all the way to beautiful—sandy light brown hair, mid- to late twenties, average figure. She looked like the kind of woman you might take to a play or share a sandwich and cup of soup with somewhere.

The invitation drifted across the room with a smile. I felt just a *little* better. "Sure, you bet."

It didn't appear there was a whole lot of choice in the matter, and being raised in a polite household I wasn't about to say something like, "Hey, kiddo, are you the only one here?" As I walked across the room toward her, my adrenaline went off the chart, causing me to lose track of what my feet were doing. I tripped on the upturned corner of a threadbare Oriental rug, but I told my feet to keep moving. I thought about the first time I had stood on a high-dive platform, thirty feet above the water. Do you take the plunge or not? All you need to do is step off headfirst. The fall may not be fatal, but I was unsure of what would happen when I hit the water. That's the way it felt.

"It's a rough night to be out. Come into my room," she said, indicating a doorway across the hall.

I don't know what I expected to see when I entered the room, but again I was surprised. The trappings resembled any college girl's dormitory room I'd ever seen. A large vanity stood against one wall holding lipstick and assorted perfumes and cosmetics. Pictures of friends and dogs and cats were tucked under the glass in one corner of a huge semicircular mirror. "C-A-R-O-L" was strung across the top in big letters cut out of red paper.

Desperate for something to say, I looked up at the mirror and said, "I guess your name is Carol, huh?"

"Yes."

I glanced around the room hurriedly. An advertisement for the U.S. Marine Corps with their motto "Semper Fi" was stuck on a closet door. Always Faithful? A single bed stood against the outside wall with the covers turned back. A table lamp turned on and likely to remain on sat nearby on a nightstand. Some hygienic-looking accessories were stashed nearby: a washbasin, a pitcher of water, some towels. It looked to me like she worked and slept in the same room—odd, but hell for efficiency. It also appeared that there was no backing out of the deal at this point no matter what.

She said, "I don't think I've seen you before. Do you know the routine?"

"Oh sure, no problem," I lied through my teeth. "Other places though."

"What would you like to do?"

"Oh, you know, just the regular thing."

"The regular thing is five dollars. You can stay a half hour if you want. That costs fifteen. Positions are an extra three dollars."

"Oh."

"Well, first your money, then your clothes," she replied carefully, probably thinking, this *must* be a green pea. Then, in a single well-coordinated movement, Carol stepped out of her lime green tutu and stood there about as naked as a person gets. I thought, Holy sweet Jesus, we haven't even shaken hands and here we are! Following instructions, I grabbed a five-dollar bill from my wallet, laid it on the dresser, and stripped down to my socks. The room suddenly felt very warm. She handed me a damp washcloth.

I cleared my throat. "What's this for?"

"That's for you," she replied with a nod toward my private parts.

So much for external stimuli and cozy surroundings. There I stood with a washcloth in my hand, wearing a pair of sweat socks. The next thing in my life was sex with a woman I had known for five minutes and her name was Carol. The conversation, which I had thought would be very important, amounted to a total of about sixteen words. Well, that is a start, I reckoned. Bizarre, but a start. The need continued.

She walked over and jumped on the bed, assuming a position on her back while propped up on one elbow. "C'mon over. I'm ready if you're ready."

I think our commercial union lasted all of forty-five seconds. Not nearly enough time to establish a long-term relationship. But it held an element of humor and compassion, a humanitarian exchange between buyer and seller. The Greek symbol *mu* crept into consciousness somewhere along the way to a climax. *Mu* represents the coefficient of friction in engineering formulas. I kept my eyes closed the whole time, because being six inches or so from a complete stranger, in that activity, was more than my psyche could handle with my eyes open, nor did I know what to do with my hands.

The engagement came to an end in just about the same way it does for everyone, but a lot of things were different after that. I heaved an outward sigh of relief because I knew my soul had crossed over into new territory and not only remained intact, but acquired a whole new perspective. I understood without using too much imagination why this diversion had become so popular for such a long time and why the earth had so many mouths to feed.

"Are you all right?" she asked.

"Sure, you bet. Thanks."

I walked over to collect my clothes stashed on a chair.

"Next time don't wait so long. You need to stop by once in a while."

I didn't know whether to take that as a compliment, a marketing ploy, or some sort of incipient friendship, but I settled on marketing. I said, "OK. Next time I get five bucks put together I'll look you up."

As I slipped my jacket on she handed me a neat green and white ballpoint pen. "Your friends will get a kick out of this."

The inscription read:

MABEL'S WHOREHOUSE—DRY FORK, ARKANSAS
Where the customer always comes first
We give green stamps

She opened the door to her room, and ushered me down the empty hall toward the dignitaries and VIP stairway exit. I turned around.

"See ya."

"Bye, hon. You know the way now."

And that's the way it was. I never went back, and I never saw her again. I decided I had had a pretty interesting experience and been exposed to some singularly polite company.

That was forty-five or so years ago. Looking back, it's difficult to say whether prostitution as practiced at that time in the Silver Valley was a good thing or a bad thing. Its presence no doubt softened a few problems for the community, possibly created others at the same time. Most would say, "Well, it was what it was. For the most part we all got along." The establishments were part of the deal; part of the warp and weft of western mining camps.

One way or another the houses poured a lot of cash into local coffers. If you've never run a small business in a small town, it's hard to understand the importance of cash in local coffers. There's no Microsoft or Boeing around to take up the slack. The madams kept their political fences mended and maintained a low profile in the community. Over the years they have bought high school band uniforms, street maintenance equipment, and a police car for the city of Wallace. In the 1960s they passed the hat among themselves and raised $5,000 in cash to pay for a local woman's lung transplant.

They made sure the girls understood the code of conduct. No soliciting on the street, no pimps, no drugs, and no drinking on the job. Buy clothing and cosmetics only from store managers. Dress appropriately, and well. Take care of the customers so they come back. If they're drunk or troublemakers, call the madam and she'll take care of the problem. Checkups every two weeks. No dating or off-hours fraternizing with the customers. No exceptions. The "company rules" were more stringent than those of most multinational corporations. What's more, when it came to enforcement, the madams talked the talk and walked the walk.

I can't say my brief encounter was definitive, but I've always thought it unfortunate that these women and their mining camp predecessors were referred to as whores, hookers, or prostitutes, although I guess the handles fit in a *Webster's* dictionary kind of way. But they are titles deprived of any trace of gentility. On the other hand, descriptions like "soiled doves," "ladies of the night," and "sporting women" seem like phony contrivances. The *Spokane Falls Review* issue of February 9, 1884, refers to them as "Women in scarlet whose footsteps take hold in hell." The reality is fairly simple: they were women willing to provide some temporary relief to a raft of lonely, single men and make a few bucks in the process. For many, it was a ticket out of a condition called "being poor." Perhaps it's a shame that the word *courtesan* or the Italian *cortigiana* didn't stick. I have no suggestions.

One day I shared a Coke with a guy who worked at the post office. I asked him how the houses got along in the community, because, technically, prostitution has always been illegal in Idaho.

He said, "Well, they're sort of legal and sort of illegal. People just accept them as part of the community. Some of the clergy have taken a stand against them in the past. They didn't get much support. The city fathers will say, 'I hear they exist but I don't actually know it for a fact.' That kind of thing.

"If you really want to get an idea of how things work, go out on the streets at Halloween. The madams pass out the greatest treats you can imagine—doughnuts, cider, homemade brownies, and cookies. All of it first-rate stuff. The kids know where every house is. They flock to them from all over town. Everyone seems to get along fine. The kids are safe and the parents know it."

Many will argue the morals of the situation. In her recent book, *Anatomy of the Spirit*, Caroline Myss wrote,

"The oldest form of sexual currency is, of course, prostitution, the most disempowering act in which a human being can participate. [But] within each of our psyches lives an element of the prostitute—a part of ourselves that could possibly be commanded by the right financial figure. Whether . . . in business dealings or in personal relationships, we will inevitably meet up with it."

For my part, I see little difference between money-for-sex or money-for-influence as we've come to know it in terms of political action committees. Maybe it's only a matter of scale. "Here's a hundred thou for your campaign, Senator. I know you'll remember to vote for the Timber Salvage rider, or the tobacco bill. You understand this is soft money, of course."

There's a joke going around that the only difference between a whorehouse and Congress is that in a whorehouse you get a lot more bang for the buck, and, they change the piano player more often.

I think these women served the commonwealth in one way or another. They certainly made a contribution to keeping the community's testosterone level at a manageable level. Whatever we think of the profession philosophically, as an investment you can't beat it: low capital outlay, high return on investment (ROI in Wall Street parlance), price-to-earnings ratio of about 2.0, plenty of yield, just-in-time inventory, low debt, and high customer satisfaction. And tax-free. Not bad when you do the numbers.

18
The Hoistmen

The boss says we need more production. We gotta get up and down faster. We'll see—we have men beneath us.

—Dave Nicholas, hoistman, 1984

Some structures are taller, wider, longer, or heavier than we think possible. They expand our sense of perspective, our view of the world. The Boeing 747 airliner is one. The Golden Gate Bridge is another. Its piers were poured under water—in the middle of a tide race—and men walked on top of the swooping catenary cables without safety belts three hundred feet above the water. There were no other jobs during the Great Depression, and that's what you did to survive.

Another, closer to the heart of this story, is the Nordberg hoist, whose twenty-foot-diameter double-drum windings still sit like the queen of the fleet atop the #1 shaft at Bunker Hill. To sink the shaft in 1904, mining crews moved cast-iron sections weighing one hundred tons or more through the Kellogg Tunnel's ten-foot-wide cross section. Bone-crushing danger lurked at every turn of the wheel and at every inch of careful jacking, tugging, and lifting it into place.

In every underground mine that has a shaft and a hoist, a hoistman sits or stands somewhere next to a set of controls, signed up for a daunting responsibility. Some hoists are no larger than a bass drum with one hundred feet of skinny, frayed cable on it. But the Nordberg was the largest, most powerful underground hoist in the world in 1958.

The operator, called the hoistman or hoisting engineer, lives an insular work life. There is a reason for this. As you approach the "office" where they work, you encounter a sign that is anything but ambiguous: Do Not Talk to the Hoistman. He must not be distracted. To do so is to run too far down or too far up with a load. On the Witwatersrand in South Africa, someone ran a cage full of men into the headworks. The impact broke the wire rope, sending the cage ten thousand feet to the bottom in free fall. They said the aftermath looked like red jelly. In 1959 the hoistman occupied the top of the underground hourly wage scale—$20.23 per day, or $2.53 per hour.

He sat at a control panel containing two throttle levers, two brake levers, and a safety that stopped the load in case he had a heart attack. A handful of gauges indicated the power settings. Communication with the rest of the shaft took place by virtue of a system of bell rings and horn squawks. A bell ring meant the load was ready to go and indicated the destination. A horn meant someone wanted to go up or down and indicated where he was. There were no video cameras, LED displays, or electronics. The most advanced piece of equipment in use was a telephone, which for some reason was seldom used except to summon the fire team or an ambulance or to let someone below know the power had gone out. An indication of where the load happened to be at any particular time came from a white pointer slowly revolving past station numbers like hours on a black clock face. The payload might be twenty-one men in a skip, a timber slide full of posts and caps, dynamite, or ten tons of ore. It is not a job just anyone can do. It requires a bush pilot's calm and cool and the memory bank of a short-order cook. Requests came from all levels of the mine any time the need arose because everyone was in their own hurry. They don't call the job "riding the hoist" for nothing.

The lives of everyone underground depend on who's in the big chair and what kind of a day he's having. Though each shaft contains a manway and a ladder, in reality these provide more mental comfort than any-thing else—a last-gasp measure to reach the surface. But no one really wanted to climb six thousand feet of wood ladder on a pair of tired legs and leaden rubber boots.

Normal traffic, if "normal" is the right description, consisted of men going down or up, ore coming up, waste and garbage coming up; air hose, pipe, pumps, fuse, and drill steel all went down. Traffic can proceed as a series of planned events, stop altogether, or turn into chaos depending on how things are going in the shaft. The shaft is the mine's vascular system, the organ that pumps life to every cell and extremity. When it under-goes an autoimmune response, like a power outage or a skip jumping the tracks, the body goes into shock, for there is no backup system and no parachute to pop at the last minute. It is the one job in the mine requiring endless, nonstop concentration and with more potential to cause multiple deaths than anywhere else but on the flight deck of a commercial airliner. But no copilot is available to back up the hoistman, or computers to guide the way. It is all up to the head and hands of one man.

A great many hoistmen sat in those chairs; Virl McCombs, Lee Curly Seufert, Gary Hoffman, Charles "Tony" Tawney, and Jake Hallman, to name a few.

Twenty-four hundred horsepower drove the Nordberg hoist, sucking electricity from a 13,000-volt main line coming in from the outside through the Kellogg Tunnel. Each of the Nordberg's two drums contained a mile or more of 1⅜-inch cable winding. Either drum could be operated independently of the other, but the greatest efficiency came from operating them in counterbalance, one side ascending and the other descending. Winding the cable overshot from one drum and undershot from the other made it possible to do this with the driveshaft turning in only one direction.

No operator approached the concept of counterbalance lightly—for good reason. If it is carelessly done, a dynamic harmonic oscillation, called the yo-yo, develops on the way up. The only way to cancel this oscillation is to stop the hoist entirely, at which time the skips roll up and down the shaft rails all by themselves for a few minutes until the energy is depleted and the process starts all over from scratch with different parameters. The hoistman will tell you that a yo-yo is always too exciting by half regardless of the nature of the load. If it happens to be a skip full of miners, it is sweaty palms on both ends of the rope, for the miners will spend some time bouncing up and down a hundred feet or more between levels, listening to the wire rope stretch itself out, wondering every time they pass a station if it will be the last thing they see. The hoistman will pray for forgiveness and that the skip is still attached.

Two other shafts started on Level 9: #2 nicknamed the "White" after some forgotten boss or event; and #3, to the west. In the lower levels of the mine the company excavated smaller-scale pipestems of supply to nourish the work: the Service, May, and Cherry Raises and one called simply the Auxiliary. These installations depended on hoists less grand than the Nordberg, but the rules for operation were the same.

As we started to pick up our tools one afternoon, a light from far off down the drift came our way. It bobbed along with a different gait, a visitor neither one of us could identify. As the light grew closer we saw it wore a white hard hat and a heavy-weight tan canvas slicker.

"Name's Ralph Cote. I'm foreman in the Ike and Truman countries. I was talking to Ted Olds today before I came down. He said there was a college student working with Chris this summer from New Mexico Mines. You must be the one."

"Sure, you bet."

"Well, glad to meet you. Every year I try and contact the college guys, especially the ones studying mining, and take them on a tour of the place—show you some things you wouldn't normally see, like the hoist rooms and some bald-headed stopes we're trying out. I'd like to have you join us if you'd like."

"As long as it's OK with my partner."

"We'll start tonight after the day shift is over. I'll make sure you get out OK. We'll catch an ore train or maybe an empty timber car. I think there're about six of you guys altogether. Meet me tomorrow where the man-train unloads coming in around three o'clock. Hope you're enjoying your job. Your lucky to have ol' Chris for a partner."

Everyone showed up at the appointed time and place. We walked back down drifts I had seen before but had no idea where they led, arriving in a few minutes at the hoist room for #1.

Ralph said, "We might as well start here. We'll go up on the platform there, where the sign says 'Do Not Talk to the Hoistman.'"

"The swing-shift hoistman will be operating, but Virl McCombs agreed to stay over and talk to us about what's happening and about the hoist.'

Banks of fluorescent lights overhead lit up the room like sunshine. The hoistman sat at the control console. The size of the hoistman's chair struck me as odd; it seemed to swallow the person sitting in it. It had a big foam rubber cushion to ease the pain of sitting eight hours, and curved armrests wrapped with black electrical tape to keep the padding in place after years of use.

The hoist room was spotless. A mechanic stalked the machinery looking for oil flying off the rotating parts, and the floor was swept clean. The hoist sported a coat of bright white paint, in stark contrast to the wire rope, black as coal from the gallons of sticky lubricant applied over the years to keep the tight windings from fretting against each other and wearing out.

The thing that's so memorable about the hoist's opera-tion was the great humming that goes on as the two twelve-hundred horsepower electric motors picked up a load and started moving it. That is, no one had any doubt about the amount of work being done by that cable as it traveled back and forth across the drum as the skip came up, staying neat and orderly like the line on a level-wind fishing reel.

Virl, a slender, soft-spoken chap with a rapid delivery, said, "I guess the first thing you might wonder about is how we communicate all day with people we can't see. It's not easy, but it's not hard when you get used to it. You've all seen the skip tenders or bosses signaling us from down the shaft. Those bells ringing are the code we use, which is listed on that board in plain view over there. The bells are for ore, men, or materials. The horns are mainly for the bosses or skip tenders when they need a ride somewhere. If all else fails, we have a phone in the booth here and one on each station."

"So, for instance, a ring for Level 9, where we are now, is two shorts followed by a pause and one short. Then the ring for Level 10 would be two plus two, and so on. When we get to 14, it changes to three short rings fol-lowed by one. Fifteen is three and two. One bell by itself means "stop." As you get off at the station every day, you notice the shifter give one yank on the lanyard when it slows down to the right elevation. Two bells mean "up" and three mean "down."

I said, "I don't know how you do it. What if you were thinking about something else when the bell rang and you couldn't tell if it was two and one, or two and two, or whatever?"

"I don't know, you just get so you can do it. It becomes second nature. Of course, sometimes there's a genuine problem, in which case we ring the skip tender back what we thought was the ring and then they ring back to verify. Sometimes, they'll use the phone. But the one unbreakable rule is that we don't ever move the skip until we know for sure. If the ring was too fast to decipher or there was any question, we just hit the horn button and tell them to do it over again. It says, 'I'm unsure of what you want.'" We used to get people to train who came up on the bid list. Some of them would make it, and some wouldn't. You can tell within four or five days whether they'd ever make it. After a while you get so you're just part of the machinery. When the vibration changes or the hum changes, you know what's going on. It's like a motion picture inside your head. Actually, you get to concentrating so hard the shift goes by just like that.

"See, he's hoisting ore from 23. They're probably filling the skip right now. When it gets about half-full of muck, it'll stretch the rope a few feet and he'll have to make an adjustment. The ore pass is about 6,900 feet from where we're standing. The skip tender is standing on a twelve-by-twelve timber above the ore pocket. When it stretches, he'll step on a switch that lights that red light next to the operator. That's the signal to raise it up a few feet so we can fill the rest of the skip without spilling it down the sump."

In a few minutes, the bell rang: Two—one—two, translated "Level 9. Take 'er up," "It's all yours." The hoistman eased off the brake ever so slightly and gently pulled back on the throttle lever.

Virl continued, "Everyone that's on the hoist has probably spent some time as a skip tender. That's important because you have to be able to visualize what's going on down there, how long it takes to unload or load certain things. Just never move the skip until there's a signal to do so."

"What happens if the skip tender sees something going wrong—like a timber is across the rails or there's a cave-in?"

"You grab the bell cord and just hang on it until the skip stops. The operator knows right away something's wrong, and he'll just slam on the brakes and leave it there until there's a clear signal about what to do. A long bell means only one thing—pay attention to me. Then someone would get on the phone and call us. Something might be wrong, or it could be what we call a parade flash. That means the company president, or a bunch of senators and their wives are coming through and we need to get everything shipshape."

Virl pointed out the two big dials, one for each drum, directly in front of the flight deck. One dial, white on a black background, began moving off the mark at 23; the other began unwinding from 9 toward 10.

"He's in counterbalance now. That's so the hoist has to do less work with this kind of a load than if you tried to do it by just using one side. What you do is pull the empty skip up into the rope raise just above us there, and the skip to be loaded is wherever it's at. Now you watch, as he starts up with the load the other one will start going down and the two skips will pass each other in opposite directions somewhere close to Level 16. He has the throttle pulled all the way back. He's moving about eighteen hundred feet per minute. As he comes up to our level, he'll ease off on the throttle, and when it gets to the tipple on the ore bin, he'll pull the brake on while the load dumps.

"What happens if the hoistman has a heart attack or a coughing spell or some emergency like that when you're lowering or hoisting?"

"That lever next to the brake is called a safety. When you have that pulled all the way back it signals the hoist to slow down and stop automatically if you go past a certain point without slowing down—either the top or the bottom. And I'll tell you what, it just slams on the brake and it stops with a BANG. There is no doubt what happened. We check the safeties for operation everyday.

"We have some special rings too. One is a ring from the bosses, or a skip tender, that they want to ride the muck-skip up. They climb onto the top of the skip full of ore and kind of scrunch down into the top and hang onto the sides. If you forget they're on there, they're going to go right on up through the raise and tip over along with ten tons of muck dumping into the bin. Well, that's not supposed to happen. But if it should happen, there's been a case where the guy riding up realized they weren't going to slow down and he reached over and gave the bell cord a yank as he went by on the fly.

"The tough part of the job is keeping track of where everything is and what's stacked up behind you in your head. If you're hoisting ore all day, it's not so bad. But, over on #2 or #3, or down on the Service or Auxiliary Raise, you've got every kind of supply the mine uses including 30-foot-long rails, and you've got garbage and all kinds of stuff coming back up. On top of that there's all the bosses and everyone moving around from level to level, maybe four or five rides stacked up waiting to go somewhere. That's when you have to keep everything straight."

We thanked Virl and climbed into a skip headed for Level 12, where we took off in some god-knows-where direction to see the biggest opening in the entire mine. Ralph knew his way around this country we were in, and after a twist or two we came to an opening in the ground that left me dumbstruck, for no timber, square-sets or otherwise, held the thing up. Ralph explained that this production stope was something of an experiment, a cavernous opening carved out of pure quartzite. No one was inside. An eerie quietude pervaded the place. It was so far across that my light didn't even pick up the opposite walls, like shining a flashlight into the night sky. The experiment seemed to work. The ore was low-grade, finely disseminated zinc, as opposed to the heavy, high-grade veins down in the Emery and May country where Chris and I had been working.

I had a tough time imagining how anyone decided that this was a good thing to try, or that in the trying of it someone might be killed. If it were my decision in later years, how would I make it? People would say, "Well, you're a mining engineer ain't you? You should know if it'll work or not." But I didn't have any information, and maybe the mine management did. Maybe they had diamond drill core that suggested it was massive intact ground that would stand. If you open up a little rock and it works all right, does that mean opening up a lot is all right too? I already knew the truth lay in a universal law called "too much of a good thing," as in gin and tonic or rum and Coke. What if there's a fault line or parting plane just outside of what you can see that will bring the whole thing crashing in at an unexpected moment?

We took pictures of each other on cheap Kodak cameras with the empty blackness in the background. I remember the camera flash and the color prints. But now, forty years later, everything is gone. Thrown away in some moment of being neat and tidy, thinking, I'll never need that again.

Ralph said, "Well, that's about it for here. No tour of the Bunker Hill would be complete without a stop at Curly Seufert's hoist room on the Service Raise, down on 23. I made an appointment with him so he could let go of the shaft for a few minutes and talk with us. Let's give it a shot."

It turned 4:30 P.M. as I glanced at my watch. Tired after a day of work, still this trip for the dedicated mining mind was a good thing to do. We had seen things few people were ever privy to.

I could tell we were in for a few stories when we approached Curly's place. He obviously had a way with words and enjoyed showing visitors around. It wouldn't be fair to say Curly was completely bald because sideburns halfway up still count as hair. But as he pushed his hard hat back to wipe a bead of sweat from the ninety-degree heat, it was clear the top was not festooned with growth.

Curly's hoist looked like a shrunken, unsanforized version of the Nordberg. It had double drums but much smaller in diameter, and the cab or office where Curly operated was just chiseled out of the surrounding rock. The Service Raise opened up the country from 23 to 30;

two compartments down to 26½ and one from there down to 30.

Ralph poked his head in. "Curly, I've got some visitors. Is this a good time to stop or should we come back?"

"No, c'mon in. You've got an appointment, and I always keep my appointments."

"Who ya got. College guys?"

I sensed Curly was ready for some entertainment, or a chance to do some. He pushed his hard hat back again. "Well, the main thing here I like to talk about is my garden."

What do you call a garden thousands of feet underground? Surreal? The room looked like a hothouse nursery making preparations for a flower and garden show. Roses, bleeding hearts, fuchsias—flowers of every kind stood piled in buckets or planters around the perimeter. A tropical fish aquarium occupied space on a shelf. I noticed the temperature pegged at ninety degrees on a wall thermometer; the humidity must have been the same. An orange tree grew out of a bucket in one corner. It had tangerines tied on to the branches with blasting wire.

Curly showed us all around, beaming with pride for what he'd accomplished with five-gallon buckets and soil he'd brought from home. The roses looked like candidates for the Jackson-Perkins catalog. Nasturtiums vined up along the back wall.

"Here's my prize bean plant," he explained. "I planted it yesterday, and now you can see it's about eight feet long. But you can't touch 'em for some reason. If I were to touch any part of it now, it would disappear. Shrink right up to nothin'. No one knows why, but that's what happens."

"It just doesn't seem possible," I said. "I thought plants needed ultraviolet light or something. All you've got here is that lightbulb."

"That's what the guy from New York said. There's this guy from New York University. Had a Ph.D. in botany or something. He heard about my trees and plants and stuff. So someone brought him down here, and he looked around for a while, and pretty soon he said, 'You can't grow anything under a 150-watt incandescent light bulb.' And I said, 'Well, there's proof right in front of you. Here's a nasturtium. Want to taste this? You ever eat any before?' 'No, I never,' he said. 'Well, I eat 'em all the time. Here, try some.'

"So he did, but he still didn't believe me—kept on saying, 'That's impossible.'

"Only thing we ever did was tie the tangerines on the orange tree. Everything else growing down here just grows that's all.

"I'll tell you what else happened last week when I was on day shift. You know Dick Target? Well, he gives me a bunch of squawks on the horn. I can tell who it is because I know how he rings. But I was real busy getting timber and rail down to 24. So I didn't answer right away. Pretty soon he calls me up on the phone.

"'I want a skip!' he shouted into the phone.

"I said, 'I'm busy for the next fifteen minutes. Have you got an emergency?'

'No. But I want a skip!'

"So I said, 'I'll get you a skip as soon as I can.'

"'I don't want one in fifteen minutes. I want one now!'

"'I'll get to you as soon as I can. I'm busy.'

"'Damn you, Curly!'

"Well, I could tell he was plenty pissed off, and when I finally got free I hauled him up from 24. He comes stormin' into the room here, saying, 'You're canned, by God, you're canned.' "And I said, 'Get outa my hoist room.'"

"He hollered right in my ear, 'You know who I am?'

"'Of course I know who you are,' I said. 'I've known you all my life.'

"'Well, you're canned.'

"So after the shift was over, I went down to the office and told Joe Gordon what happened, and he said, 'Curly, you ain't canned. I don't care what anyone says. We need you ridin' that hoist tomorrow. I'll take care of the rest of it. You just let me know if there's any more trouble. Anybody thinks they can can Curly Seufert got another think coming.'"

The Sunshine mine lies about two miles southeast of the Bunker Hill. All the miners in the valley worked at one or the other or both. They all knew each other. The Sunshine has a number of vertical shafts, but the Jewell shaft starts at the surface and descends to the 3100 level, and another, the #10 shaft, starts underground and descends to the 5400 level and beyond. The two shafts are a mile apart, connected by a haulage drift. On May 2, 1972, Norman Ulrich and Arnold Anderson detected smoke on #10 shaft's 3700 level. The time was 11:40 A.M. Because the mine's ventilation fans were going full force, carbon monoxide gas and smoke began infiltrating openings throughout the mine. The stench warning system was armed at 12:05 P.M. and the order to abandon given as fast as word could travel. Hoistman Ira Sliger rode the hoist in Ten Shaft, evacuating crews until 12:35 P.M., when he could no longer breathe. Hoistman Robert Scanlan took over. He stayed on the hoist controls until 1:01 p.m. He died as he brought the last cage of men up from the 5400 level. This meant that crews on the 5200 and 4800 levels couldn't be evacuated. Skip tenders Greg Dionne and Doug Wiederrick succumbed while helping to load cages during the evacuation. The last survivors made it to the Jewell shaft's surface at 1:10 P.M. Of the 173 men underground at the onset of the fire, 82 survived to tell the tale, in part because hoistmen stayed the course. This is a very abbreviated version of what happened. Countless other acts of heroism took place in that one hour, some no one will ever know about.

19

Two Miles to Riches or Bankruptcy

The inscription over the concrete portal reads "Kellogg Tunnel 1893–1902." It's a solemn heading, like those adorning tunnels and bridges everywhere. These inscriptions don't tell the story of what really happened because there isn't room. But mistakes were made, men were killed more often than not; hubris, hangovers, politics, warfare, and any other human foible one can think of all played a role. Tunneling is tough work. It's always loud and usually wet; the powder fume–laden air sucks and distracts; large and small surprises await every advance. The cycle—drill, blast, muck, timber—repeats endlessly. But in spite of the repetition, those who've driven one say it's not dull work.

Every day as Chris and I joggled over the two miles of rail to the underground shafts, I wondered who had made the decision to drive the tunnel. Who did the work? How much did it cost? Why did it change directions? What was going on in the world outside? What did the men think about, and what was on their minds as they went to work? And why was the starting date shown as 1893 when the first round wasn't fired until four years later?

It's not always possible to answer these kinds of questions. The information trail freezes overnight, floods occur, fires start, records disappear, companies change hands, and the truth, if it survives at all, is dependent on what someone happens to remember. But we are fortunate. In the 1890s two articulate managers at the Bunker Hill mine wrote weekly reports to the company offices in San Francisco describing Kellogg operations. Ray Chapman, a latter-day personnel manager for Bunker Hill, had the good judgment to haul the files to the University of Idaho's Special Collections Library. Otherwise the information would have wound up in the Shoshone County landfill.

The tunnel's story really begins on a hot summer day in July 1885, when an out-of-work carpenter, Noah Kellogg, discovered the original outcrop. He was prospecting for gold and probably didn't report anything more sophisticated than "It's dark gray and there's lots of it." But his grubstakers knew. In a matter of months a virtual forest of claim posts sprouted on the steep slopes around Milo Gulch. Although the discovery labored through a dense swamp of court battles for two years, it became the centerpiece of a new mining district and home base for the Bunker Hill and Sullivan Mining and Concentrating Company. As the labor union movement spread westward, the company engaged in a violence-filled, decade-long battle with the Western Federation of Miners (WFM), a battle that profoundly affected the tunnel drive.

It became obvious a few years after the discovery that the unfolding prospect clearly exceeded the know-how and resources of a few argumentative prospectors. Real management and venture capital were needed. But where would it come from? In 1887 Simeon Reed, a Portland financier with connections to Crocker National Bank in San Francisco, paid $680,000 for the property and, to turn the fledgling property into an economic producer, hired the best engineering talent available: Victor Clement, the mine's first superintendent, followed by Fred W. Bradley and Frederick Burbidge, an English mining engineer educated at the Royal School of Mines.[1] As events unfolded, serious constraints imposed by the mountainous terrain—no storage room for waste or mill tailings and reliance on a problematic Bleichert aerial tramway—extracted a heavy toll on the operation's viability. Something had to be done. Would the life of the mine depend on a hoist and shaft perched precariously on the side slopes, or on a haulage tunnel driven from a point two miles away on the valley floor?

On September 12, 1892, Clement, sitting at a desk in the embryonic company's unpainted clapboard office, penned a longhand report to the company president, John Hays Hammond. This letter is the first mention in the correspondence rescued by Chapman that the ultimate development of the mine depended on driving a lower-level tunnel to intercept the expected continuance of ore at greater depth. He was straightforward about what needed to be done:

My Dear Jack,
    . . . We should push for the big tunnel. I am getting bids for a small compressor . . . we will be able to run for a considerable distance for $10 to $12 per foot.[2]

But two years passed without a decision on the tunnel. By May 1894, the logistics of handling material—supplies going in, ore going out to the tram and down to the mill—strangled production. In addition to tramming ore by hand 2,900 feet from the farthest advance along the vein, the aerial tramway to the mill proved more troublesome than originally thought, sometimes working as advertised, often breaking down or prematurely showering tons of high grade on residents living two hundred feet below the drooping cables in an understandable state of anxiety.[3]

Delay on the tunnel continued for two more years, by which time the total cost was estimated at $200,000— roughly equivalent to $4 million today. So the gamble to proceed with the project, or not, became a pivotal decision for a young company struggling for survival in an era of depressed metal prices, along with increasing harassment from the WFM on wages. Deep-pocket investors notwithstanding, everything was at risk: cash in the bank, future dividends, capital to build a smelter, to develop markets. What if it didn't work? What if the vein faulted off or terminated before reaching the tunnel elevation? A ten-thousand-foot tunnel is a hard thing to undo. And more important, the history of the West is replete with tunnels, real and imaginary, put forward just to sell stock. But the Bunker Hill management of the day meant to make an engineering decision and do the right thing. To be sure a lot of big-name reputations rested on the outcome, but they bet the company's net worth and all its resources on the distance anyone could see into the earth, about a molecule deep.

It's understandable in retrospect that the Bunker Hill management did what many corporations and governments do today: they hired a consultant. If it works out, the company takes credit for being right; if not, the consultant gets credit for being wrong.

The company hired C. R. Corning as a consultant. His reports crystallized the issue for management in support of Clement's proposal, coming down strongly on the side of the tunnel as opposed to the shaft option. In July 1896 Corning wrote a lengthy report outlining the pros for a tunnel and the cons against an inclined shaft:

> As matters stand at present, I deem it highly advisable that preparations be made for the active pushing of the deep level tunnel so long since proposed, starting from the mill at Kellogg. I decidedly favor the tunnel for several reasons. It will permit of our extracting practically as much ore as may be desirable: whereas, a shaft will be limited in its output to whatever the present tramway may be capable of carrying (scarcely over 600 tons per diem). Again, a shaft means placing the company much more at the mercy of a Union, as the works would have to be kept dry. Such a tunnel would be ten thousand feet long providing the vein maintains its present dip. It would cut the vein near the northern boundary of the Bunker Hill claim, probably between the Last Chance and Stemwinder ore shoots, neither of which is definitely known to encroach on our territory.[4]

Corning's prescient statements were on target, given that we know now that the tunnel became the lifeblood of the mine for the better part of a century. What he could not foresee was the heightened state of anxiety suffered by Bunker's management at the tunnel's closing hour.

Corning knew that commandeering the necessary real estate for right-of-way posed a vexing problem. He recommended locating a long string of "quartz claims" across the countryside to gain ingress for the tunnel's centerline, "as a means of insuring title to ground over which the company has no control."[5] (A quartz claim in the parlance of the day was a convenient subterfuge for a standard 600-by-1,500-foot lode claim with no mineral on it and, quite possibly, no quartz.)

Another imperative was the purchase of two land parcels near the proposed portal. The first posed no problem, because it was owned by the cash-desperate Noah Kellogg, who had by that time given away or drunk his way through most of his $150,000 share in the discovery. On the other piece, foundations for two saloons had been laid, and the company feared that a town would spring up on the site. Another claim, the Jackass, lay in the center of the proposed right-of-way. A remark made by management at the time reminds us that the world of communication has changed beyond anything imaginable in 1897: the principal owner was a Catholic priest "who is now at a mission on the Yukon River, and cannot be reached until [the] Summer [breakup]."[6]

In a series of end-justifies-the-means moves, enough real estate to start the drive came into company hands. After drilling and loading the first tunnel round in mid-May of that year, the mandatory shout "Fire in the hole!" echoed across Jackass Flats. (This hallmark event took place within a few hours of the Castle Gate coal mine payroll robbery, eight hundred miles away in Utah, where Butch Cassidy and the Sundance Kid lifted $8,800 in gold.)[7]

As the new superintendent of Kellogg operations, tough and loyal Frederick Burbidge assumed responsibility for driving the tunnel, along with other Bunker Hill mining and milling operations. The tunnel got off to a slow start, and after six months of intense work Burbidge wrote in his October report: "Progress in the tunnel is much slower than we have expected—the rate of advance being only 5 or 6 ft. per day—of 3, eight hour shifts. The chief trouble is the bad air, which causes a great loss of time and makes the men sick."[8] This condition arose because the water level in the creek was sufficient to turn the Pelton wheel generator only for a few hours in the early morning, leaving the electric exhaust fan mute most of the time.

Burbidge reported serious problems with the available blasting caps, the fuse, and even the powder itself, which in those days degraded rapidly in wet holes. This meant that only a portion of the round might go off, leaving the rest primed and loaded with powder.

We have lost three rounds through misfires. Whether these are due to poor fuse, poor caps, or poor powder, or all three, it is hard to determine. The fuse occasionally goes out before reaching the cap, and caps have been heard to explode without exploding the powder. An accident occurred last night. . . . One of the men had spit his fuse and started out, and had gone a little way when the charge exploded. A large piece of rock hurled down and struck him breaking one or more ribs. Some tests made by Mr. Burch today show the fuse to burn at 3 ft. per minute, whereas it should burn at less than one foot per minute. Again, the fuse is so brittle a great deal of it cracks in uncoiling, even though it be fairly warm.[9]

The next crew faced an ugly sight—a piled mess of broken rock and live dynamite lying on the tunnel floor. Chris and I would have had the same problem fifty years later, but our caps went off, the powder exploded, and the fuse burned at exactly forty-five seconds per foot as advertised.

Since compressed air–powered equipment was still in the offing, shot rock from the face was lifted into cars by hand shoveling and trammed to the surface. This work took so much time that Burbidge attempted a now politically incorrect ethnic solution to the problem: let the Italians try it.

We lost considerable time during the week . . . preparing to run the heading full size[,] . . . partly on account of trouble with the shovellers. I let a contract to some Dagoes, but the drill men and others at the tunnel threw every possible obstacle in their way, and abused them to such an extent that they quit. What little they did was the best and cheapest loading we have done at the tunnel, and I am trying to induce them to return to work with the guarantee that they shall have proper treatment. Failing this, I propose to let a contract for 2,000 feet of tunnel, and let all of our present crew go.[10]

Progress through 1898 and 1899 went more or less on schedule—a good month advancing 354 feet; a bad one, February 1899, only 53 feet.[11] An unforeseen event related to union demands stopped progress altogether in spring

1899. The issue was relatively simple by today's standards: should muckers be paid $3.50 per day, the same as machine men and timbermen, or $3.00 per day, as was the practice? The wage levels had not changed in seven years, and the backbreaking workweek consisted of ten-hour shifts for thirteen consecutive days. The men were given Sundays off every other week.

Fearful of what wage demands might mean to the company's profits, and unionization in general, management fought all attempts by the WFM to organize the workforce. Pinkerton Agency detectives, working covertly as miners, infiltrated union membership meetings and offices at considerable risk of having their necks stretched. One agent, Charles Siringo, was elected secretary of the Burke local. Daily reports from the agents on union activities were signed "Operative 15" or "Operative 108." The company used coded telegrams to convey sensitive information. A new code and deciphering sheet was carried every month by courier to and from San Francisco. Mysterious messages left at specific drops added fuel to the smoldering fire. One such message was a piece of foolscap tacked to the mill flume. It read, "Who are those guys? Where did they come from? What do they want?" Tension mounted.

On April 29, 1899, the situation fell apart.[12] An angry mob of eight hundred WFM miners congregated at 10:00 A.M. near the Gem mine in Burke and commandeered the Northern Pacific's engineer, Levi Hutton, holding two Winchester rifles to his head. "Pull out for Wallace, and be damned quick about it," he was told. Fortified with sixty cases of dynamite stolen from the Frisco mine's powder house, guns, and a generous supply of Periwinkle rye whiskey, the Dynamite Express's two passenger coaches and three boxcars sped down-grade toward Wallace, ten miles away. There an astute telegraph operator realized what was taking place and wired ahead to Burbidge of the danger. Burbidge did what any good manager would have done with the news: he loaded up his family and the rest of the staff and headed for Spokane.[13]

Switching from the Northern Pacific to the Union Pacific tracks, which serviced the brand-new Bunker Hill mill, the mob placed all three thousand pounds of powder at strategic locations inside and blew it up. The time was 2:26 P.M. Lumber and cast-iron industrial shrapnel rained down on the town of Kellogg a mile away, littering the tunnel portal and staging yard. Two longtime Bunker Hill miners were humiliated in front of the angry mob, then given the chance to run for it—which they did until bullets cut them down.

The uprising made front-page news in papers across the country and became the immediate focus of intense intracompany correspondence. Burbidge wrote:

On May 3rd, the Governor of Idaho [Frank Steunenberg] proclaimed martial law in Shoshone County, and at his request United States troops were sent in to assist in restoring order. Upwards of 1,000 men were arrested for supposed complicity in the rioting, and although a great many were subsequently released, about 200 remain in prison at this date. The County Commissioners and Sheriff, who failed to take any steps to prevent the rioting, although advised of its approach, have been removed from their offices.[14]

Work on the tunnel came to a standstill until tempers cooled off and crews could be reassembled. Progress resumed over the summer of 1899, but in October the tunnelers encountered another hazard: massive inflows of water. Burbidge reported, "It has been very wet—more so than at any time heretofore—and the ground has run into the tunnel from far above the timbers. It has been necessary to bulkhead the face most of the time. Last week the progress was one foot."[15]

This was probably the point of advance approximately 6,900 feet from portal, where the tunnel intersects the great Osburn fault. It is one of if not *the* major tectonic features in the district. Like most faults, it is full of gouge, a material that slips and runs when it's wet and requires constant shoring up. (This point is where the passing tracks were located and where in 1955 Air Door Pete rammed the haulage train through the closed doors. It became the obvious choice for the double tracks as it grew larger each year and had to be repaired.)

Everyone knew the tunnel headed in the general direction of the Bunker Hill claims. But the exact bearing, S20°W, was a closely held secret, because it trespassed directly underneath the Empire State Company's Last Chance mine, run by Charles Sweeny. Sweeny was an immigrant Irishman with an unquenchable thirst for money and fame, and he wasn't above stealing a few tons of ore from the Bunker Hill claims. There was no love lost between the two companies.

With the heading rapidly approaching the Last Chance property, the Bunker Hill management decided to address the trespass issue and in the process displayed a disingenuous side themselves. A proposal was brought forward to condemn portions of the Last Chance and the adjacent Emma claims in the name of obtaining right-of-way, whereas the real reason was to expropriate ground thought to contain valuable ore. The condemnation proceedings fell apart, however, and Burbidge spelled out the dilemma faced by the company—whether to continue and go for a jury case or seek a court-appointed appraisal. The latter course of action had serious drawbacks, described in a February 1900 report:

> If appraisers are appointed, they may make an inspection of the tunnel and call for a survey which will show that *we are not heading for that ground through which we are seeking to condemn a right-of-way.* It will probably be better to let this drag along . . . until we get through the ground in controversy into our own.[16]

So the Bunker Hill management tried to sneak the tunnel beneath Empire State workings, but one of the shift bosses, Joe Klever, informed Burbidge he had heard blasting shots fired in Empire's Skookum stope directly above them, which meant the converse could be equally true. Burbidge worried about this potentially dangerous turn of events, given Sweeny's keen desire to thwart Bunker Hill at any cost:

> The fact that we hear the reports of their shooting shows there is very little chance of our getting through to the vein without the shots in the tunnel being heard by them. If they hear us . . . they will probably try to enjoin us or head us off in some way.[17]

No one knows for sure what happened at this juncture. One might assume that a full year after the mill was dynamited some slackening in labor-management tensions would have taken place, but martial law still ruled the day, and threats from radical elements in the WFM tyrannized the camp. A pall of fear hung over Kellogg like a blanket of smelter smoke. In a letter to Bradley dated June 22, 1900, Burbidge described an attempted shooting of Joe MacDonald, his friend and a fellow member of the Mine Owner's Association:

> I learned just as I was leaving Wardner today that an unsuccessful attempt was made this morning to assassinate Joe MacDonald. I did not get much detail—but understood that four shots were fired at him as he stood outside his office by parties concealed in the brush on the mountainside opposite. None of the shots struck him very fortunately. It is highly improbable that the miscreants who did the shooting will be captured. It is an important occurrence as indicating the desperate character of the dynamiters who made such an attempt despite the presence of U.S. troops. Tom Greenough, who came down today said that he was warned . . . to keep a watch out for himself as similar attempts would be likely made against him and me. I should think this last outrage will have the effect of rousing the law and order people to active work for carrying the election.[18]

As the tunnel drive advanced to within a few thousand feet of the much-anticipated vein intersection, Burbidge and his right-hand man, Al Burch, scrutinized every round, looking for some indication that the big gamble had paid off. Not a glimmer of ore showed up until December 1900, when a narrow ore stringer several inches wide was cut at 8,259 feet from the portal. This occasion gave some credence to the company's statement, "*The* vein was cut on December 24."[19] But it's not quite the same thing as saying "We have cut the downward extension of our rich ore veins from above." The former statement keeps the stock price up; the latter was what was hoped for.

But the drive continued into totally barren ground, dead-ending 10,800 feet from the portal in the same hard, flinty, quartzite drilled and blasted so laboriously during the previous three and a half years. One can speculate it might be very quiet at the end of a two-mile tunnel where ore was supposed to be but was not;[20] $200,000 had gone up in smoke.

You can't help but wonder what these mining men said to each other. Whatever it was, it's not in print today, lost—either accidentally or purposely. A concerned group gathered at the candle-lit terminus must have deliberated some time over what to tell the stockholders, or indeed whether to tell them anything at all. The likely question of the day has been heard many times in the history of underground mining: Where do we go from here?

Since the tunnel alignment had aimed at the westward trend of the upper veins, still nine hundred feet above the tunnel level, the crew was directed to back their machines several hundred feet toward the portal and begin excavating a curving exploratory drift to the southeast. (This intersection was the place where our crew unloaded each morning, near the Nordberg hoist.)

When hunting for elephants, go where elephants have been, proved a wise strategy. Round by round, each day's work throughout 1901 revealed an increasing degree of overall mineralization.[21]

Then the persistence and patience finally paid off when miners in the 909 West Crosscut cut a thick vein of silver-rich ore.[22] This was the top of the famous March ore body that enriched corporate coffers single-handedly for twenty or more years, paving the way to develop ore bodies far below the tunnel under the Cate fault: the Shea, Emery, Truman, Ike, and Quill.

Burbidge stayed the course until the real vein was found in 1902, displaying uncompromising determination and courage in the face of tremendous upheaval and personal danger. Burbidge, in conjunction with other Bunker Hill managers, made working conditions in their mine the envy of many in the district: good tools, attention to the quality of shift bosses, a heated dry house with showers, improved wages, and eight-hour shifts. These improvements struck at the heart of what the WFM intended to offer but without unionization and without monthly dues. In taking these steps, management earned the everlasting animosity of union organizers and pro-union workers. A report from Pinkerton Operative #15 gives us an indication of the strength of that feeling, suggesting that for these managers showing up for work every day was anything but ordinary:

Burkbridge, or a man of a similar name, formerly superintendent of the Bunker Hill & Sullivan, is in danger every time he goes up the Burke canyon. If he ever goes down into the Frisco mine he is, in the vernacular of the men, a "goner." They are going to kill him on the cage if they have to run it into the head sheave. They are bitter against him.[23]

So I used to think about those men, the bosses and the crew both, and what they accomplished. Riding over the same ground every day on that narrow-gauge track helped me to better understand the meaning of words like *tenacity* and *determination*. No electricity. No batteries or headlamps. Candles stuck on flimsy felt hats. Ten-hour days. Work, eat, sleep. A big night's entertainment might be a nickel cigar and a two-bit shot of whiskey or a visit to one of those "women in scarlet whose footsteps take hold in hell." I suspect tunnel drivers the world over feel a well-earned pride in having met Mother Nature on her own terms and brought the project home. The Kellogg Tunnel made the mine. Over the tunnel's century of existence, 4.5 million tons of lead metal and 430 million ounces of silver have been hauled through it to the outside world. If you could put it all on one train, the total production would make up a string of flatcars stretching from Seattle to Bozeman, Montana. Victor Clement may have relied on instinct or made only an educated guess, but he was dead right in 1892 when he wrote to John Hays Hammond: "We should push for the big tunnel."

20
Timber Repair

I overheard the bosses talking about the amount of catch-up work needed all over the mine to fix rockfalls and cave-ins. Some of the timber in place was fifty years old and starting to rot. Squeeze blocks put in to act as shock absorbers had been squeezed out of existence. "Let's send Chris out for starters. He's good at that kind of stuff," they said.

So I wasn't surprised when Jim Cantrell stopped by at noon the next day to talk to us. "We've got some bad spots up on 15 and 21, and a few others. What do you think about taking on some timber repair for a month or so?"

Chris laughed. "Yah sure. We're gettin' tired of stope mining anyway. Sure. Let me know tomorrow where you want me to go."

Timber repair was a job reserved for the experienced and the careful, a perfect fit for the crop duster's motto: We have old pilots and bold pilots, but we have no old, bold pilots.

A few days later in an ancient part of the mine we wound around this or that drift for the better part of twenty minutes accompanied by the shifter who knew where the ground had collapsed. All he said when we got to the site was, "This is it. See what you can do." And with that he turned on his hard-toed boot heel and disappeared into the dark.

Damn nice of you to explain the situation, I thought. It looked like a rockery contractor had dumped a truckload on a chicken coop. Splintered timbers lay all over the place. Runny muck and chunks of soaking wet quartzite the size of truck tires blocked the entire eight-foot-high cross section of the tunnel. We didn't know if the damage strung out ten feet or fifty feet, nor did we know if it was through caving, but we did know that no one was underneath when it let loose and that no one was trapped on the other side. It was also impossible to tell how far above us the caving had started, or what it would look like even if we were able to get all the rockfall cleaned up. Good work for optimists.

For a while I just stood there and stared at the mess before us, refusing to believe that those great god-awful heavy posts and caps could have failed—that for all the apparent strength and safety they presented to the eye, some force unseen and unfelt had torn them asunder. And I couldn't imagine how a couple of pissant human workers could undo all that trouble and make it well again.

Chris looked at it for a few minutes too. He muttered a sad commentary on the day ahead: "Ooh, ooh. Aye yi yi."

Occasionally a new piece rolled down from the top of the pile. It was disconcerting, because it meant the thing wasn't through. This had the effect of roller-coastering your thought process from We can do this to I'm not sure if we can do this.

Finally, Chris turned to me. "What you think, partner? Where do we start?"

"Well, just pull that big chunk of cap out of there and dig into it. Maybe we could bring up a mucking machine. We'll be done in no time."

"Partner, sometimes I worry about you. No, no, no! First thing we got to do is shore up this last good set with some stulls—make sure what we're working under is OK. Then start with the small stuff. Just bar one or two of those chunks out of the way, and wait and see what happens. Then take a few others, and wait some more. That overhead lagging hanging there? Just take one piece out at a time—wiggle it first. You need patience, because if you get in a hurry we'll both be dead. They tell me it lasts quite a while."

We filled up a timber truck with everything we thought we'd need—the lagging, stulls, scaling bars, wedges, shovels, double jacks—and rolled it down the track to the site. We tested the timber in the set next to the cave-in. It sounded OK, but we shored it up with two stulls anyway. At first we concentrated on the one- and two-man rocks, getting them out of the way and loaded onto the timber truck. We pulled pieces of timber out when they appeared not to be bearing weight. And we waited and listened—stopping for a minute or two in case more stuff decided to fall.

Around noon we looked up through a small opening at the top of the pile and took a squint at the cavity formed during the slide. It looked like a big slab had broken out of the back along a fracture face dripping water and had hit the drift cap full speed, crushing it.

We whittled at the chaotic jumble all day, finally clearing out enough room for a new set on either side of the track. But rather than put the posts in first, Chris said we needed to get the cap up in the air, then slip the posts in underneath and lower the cap. The particular piece he had in mind was a fourteen-by-fourteen, ten feet long. It weighed about four hundred pounds.

"And just how the heck will we lift that sucker up in the air?" I asked.

"Old trick. I'll show you."

We drove rail spikes at four-inch intervals up the two posts spanning the drift's left and right sides. They started at about the same level as the cap, which lay massively recumbent on the timber truck. Then Chris laid a scaling bar on two spikes at about the same level. We slid the cap over on top of the bar in the center and lifted one end, then the other. It took both of us standing side by side, straining and lifting simultaneously, to move the bar more than one notch up the ladder of spikes. Had the steel bar snapped under the weight while we were lifting, I knew what would have happened, but it was the kind of thing you don't want to think about too hard while it's taking place. We crossed over to the other side and did the same thing. I got the idea. After many repetitions of this incremental resurrection we had that wooden monster at the same height as its neighbors. I just didn't want to stay underneath it very long.

We measured the posts and cut them to length as fast as we could, like two guys outrunning a twister, and gingerly slipped them into place, all the while keeping an eye on the overhead for signs of more spalling. All remained quiet. We lowered the cap so that it rested on the posts. Its weight steadied the whole setup while we set squeeze blocks on each end, then wedged the assembly tight against the walls.

"There, you see. Nothin' to it," Chris piped up.

"Oh absolutely nothin' to it. Someone might think it was coffee and brownies at Pinehurst Lutheran. But that stream of sweat drippin' off the end of your nose gives you away."

After catching our breath, we nailed a cleat to the cap's bottom so the two posts couldn't slide toward each other. We built a bulkhead with Chris balanced on the rim of an ore car while I tossed up the three-inch lagging, which he crisscrossed clear up into the opening until it was all caught up and closed in.

After that we sat down and took a long drink of water, admiring the work. It looked pretty good. The posts were straight and true, the cap nicely centered. It even smelled better.

Over the next month we tackled six or eight bad spots. Sometimes we had another crew helping us. Mostly we worked by ourselves, which was easier because only one guy's opinion mattered on what had to be done next, so we got more work done, it took less talk, and it didn't seem like a committee meeting.

The worst one took place in what I thought must have been a fault slip. The walls resembled mushy oatmeal and the water streamed in from above. We were soaked to the skin in the first five minutes, and the mud came halfway up our boots. We staggered and slipped around like a couple of drunks, trying to fix the damage. My diggers got so heavy I couldn't keep them up, or do anything more than duck waddle on the surface after they started to dry out. We worked on it three days. In the end we had to breastboard the walls tight with lagging for thirty feet along the drift to keep the muck from running onto the tracks. Even then the hydraulic pressure pushed the muck through the cracks so bad we were forced to toenail the whole thing together. The situation is like building a boat from the inside after it's in the water.

We saw some strange things too. On Level 15 a crew running a development drift hit a pocket of sand. "*Sand? There ain't no sand in 21,000 feet of solid quartzite,*" someone said. And that's what I said, and the chief geologist said, and everyone else said. But there it was. The finest-grained, slightly rust-colored sand anyone can imagine. It ran out of the back like water and flowed down the drift for fifty feet. We had trouble stopping it. Finally they shot-creted it with cement and wire mesh. This looks like the kind of thing you pick up in a sand dune, had been my first thought when holding it in my hand, and it might be true. But it's tough, really tough, to visualize a sand dune surviving two billion years of metamorphism that turned every particle of sand and mud into a mass of rock so hard it almost breaks your heart. Today, with the mine flooded, it's under six hundred feet of water. I wish I had some just to ask it a few questions.

21

Misfire

Leadership is an odd thing. During the school years, the jock, the tallest guy, usually the football quarterback, embodied leadership. It helped to be a jock *and* funny. Then you were sure to be the leader and get all the girls. Next came the class officers and student body president. Did these people turn out to be leaders in later life? Maybe. If you sit in on high-level meetings at large corporations, you find things like "Tiger Teams" and other sports analogies because the old ways die hard. And if you invite enough people, someone is bound to show up who talks all the time, and when he or she is through talking the meeting is over. You assume the fast talkers must know something the rest don't because they talk so fast. This may sound like leadership, but it doesn't feel like it. It doesn't feel like it because you're being pushed instead of pulled. Then there is the side of leadership that relies on invoking fear. I've seen grown men pound the table, scream, shout, and weep in the name of leadership—and showmanship, just in case their boss happens to be in the same room.

But there's a quieter brand of leadership that seems to seep out of the woodwork when those who pound and shout least expect it, and it overpowers them. This is a leader who defines reality in such a way that no one can argue. Chris was a leader but never thought about it, wouldn't have known what you were talking about if you had mentioned it. But I noticed the other men asking him a lot of questions about how to do something, and one day in particular it occurred to me that leadership at its finest moment is an art form, emerging naturally from a place deep inside—knowing what to do and then doing it.

We had spent the better part of three days replacing two drift sets that had been crushed to firewood. We cribbed up ten feet to reach solid ground, looking up all day long to avoid any more of it coming down, if that's what it decided to do. So after driving the last wedge in place and making sure all was as it should be for those in the future who might pass under this place, we sat down on the wet steel track and admired the straight, clean lines of the new timber and the long spikes driven home with three blows and no misses.

"Think it'll hold?" Chris asked.

"I think so."

"So do I."

"Well, it ain't much for looks, partner, but it's hell for strength. Let's go. I've seen enough of this place for right now."

We walked along side by side, heading toward the station at the May Raise, a hundred yards away, each absorbed in our own thoughts with no premonition that the next five minutes might leave cold sweat sticking to our respective skins like thick fog.

As we approached the shaft and our eyes grew accustomed to the light we came upon a group of five or six miners standing around in a huddle looking down. Their gaze focused on a knife switch that should have fired a drift round somewhere but hadn't. Confusion reigned—furrowed brows, hardhats tilted back, a great scratching of foreheads.

"What's goin' on?" Chris asked.

"Gypos told us to fire the round," someone volunteered, "and just took off up the shaft so's they could catch the gravy train. Stogey John just put the juice to it and nothing happened—didn't fire, for chrissakes! Goddam gypos anyway. Shifter ain't here neither."

Deep in the earth, especially at the end of the shift, a misfire is what you call a *big* problem. One crew is leaving, another coming in; communication is difficult; there's a lot going on; messages get scrambled. The unspoken but understood work ethic is simple: We won't leave you any problems we know about. No one wants to walk off and leave a loaded cannon for someone else to discover by accident. The situation required resolution in the few remaining minutes before everyone caught the skip, or else someone had to stay behind and make sure the night crew knew what was going on. The top half of the hourglass was almost out of sand.

The crew explained to Chris that contract miners were driving a nine-by-twelve-foot haulage drift leading off into the darkness toward the north. The big drift round they had drilled and loaded with one hundred fifty pounds of powder was supposed to detonate with electric blasting caps, but nothing happened when the switch was thrown. And no one wanted to go fix it. The request to the day's pay crew was simple enough if everything had gone the way it was supposed to. But something had gone wrong. There was no fire in the hole.

The hands looked down at the ground, then at each other. The gaze shifted in Chris's direction.

"Yah then, maybe I'll go up there and see what's going on."

I had read the chapter on electric cap wiring in the *DuPont Blaster's Handbook* and asked enough questions to hazard a guess on what had happened. But I wasn't completely sure. I knew the lead wires where we stood had to be shunted to each other so stray currents couldn't introduce a voltage across them. But I decided to keep my own counsel, since not being sure about blasting is the same as not knowing.

Chris said, "Disconnect the two lead wires and twist them together. Now, don't anyone touch 'em until you see me come back around the corner." He walked off up the drift, dwarfed by the size of it, his tiny light bouncing along as he ventured into unknown territory.

I wasn't about to be left out of this great adventure, so I shouted after him, "Hold on, partner, I'm coming with you." By now we had been working together so many shifts in so many situations that I knew Chris didn't do stupid things. And I didn't think he was about to start now. As we walked along up to where the trouble lay, a tiny river of sweat, not due to the temperature, ran down between my shoulder blades straight through that part of us referred to in *Gray's Anatomy* as the "glutial cleft."

"Broken wire?" I asked, trying out the sound of my own voice. The words sounded like they came from someone dying of thirst.

"Yah—I think. Gotta be outside on the face where we can see it."

We slowly approached the heading and stopped some distance away to take stock of the situation. Chris might have been ordering a short beer for all the concern he showed. Ahead of us a conglomeration of yellow and red wires hung out of each blasthole. Yellow hooked to yellow, red to red. All appeared in order, but that was all that could be said at first glance. I remember only two sounds emanating from that hobgoblin enclosure: the steady drip from a trickle of groundwater in one corner and the sound of our own breathing, which struck me as an odd thing to be listening to. We flashed our headlamps around the Stygian darkness seeking some clue to what had gone wrong.

Chris said, "Why don't you start up there at the back holes and work your way down that side. I'll do this one. Let me know if you see anything."

I got up close to the face and inspected each connection, one by one, making sure that connections that looked solid really were. My subconscious sent a strong message: Run, Bucko. My conscious voice said: Stay. Stay was winning, but it was close. Half a minute went by, then a whole minute. I told myself twenty times to forget the fear and concentrate on the task at hand.

I was on my knees near the lifter holes on the floor when I saw what had happened. There on the ground lay a bare wire termination. A piece of rock must have fallen out of the back and hit a connection, pulling it apart.

"This must be it!" I sputtered.

What to do next was the hard part. Theoretically, nothing would happen when we hooked that wire back up. But after two years of technical training, I had seen lots of theories I didn't care for, and furthermore, this wasn't exactly what you'd call a lab experiment.

Chris strode over and looked at what I had found. Finally he said, "This lead has to go to this one here. I'll do it. You can duck down around the bend if you want before I hook it back up."

"Well, I don't think you're about to leave Lucille a widow. So go ahead."

If this was the wrong thing to do, it would be the last thing either of us ever did. Tiny pieces of ourselves would soon be flying down the drift at about the speed of sound and impinging on timbers along with a lot of rock fragments, muck, and smoke. Would there be a roar and firestorm?

Chris reached down and twisted the loose wires together.

Nothing happened.

He looked up smiling. "Yah, for sure, that was a good one."

I felt relieved and very, very tired. The sweat stopped running down my butt.

On the way back to the station, Chris talked about the last time this had happened and why he knew what to do. I listened to him superficially. I was really thinking whether I could answer the same call sometime and maybe show some other youngster how things were done. And I was thinking about leadership, though the first book on the subject hadn't been written.

I also learned that fear, run amok, can get you killed. I kept saying to myself, One thing at a time, one thing at a time. Easy. Easy. It starts in on you and then you have to kick it out. It changes your perception of reality. You force yourself to make a decision, but the decision has to be based on the right information: do the right thing right the first time. Your best friends in tight spots are knowledge, process, and discipline. Then, can you trust and accept a colleague's judgment? Big decision. I would think about that in the years to come.

If Chris had said, "Partner, I think we should dig a ditch to the North Pole," I would've grabbed a shovel and started in.

When we got back to the shaft, the miner guarding the short-circuited lead wires still attended the duty. All the hands were understandably relieved to see us. Chris told them, "Partner found the problem and fixed it. Let him fire the round."

So I hooked the leads back up and hollered, "Fire in the hole!" When I closed the switch, the blast concussion thundered toward us down the drift like Beethoven tympani. Carrrrrrrooooomppp.

Somewhere in the distance where the two of us had stood minutes ago, a chunk of St. Regis quartzite the size of a dump truck blew apart in the space of fifteen milliseconds.

♠ ♠ ♠ ♠ 22

Terrible Edith

[A]nd some rin up hill and down dale,
knapping the chunky stanes to pieces wi' hammers,
like sae mony roadmakers run daft—
they say it is to see how the warld was made!

—Sir Walter Scott, *St. Ronan's Well* (1823)

At night I spent a lot of time reading and rereading a tome titled *Geology and Ore Deposits of Shoshone County, Idaho,* by Joseph Umpleby and E. L. Jones. The book describes all the known mines in the area in great detail, with maps and cross sections, and identifies where they lay in the mountains. U.S. Geological Survey Bulletin 732 had been brand-new in 1923. Now after years of use the cover was torn and brown tape reinforced its crumbling binding.

I had found the bulletin in the box of stuff Wallace Woolf gave me when I moved into his home. The box also contained a huge chunk of gold-infested quartz from the Smuggler Union mine in Telluride, Colorado. (The dump at the Smuggler Union has been subdivided and now supports a condominium.) Umpleby and Jones were old-time practitioners of the craft, tramping the backcountry in person, performing real fieldwork. That takes a lot more effort than dry-labbing other investigators' reports and calling the new report new, a process known to have happened occasionally in scientific circles. This information-rich bulletin contained a geologic map of the entire Coeur d'Alene mining district in color, displaying grandly drafted detail in rich hues of sienna, ocher, and mauve. Features like the Placer Creek and Polaris faults took on the familiarity of old friends. Historic trails, by 1959 overgrown and barely recognizable on the ground, were shown, and even minuscule prospects that never had more than a hundred bucks spent on them. The map depicted the gigantic Osburn fault that slid the north side of the valley fourteen miles toward the Montana border like a machete stroke; or depending on which side you happened to be standing, slid the south side fourteen miles toward Spokane. Did this mean ore at the Lucky Friday mine near Mullan was once part of the Bunker Hill where I worked? If that were true, I reasoned, then there must be a lot of ore-bearing mysteries buried in the intervening stretch of real estate. I fancied my newfound knowledge of geomorphology leading to the discovery of hidden splendor overlooked by the other guys. I dreamed up names for my own prospect and imagined riches flowing to my counting vault. More important, I knew I would have the thrill of putting keen geologic reasoning to work and of watching the discovery breathe life into my theories—the joy of daring to think what no one else had thought and being right. College kids with three-hundred-dollar bank accounts can think those thoughts if they choose;

no one will listen to them anyway or pay for them if they prove wrong.

I stumbled across a write-up on the Terrible Edith mine in the section of the report devoted to zinc deposits. Given that this was big-time mining country, there was nothing particularly remarkable about the description of the ore, but the name itself struck me down. It was a piece of local history to be unraveled.

Perhaps this particular Edith had been the shrewish wife of some ragged-ass miner coming home to a litany of directions and complaints in a voice shrill and sharp, like a chainsaw in high gear. "Do this. Do that," she said. Or, "What are you doing here? You're supposed to be at work." Or possibly Edith was an incorrigible two-year-old daughter. Maybe neither one. Maybe a sister or an aunt to be immortalized as the mine's namesake for purposes of long-simmering revenge. But I smelled a story and vowed to find out everything possible and go there.

First I did my homework. Umpleby described the mine's location as "at the head-end of Wesp Gulch northeast of Murray" and said that an 825-foot lower tunnel had been driven to intersect the vein below the discovery outcrop. I knew Murray had been a wide-open 1880s gold camp, self-proclaiming a population of twenty-five hundred souls. It lay on Prichard Creek about twenty miles north of Wallace over the Dobson Pass road.

I told Chris about the report. He said he knew right where the mine was because he had lived in Murray for many years. He suggested I look at the claim records in the Shoshone County courthouse at Wallace. The day being Friday, he arranged for me to take the early gravy train so I could get there before closing time.

The courthouse turned out to be a stately white structure with classic Greek lines and a marble-tiled entry. It had the comforting odor of official volumes, an atmosphere of the keeper of the kingdom.

I explained my quest to an assistant in the Recorder's Office. She directed me to two enormous binders, one titled "Index of Lode Claims," the other "Index of Locators." Dates for both were marked 1876 through 1895. I had to guess at the approximate date of discovery because a mining map, hand drawn in 1892, provided the thinnest of clues. At first, poring over hundreds of different entries, I didn't have much luck, but my persistence paid off. About halfway through a multitude of *T*'s I discovered a claim called the "Terrible." The locators were John H. Clark and Mike Kirlin. The names sounded English enough to qualify as a couple of Cousin Jacks— the local vernacular for resourceful hardrock miners who had brought their much-needed skills to this country from tin mines in Cornwall.

The date of discovery and the date of recording for the Terrible claim—usually two distinct days because you don't come out of the woods all mosquito-bitten and brush-beaten and head straight for the county Recorder's Office— were the same: January 1, 1887. Because the name of the claim wasn't a perfect fit, I kept studying the records. Then it struck me as a very odd thing indeed that the county offices would be open on New Year's Day or had opened in the midst of the usual northern Idaho blizzard to take care of two prospectors. I thought maybe they decided to have a hot buttered rum the night before and fudged a little on the date in the interests of good business.

The next clue, the notice of location in the other index, had been entered by hand in a flowery script with official-looking seals and testaments. Pay dirt: The "Terrible Lode" was an extension of the "Little Edith" lode, recorded by the same men on May 25, 1885. The claim description fit perfectly: "at the head of Wesp Gulch in the Summit Mining district, 3 miles NE of Murray, Shoshone Co, Idaho Territory."

Denied statehood until 1890, Idaho was still a territory in 1885. The word conjures up a picture of life as pretty rudimentary, close to rawhide for lack of a better term. How many grand pianos graced homes in Boise at the time? I wondered. How did anyone smell after two weeks prospecting in the backcountry, or working underground without a bath, or stuck in the middle of Utah's San Rafael swell on horseback in hundred-degree heat? What else was happening when Mike and John crawled up the creek in Wesp Gulch looking for gold?

Later I delved into some general history books. Only six years had elapsed since the Northern Cheyenne bands led by Dull Knife and Little Wolf crossed the southern border of Kansas in a desperate attempt to get back to their homeland in Montana. The 353 men, women, and children with them knew what lay ahead. But they preferred death to living out their days wearing white man's clothes and watching their children being whipped in Indian Agency schools.

Six years on the other side of 1885, Butch Cassidy and the Sundance Kid robbed their first bank, just down the street in Telluride about a quarter mile from the Smuggler Union mine.

And close to the very same day that the two prospectors walked into the Wallace courthouse to record their claims, a Chiricahua Apache chief named Geronimo had gathered up ninety-two women and children plus thirty-four surviving warriors and headed for their old Sierra Madre sanctuary in Mexico. Ahead the Mexican army lay in wait, wanting to kill them; behind lay General Crook's garrison wanting to make them prisoners one more time. For the next twelve months, while Mike and John drilled and blasted the Little Edith outcrop, the Chiricahuas ran and hid in country so rough that only snakes like it, finally to be crushed the following spring by Brig. Gen. Nelson Miles's force of five thousand regular cavalry.

Whether we think of the world in terms of 1885 or 1985, it is remarkable that an entire year and a half transpired between the filing of the Little Edith and Terrible claims. In mining country a strike is a strike. Greed and avarice are pervasive. History fails to record hesitant prospectors standing around, pure of heart and purpose, unwilling to stake adjacent ground—legal or not, mineralized or not. This is what keeps mining camp attorneys busy in perpetuity, transplanting wealth in the ground to wealth in the bank. But at this juncture apparently there had been no hurry. A lode claim four thousand feet above sea level stuck in the middle of roadless mountains may be one reason. It takes more than a strong back and lots of water to put a hardrock mine into production: build a pack trail; haul in tons of steel track, ore cars, drills, and dynamite, as well as toilet paper, beans, coffee, lard, beans, pork bellies, butter, bread, and beans. Planty of beans. Every diamond hitch, every moment of every trip its own adventure. Whatever the reason, Kirlin and Clark had time to tie up their own adjacent ground, and in the short space of eighteen months Little Edith turned Terrible.

It took a while to digest all the mining trivia I had acquired at the courthouse, but the stage was set. At dawn the next day I got behind the wheel of my 1949 VW, which had replaced my 1939 Chevy. Well, upward mobility is upward mobility. It was the thirty-six-horsepower model with no gas gauge, plus a heater, which provided warmth in name only. The road meandered along the bottomlands of Ninemile Creek, then I ground away in first gear over the top of Dobson Pass, where the blacktop ended and gravel began. The road down the pass's north side is nothing less than a short course in hairpin-turn survival; some even slant the wrong way. The angle of repose is such that to stop and pee over the side might have nourished saxifrage four hundred feet below. At times of great anticipation we tend to hurry. Equally true, quite often we learn something in the process. I carried too much speed into one of the curves, which I recognized at precisely the same time that I started bouncing from peak to peak over the washboard surface. With all four brakes locked up the VW slid sideways out to the shoulder's edge but clung to it like a pit bull on a mailman's pouch. If it's possible to have more than one emotion at a time, I felt lucky, foolish, and scared all at once.

A junction in the road a few miles farther down has a name: Delta. Nearby there stands a barn and a cabin in the midst of a grassy field filled to overflowing with summer daisies. It was and is a quiet junction. I thought it the loveliest spot on the whole planet. I still do. A hand-painted road sign nailed to a leaning fence post read "Murray 6 mis."

For all its former glory, even in July 1959 Murray resembled a settlement straight out of a Hollywood Western—like the set used in the great classic, *Shane*. Town consisted of one city block. The Catholic church's steeple stood sentinel over the Prichard Creek Bridge. An ancient two-story hotel occupied the opposite corner. Six rooms with shades drawn peered out from yesteryear over the first-floor bar. The elements had weathered the whipsawn lap siding into driftwood. On the north side of the lone street, empty of traffic save for one car, a structure called the Sprag Pole Inn seemed to hold the place together. Depending on how one looked at the sign over the entrance, it could be (a) a watering hole, (b) the town hall, (c) a general social hour meeting place, (d) the post office, or (e) all of the above.

Upstream and down, heaps of dredge tailings cluttered the floor of Prichard Creek as far as the eye could see. The piles were the enduring result of 1917 dredging sponsored by big money,—the Guggenheims. Ignorant of being turned inside out, the creek rushed along westward, cold and clear, jammed tight against the valley's south bank.

The scattered one- and two-room cabins looked rusty, like the old mining equipment standing mute in vacant lots. Tires on old trucks oxidizing in the fields were cracked and flat, and weeds sprouted up in isolated patches over taillights and mossy fenders. Long unused but not for-gotten, I imagined the owners saying (with optimism and determination), "Some day when the price is better, we'll take that bygod-sonofabitchin' drill back up on the mountain and open 'er up. We'll be richer'n stink because we know its there. The gold is there."

I stopped and sat on the VW's front fender for a minute, taking it all in. Trying to get a feel for the country. Logged, burned, or used up, for the time being the steep mountain slopes all around rested, deep green and timbered, plunging into the valley like ski jumps. The air ran heavy to oxygen combined with the opiate perfume of inland fir and cedar. I filled my lungs, wishing for more holding capacity. My system seemed impatient to get enough of it, fast enough, like a cold beer at the end of a day on the Mojave.

I drove east of town about a mile until I reached the second drainage to the north, which according to my map and dead reckoning was Wesp Gulch. Every drainage in this part of Idaho is a "gulch." I vowed to take measurements someday of the average width, depth, and length of gulches to define their geometric ratios, because a gulch is not a draw, a draw is not an arroyo, an arroyo is like a gully but not quite a ravine, and so on.

I spotted a half-road and half-trail opening in the brush that slanted up the mountain in the right direction. I decided to walk since the thrill of being high-centered and out of forward motion was fresh in my mind—not to mention the wrenching process of backing down the same track through the rearview mirror and listening to the bending sound an oil pan makes when it encounters boulders that weren't there on the way up.

I discovered a log cabin tucked beneath a cedar tree and perched on a tiny bench above a stream. I stepped inside gingerly, not wanting to go through the floor. It had the moldy smell of all structures that stand in the forest, slowly being eaten by bacteria to return bit by bit to the soil. It was in pretty fair shape, due in part to a hand-split tamarack shake roof, supplemented by pieces of strategically placed sheetmetal roofing. An iron-spring bed frame, black and rusting, stood against one wall. Rodents had scattered tufts from a long-departed mattress all over the floor.

Cupboards made of dynamite boxes, designed to carry fifty pounds of explosives, occupied part of one wall, the signature autograph of all mining camps from the 1920s on. The sides and dovetailed corner joints made from half-inch clear yellow pine were so elegant that if it weren't for the black stenciling you might confuse them with kitchen cabinetry. The long sides were stamped "High Explosives—Dangerous," and product names such as Red Cross Extra, Gelex, or Special Gelatin showed on the ends. Burned into the center of these was the elliptical DuPont trademark and underneath, "E. I. Du Pont de Nemours & Co., Wilmington, Delaware." The boxes had been used for everything from kitchen tables to wine racks. But by 1959 the wheels of progress had turned away from pine boxes, and all our powder at the mine was packed in thick fiberboard cartons. They were strong and serviceable and cheap but devoid of any endearing qualities. A great loss.

I wondered if Kirlin and Clark had built this place. Probably not. Seventy winters in this country is a long time for a log cabin to stand without continual maintenance. Maybe some follow-on miners working the Edith built it. I wondered who they were and where they were now.

A cast-iron cookstove stood watch on the west wall, the kind made by the Malleable Iron Range Company in

Beaver Dam, Wisconsin. This appliance kept long-departed occupants warm in midwinter, cooked their meals, and provided snap and crackle to break the silence of long nights without radio or television. On occasion, even cheaper entertainment arrived when the creosote inside caught fire, turning the stovepipe cherry red, followed by an awe-inspiring, roaring, sucking sound.

With pieces of the late morning sun slanting down through the green canopy overhead, this place smelled good. Somewhere the world was at war, but here in the woods it was only peaceful, a place of safety. Some day, I thought, when I'm old I'll come back here. But today I have to find the Terrible Edith.

I continued up the adverse grade, heading west along a hot southern exposure toward a distant switchback. On each side of the track one patch of wildflowers followed another. First Indian paintbrush, then in a few yards deep blue mountain gentian, named after the king of Illyria by Pliny the Elder. Farther on, in a hot, rocky area devoid of brush, stood a willowy red penstemon.

In about a mile the trail curved around to the northeast and gained elevation rapidly. Stinging sweat began to drip into my eyes as the temperature headed into the high eighties. I wrapped my forehead in a red bandanna to keep the stinging down.

At this point I began to imagine what the country had been like at the turn of the twentieth century, attempting to re-create what the two prospectors saw as they blazed the trail that ultimately led to the building of the road on which I stood. The trees surrounding the road were small by western Washington standards—twelve inches at the butt, probably growth that sprang up in the aftermath of the great fire of 1910, which burned three million acres. Small fires in the Salmon River country far to the south had fanned into bigger ones on August 10, causing ash and embers to fall as far away as seventy-five miles to the north. On August 20 a gale blew up out of the southwest, uniting all the smaller fires and turning all of northern Idaho and parts of western Montana into one gigantic conflagration. The entire east half of Wallace burned to the ground, leaving a Hiroshima-like landscape behind. When the Sunset Brewery went up in flames, two thousand barrels of beer flowed down Seventh Street in a frothy tidal wave. Heat was so intense in the forest that some trees simply exploded. Ashes lay everywhere, ankle deep.

Something caught my eye a few feet downslope, another trail heading in the same direction as I was. Not over three feet wide, covered with windfall, and obviously old, I guessed it was the first one used by the old-timers. I slipped my pack off and dropped down to examine a stretch of it. The wheezing and sweat of overloaded pack-horses were long gone, along with the packers, cussing and checking for shifting loads. Still, I spotted something man-made tucked away in the slough along the trail's edge—a flat slender can. A remnant of orange and black paint, "P _ _n _ _ A _ e _ t," was all I could make out. With a little imagination thrown in, I made it Prince Albert pipe tobacco. A good smoke in those days but also a superb weather-tight container for claim notices nailed to witness trees. Momentarily, I thought I'd stumbled across an original-issue discovery notice. I opened it with great excitement. There was only sand.

I crawled back up the slope and continued, keeping an eye on the parallel trail. After another switchback the two treads came together. I shot up a steep pitch and stared straight into the lower tunnel described in Umpleby and Jones's report. The adit was still open but only slightly. I poked my head in and shone the flashlight down the centerline. The light went out into the darkness until there was nothing to see but some distant broken timber sets. Finding it uninviting, I ducked back outside, blinking in the sunlight. A rough-hewn log covering the entrance had collapsed, and a trickle of water came out of the opening. In the yard in front of the tunnel I discovered an assortment of old drill bits and some steel rail. A building, perhaps the mine office, off to my right had collapsed and a lean-to was about to fall over. But there was nothing on the rock face just above the tunnel entrance to suggest mineralization, and precious little stuff in the dump. Whatever ore came out of this tunnel had been carefully sorted and hauled away.

I tried to figure out what was going on here. Why a tunnel that doesn't follow a vein? The answer came after a little walking around.

A path leading uphill from the mine yard circled around to the north. Within a few minutes the path gained over three hundred feet in elevation and headed back in a direction that I knew would take me over the tunnel I had just inspected. The reward came soon enough in the shape of a big open cut. It had all the earmarks of the original strike: a cribbed vertical shaft, sealed over and caved in but with definitive minerlike qualities: a pile of spent calcium carbide from the old lamps, silvered mine timbers.

The bottom and side of the cut made an *L* in the hillside, maybe two hundred feet long. Everything was overgrown with scrub so I couldn't make it all out.

I scrambled to an outcrop of undisturbed rock directly above the excavation and immediately recognized the Prichard Slate Formation. It was very fine grained but felt gritty, like quartzite, with alternating half-inch bands of dark and bluish gray materials, reminiscent of a petrologic zebra. I held a chunk of it in my right hand and wondered what the earth was like when that ten-inch chunk of Precambrian sediment was laid down. The climate or the conditions must have changed quickly, dramatically altering what was being deposited or how fast. Why? Maybe the banding was the result of sunspot activity, or solar flares, or the oxygen content of the atmosphere. At first nothing more than sandy mud, now it had been buried, cooked, shoved around, faulted, and mineralized. It was so hard that it rang when struck with my hammer. The vibrations charged up my arm like an unbalanced tuning fork. "Harder'n a whore's heart," as Ralph Hopes, a miner from Eureka, Utah, used to say.

One band looked like it contained tiny grains of pyrite, which might explain the iron staining in microcracks and fracture faces. How many years did it take to accumulate a half-inch of pyritic sand, I wondered? Where did it come from? Why pyrite? Did it rain iron sulfide?

I knew from studying the report that these rocks are part of the Precambrian Belt Series, about 1.8 billion years old. A long, long time. If you could lay down a row of 1.8 billion copper BBs, each representing one year, they would create a line 2,762 miles long—from Seattle to Baltimore. A short walk of only 208 feet toward Baltimore would bring you to the end of the last ice age, twenty thousand years ago. At that time a Cro-Magnon artist descended into a limestone cave at Lascaux, France, equipped with a quarter cup of fat oil balanced in a shallow rock lamp along with some powdered manganese oxide. He or she managed to paint an enraged bison on the wall with entrails hanging out and tail lashing the air. The discovery of the Terrible Edith mine was only a foot away.

It was humbling to hold that piece of the earth's beginning in my hand—like discovering a ribbon-tied bundle of letters in Grandma's attic, though the rock gave me less information. Or maybe not. Maybe I saw most of what there was to see. We know there was water and iron, sulfur and silica. Wind probably. Erosion of *something*. Gravity for sure. There was no sign of a living organism, though the equator wasn't far away at the time, running north and south on a line through Newfoundland and Florida.

After poking around a few minutes, I stumbled across a chunk that appeared to be a piece of garden-variety quartz. But as the rest came out of the ground I saw it contained brecciated fragments of Prichard Formation, with perfect cubic indentations where pyrite and galena had been.

Taking a short ego trip, I imagined that I was looking at the very rock that Kirlin and Clark had stumbled across almost seventy-five years before: oxidized mineralization that dissolved near the surface, to be precipitated and then enriched below the water table. If I had been there with them I would have gone nuts with excitement. I suddenly realized that the original outcrop, now blasted and carried away, leaving twenty to thirty feet of high wall above me, had probably been a ragged outpouring of white quartz.

Kirlin and Clark would have come up the creek for a ways, like I did, panning the bottom for gold, breaking out on the ridge crest to get away from the brush and windfall. I later discovered from a *Spokane Falls Review* article that snow lay ten feet deep on the level at Prichard in February 1885. That would mean that on the day of the prospecting trip, May 25, with the temperature in the sixties, there would still be snow on the north slopes and a few patches on the south slopes. I can imagine Clark in the lead, shouting back, "Hey, Mike, look at this! By God. Lead! Silver! We're rich!" They slapped each other on the back and tramped up and down the outcrop looking for more. The next day they returned to the site, joking all the way, packing shovels and saws to cut claim posts and mark the discovery.

"What shall we call 'er?"

"How 'bout Little Edith?"

They would have packed supplies up to the discovery all through the summer, beginning with a mosquito-enhanced June. They probably made arrangements for some capital, telling the fat cats, "Just enough to get started," showing off samples of hand-picked ore with the comment, "Oh, we've got a mountain of it."

I stopped in my tracks, hoping a vision would appear, or at least a voice from the past to make a connection. I wished I could listen in on conversations recorded by the rocks in the amphitheater surrounding me, my mood quiet and humble. I tried hard, even straining, but no visions appeared. No crosses in the grotto, no Magdalene, no Kirlin or Clark. I was trying too hard. "Relax and let it happen," I counseled myself. Slowly, I began to hear a jumble of men's voices, not with my ears, but inside my head, the words unintelligible, compressed and distorted like a tape recorder on fast forward. There was *something* remaining of days and spirits gone by, but how could I decipher it? It was elusive, slippery, as if there were a presence in the absence. But after a few minutes of attempting remote mystical telepathy, I surrendered, content with the feeling that miners had been here, cussing, discussing, chewing, spitting, and breaking rock.

Brush had to be cleared and a tent platform set up on a level spot chiseled out of the hillside. A bench for washing and cooking and a privy must have followed in quick succession. Then the real work started, for no air compressors or pneumatic drills sat around on that hillside north of Murray in the summer of 1885. What was heard was the sound of sledgehammers striking drill steel. It might have been one man working alone, single jacking, with a three-pound hammer in one hand and a drill steel in the other. Swing, strike, twist, retract. Repeat ad infinitum. Don't miss the steel. I knew from having tried it once in a Forty-niners Day contest that it was no fun. In three long minutes, I had drilled a hole one inch deep that gave new meaning to the concept of infinity. I kept looking up at the timer with pleading eyes asking him to either speed up the clock or shoot me for having had the bad judgment to enter the contest. It took two days before my arms uncramped from the punishment, wherein I had time to develop an exceptional measure of respect for my mining forefathers.

Or maybe they had drilled with two-man teams, a process called double jacking. Using an eight-pound hammer, the driller swung at the steel with a truncated movement from the shoulder, striking the one-inch-diameter target held by his bare-handed partner, the "turner," standing or kneeling as far away as he could stretch. The turner twisted the bit after each blow, and every so often cleaned the cuttings with a blowpipe. The partners would switch positions, sometimes every thirty seconds, without missing a stroke. No one knows how many fingers, wrists, or forearms were broken when the target was missed. If someone missed the steel and broke the turner's arm, the occasion was more than just bad luck. No one had even thought of workmen's compensation, sick leave, health insurance, or comp time. Pay was $2.50 *per day*, and the days were ten hours long. And even that didn't apply when you were prospecting for yourself.

Sometimes a team struck a cavity in the quartz vein, wedging the steel in tight. "Thunder and damnation!" someone would exclaim, spewing out a long stream of tobacco juice as if doing so would somehow undo the predicament. Drilling resumed a half hour later after exhaustive chipping away, banging and pulling on the miscreant hardware.

Boxes of Alfred Nobel's new invention, dynamite, would have been stacked and tarped under a tree out of the way. Nobel had had the idea of impregnating collodion cotton with nitroglycerin and wrapping this potential energy in a waxed paper cartridge. It was an astounding advancement, because, unlike black powder, it would fire in wet holes, and, unlike raw nitroglycerin, it would not blow up if dropped or jarred. The real problem for my ghost miners up on the Edith was fuse quality. On occasion the fire-train burned through the fuse sidewall and went completely out. Waiting for a blast that never goes off tends to be unnerving. A prudent man might be justified in asking, "What happened?" Eventually someone had to go find out.

Sometimes the fuse from one roll burned at forty seconds per foot, the next one at five. "What's the matter with him?" the rest of the crew would ask as a miner ran by like a freight train passing a tramp. "Fast fuse!" the runner exclaimed, moving fast enough to create a Doppler effect.

And no doubt the vein played hide-and-seek on the surface. Like the rest of Mother Nature's creations, it wasn't laid out with a T-square.

"Where'd it go?"

"Damfino, can't see into the ground any further'n you can."

"Keep on a-going over there and see what happens."

Each day small blasts would have broken twenty or thirty tons of rock. Sometimes the vein was plain white quartz, sometimes high-grade galena. There was no crushing, grinding, or milling on site. Someone stood at a table all day and hand sorted every piece of broken rock into two piles, "them that has mineral, and them that don't." The ore was packed in gunnysacks and sent down the mountain on the backs of mules or horses to be shipped to a smelter in Montana.

And while the crew chipped away on the outcrop, Kirlin and Clark would have been out selling stock and talking about the obvious need to drive a tunnel into the vein from a point farther down the mountain.

"How far down you think she goes?"

"Quite a ways, I reckon."

"If we drive a tunnel, you think we'll hit anything where it's supposed to be?"

"Damfino. We got nothin' else to do anyway."

Back to the present, a trail leading away from the open cut proved irresistible. I followed it for a quarter mile, where another larger dump of broken rock came into view. Here I saw not only a shift in volume but also a big shift in technology. A steel axle with three belt-driven pulley wheels attached to it lay askew on the steep slope next to fifty feet of thin-wall pipe, bent and crumpled by winter snows. This told me that a steam donkey or early gasoline engine supplied torque to cut mine timbers in a crude sawmill or ran an air compressor. The compressor provided enough air to run early pneumatic drills, a "Wiggle Tail" buzzy or a crank Leyner. Although these drills weighed only several hundred pounds, anyone carrying one up a trail or setting one up would swear they weighed closer to several hundred tons. But the pain paid off, because they made holes in rock ten times faster than single- or double-jacking—not always in line with improved safety, however, since these brutes earned the nickname "widow maker" in short order.

An adit drifted into the mountain at about the same angle as the one I just left but higher and a few hundred feet farther north. Dandelions and sweet grass grew around the tracks leading from the opening to the dump. The adit too had partially caved in. Though I was keen to explore it, Chris's voice came from the backwaters of my mind: "Not good, pardner, not good."

My stomach sent a message to my brain announcing that my blood-sugar level had bottomed out. A soft-looking rock at the crest of the dump seemd the right perspective for food with a view. The peanut butter and dill pickle sandwich from Dora's lunch table was now squashed beyond recognition by the mineral specimens collecting on top of my pack. I thought about what must be an irrevocable fact: of all the pursuits humankind undertakes, a picnic in the woods, beyond earshot of anything but wind in the trees is one of the things we are destined to enjoy. The experience centers and succors the soul.

As I surveyed the upper dump material, I decided the bluish gray shot rock must be unaltered Prichard slate blasted loose during the tunnel drive. The opposite side was full of the same rock type but stained reddish brown, probably pyrite-laden waste rock. I reminded myself that most of what I was seeing on the dump's surface was the final material hauled out during the last few weeks of work. It looked like pretty slim paydirt.

It also looked like the Terrible Edith Mining Company ran out of ore and dough at about the same time. Why? One explanation is that a fault displaced the vein between the lower tunnel, the open cut, and this upper working— ending abruptly in a barren face. There was little evidence of a happy ending to the search for more ore. "Which way shall we go?" someone asked, the choices being up, down, or sideways. Sooner or later a decision was reached. "That way." I think they had bad luck. It was the wrong way. But perhaps there was nothing to find.

By now, the sun had passed through high noon and started down the other side of the sky. I judged it to be around 2:30 by the length and slant of shadows falling across the mine yard. Overhanging fir branches began moving around with the arrival of a chilly downslope breeze. I needed to get moving or put something on besides a T-shirt.

I had been wandering around the property for four hours, talking to myself, imagining conversations and decisions made, listening for ghosts, trying to re-create history. Who knows how the real story unfolded? I suspect it was complex, full of anguish, sweat, greed, curses, lawsuits, dreams, and stock schemes. All of it vaporized like a block of dry ice. Some of the decisions were right, some were not. Who knows what one more round in another direction might have produced?

The reality is that the Prince Albert can, the old drill bits, and the rusty shaft tell no stories. They offer only mute testimony to how much they weigh and what color they are but not much else. I wanted to know who put them there and why.

Finally, I hotdogged it down the hill with the kind of reckless abandon that doesn't consider the possibility that anything can happen to eighteen-year-old legs and ankles. Whenever I could see the trail zigzagging below me, I crashed through the brush and cut off the switchbacks.

My downward plunge came to an abrupt halt when I spotted a pile of bear scat lying square in front of me on the tread. It was big and blue, and coyotes don't eat huckleberries. The pile gave off steam. This meant a great deal even to my untrained eye. There'd be nothing to do but stop and act polite.

I peeked around with glacial slowness, as if turning my head would make enough noise to betray my already obvious presence. Though I stopped breathing for a few moments, my heart pounded like the bass drum in a marching band. Externally, there was no sound and nothing to see in all directions except trees and the late afternoon sun. Maybe the bear, probably a blackie, was equally scared. As it should be. I represent the species that occupies the top of the food chain—most of the time—and every November we carry long black irons into the woods that spit fire and hurtle half-inch-diameter lead bullets at them.

Was it watching me from some unseen vantage point? If so, it was being polite too, and I appreciated that. A few minutes of acute sensitivity passed. Still no movement. I decided to call it a draw. But I continued down the trail with wary eyes and ears, thankful that the occasion hadn't relegated my person to second place in the food chain.

When the adrenaline subsided a powerful thirst rose in my throat. I remembered the Sprag Pole Inn at Murray and thinking that it looked like it might serve a beer to an underage lad.

I parked in front of something that looked like a hitching post and stepped inside. "Like a six-pack of Oly," I said, as if the purchase were old hat. A woman behind the bar, who I assumed from the proprietor's sign was the owner, Bess Almquist, didn't give me a second glance as she pulled the stubby brown bottles out of the cooler.

"Just passing through town?"

"High-grading some old dumps up on the hill. Know anything about the Terrible Edith Mine?"

"Not much. There was a lot of excitement in the thirties. Some guy named Stapleton owned it—him and Herman Rossi down in Wallace. They tried to turn a lead mine into a gold mine. Sold stock all over the country—

to little old ladies in Portland and Seattle and as far away as Pontiac, Michigan. I don't know whatever became of the company or the stock. You could ask some old-timers around Wallace."

"Nice place you have here," I volunteered. "Murray is my kind of town. Quiet."

"Yes, it is quiet. We like it that way."

"Thanks for the beer."

On the way out the door, I noticed a small sign that said, "Welcome to Murray, Idaho. Our Motto: Never refuse a drink or kick a dog."

What about Edith? Who was she, and what kind of notorious behavior earned her a place in the lexicon of memorable place-names? Forty years after my prospecting trip on the hill above Murray, I resumed my hunt for the real Edith. I had begun to think that *elusive* was a better adjective than *terrible*. But in the summer of 1998 I happened to mention my quest to Deborah Mellon at the *Shoshone News-Press* office in Kellogg. She handed me a short piece she had stitched together from anecdotal information and oral history. Mellon's story told me a lot. I learned that accounts differ on the story surrounding Edith herself and on how the name came to be applied to the mine. But one thing all agree on is that in a short life of twenty-three years she acquired an incredible number of different last names. We know her maiden name was Bergoine. But she didn't remain a maiden for long. Next in order might be Rostele, then McGongil, followed by Arnberg. In any event, we have to honor the name inscribed on Edith's marker in the Murray cemetery, which reads McCorkendale. It's a replica of the original, but I know the folks who reproduced it took the job seriously, for it was painstakingly painted.

However many last names Edith might have accrued and for however many reasons, it is apparent that she was a force to be reckoned with from the very beginning. Her suspected date of birth was sometime during 1882, so in May 1885, when John Clark and Mike Kirlin picked a name for their new claim, little Edith was three years old. By January 1887, at age five, she had qualified for the rubric "Terrible."

Edith's parents owned and operated the Palace Hotel and Saloon in Murray, a few yards to the east of the Sprag Pole Inn. Fritz, the father, was considered reasonably refined and easygoing for the time. But the mother, Sarah, had given up a promising career in the red-light district for domesticity. It may not have been the best decision. The union fostered two girls, Edith and an older sister. After the girls came into the world, Sarah's main interest in life turned to the contents in tall brown bottles of Meyer's 150-proof rum.

Edith acquired two charming attributes by the time she was fifteen: a lovely singing voice and a lovely body. Edith figured out that there was a lot more money to be made with the body than the voice. With the ratio of men to women—regardless of eligibility—running at 100 to 1, it wasn't long before she started trading love for money with a select clientele of well-heeled mining and labor union executives. Her days in Murray's red-light district were punctuated by an occasional "We're married," which in Idaho Territory at that time was not quite the same thing as a trip down the aisle.

Jack Rostele may have been more of a "business manager" (i.e., pimp) than a husband. Not much was known
about McGongil, but he was followed by a reasonable
chap known only as Carl. His last name was possibly
Arnberg. The bonds of matrimony didn't last long. The
taste for 150-proof rum acquired from her mother, along
with the pull of easy money, doomed the relationship.

Around 1904 Edith found a husband with the nickname "Bull." I postulate he was the McCorkendale who
lies moldering in a grave next to Edith's. On the evening
of March 17, 1905, Edith was seen on Main Street quaffing
serial straight shots from a jug, then stopping at her
folks' cabin as the sun went down. Edith and her mother
had an argument. Soon afterward, Bull showed up, angry
and puzzled. He shouted into the house, "Where the hell's
Edith!" or words to that effect. A family scene ensued. Bull
beat Edith senseless and dragged her up the half-mud,
half-frozen street by the hair, leaving her lying uncon-
scious on the cold floor of their cabin to figure it all out.
Edith didn't make it. She died the next day of heart
seizure, exposure, and acute alcoholism at the ripe old
age of twenty-three. They say she's buried headfirst. I
don't believe it.

Edith remains a mysterious figure. The trail grows cold
in a hurry unless someone is there to keep it thawed out.
I researched the Bernard-Stockbridge collection of historic photographs at the University of Idaho's Special
Collections Library to no avail. Pictures of Edith could
not be found. I sought a photo that might be titled
"Everyone in Murray at the Miner's Picnic," but there
wasn't any. Newspaper offices come and go. Spring floods
and bad plumbing do their work. Some burn. Folks move,

discarding a bunch of old stuff—items we historians consider golden. History is a messy thing.

I feel a kinship with Shelley and his piece on Ozymandias when I think of the bunkhouse that has turned to dirt up on the Edith claim, the collapsed snow shed leading into the adit, the blacksmith shop where the bits were sharpened. All gone.

I met a traveler from an antique land
Who said: Two vast and trunkless legs of stone
Stand in the desert. Near them, on the sand,
Half sunk a shattered visage lies . . .
And on the pedestal these words appear:
"My name is Ozymandias, king of kings:
Look on my works, ye mighty, and despair!"
Nothing beside remains. Round the decay
Of that colossal wreck, boundless and bare
The lone and level sands stretch far away.

23

Cocktails

"They're all going to be here," Doris Woolf said one sun-drenched July afternoon as I came in. I knew her well enough to understand the abrupt statement implied a message for me to listen up; there were things coming along that concerned me. Then she said, "Here, have a Coke—there's half a sandwich in the fridge if you're interested."

I said, "Sure thing. But who are 'they'?"

"Newmont Mining's management is paying the valley a visit. So tonight Wallace and I are throwing a dinner party for all the mining people—Asarco, Sunshine, Hecla, our managers—everyone. Jeanette is coming in to help with dinner. What do you think about tending bar?"

Jesus, I thought. Newmont Mining Company, American Smelting and Refining! These are the big boys. What I said was, "Sure, you bet. What should I do?"

"The guests will start arriving about six. We'll serve cocktails until seven, and that's where you come in. Keep things liquid, and moving. Then I'm serving dinner. You probably won't want to attend the dinner"—more of a statement than anything to do with probability.

But I knew big business held sway that evening, and anything at all to do with it meant a chance for me to see the top rungs of the corporate ladder in action, to chance a sip from the Silver Chalice, a few hours at the Holy Grail. Being one paycheck away from starvation, with matriculation-induced poverty staring me in the face, the prospect of a job offer falling out of this gathering, by sheer proximity, got me thinking about the need not to be shy. Big wheels or not, I knew my chances ranged from murky to nonexistent. There would be other engineers from New Mexico they knew or worked with. The CEOs and chief engineers might say, "Here's my card, call us when you've got your degree next year." It's tough when you're eighteen and know virtually all there is to know even though you only know enough to be obnoxious, as events in the near future would prove, replacing hubris with reality.

I secretly hoped the conversation might turn to exploring for yet-undiscovered ore bodies in the district, and if I eavesdropped with caution, someone might ask if *I* knew anything. If an opening popped up, I could leap in with an opinion: "An interesting target might be a point north of the Sunshine where the Polaris and Alhambra faults intersect the Osburn." Not too determined or overbearing. Just say, "Well, that's an interesting structure."

Doris jerked me back to the moment.

"Now, I think you'll do just fine. When glasses start looking tired or nearing the empty mark, ask whoever it is if they'd like another drink. They may or may not. Keep the hors d'oeuvres flowing. You can help me make them if you want. In fact, that's what I'm going to do right now. Here, grab a spreader and some cream cheese."

"Sure, you bet."

With that as an introduction, I found myself intimately involved with snacks and drinks, 1959 style—at least as practiced by well-meaning hostesses in western mining camps who read their pre–Martha Stewart recipe suggestions in *Sunset* magazine. We left the food chain somewhere below the cocktail fare described by Thomas Wolfe at Lenny and Felicia Bernstein's radical-chic soirées in upper Manhattan: Roquefort cheese morsels rolled in crushed nuts presented with flaming water chestnuts. Instead, we sliced celery sticks on the bias and filled them with Philadelphia-brand pimiento cream cheese. We wrapped strips of bacon around stuffed green olives to be heated in the oven. Boxes of Hi-Ho, Ritz, and Triscuit crackers cluttered the countertop. We dumped tubs of avocado and clam dip into cut-glass serving dishes. Doris sliced strips of smoked Gouda cheese she'd picked up at a Spokane delicatessen and placed them on a polished silver platter with artistic precision.

As we bent to the task at hand, she asked me if I had ever mixed drinks before.

"Nope. Watched my father fix his martinis. That's about it."

"OK. Here's what to expect. The mining crowd is basically a bourbon and water outfit. But it's going to be warm tonight and someone may want a gin and tonic or vodka tonic. If that's the case, use one and a half jiggers in a glass this size, put the crushed ice in, and add the tonic and a twist of lime. The main thing is to not give someone a vodka tonic who ordered a gin and tonic."

"Got it."

"If they want a bourbon and water, they might say, 'I'd like a ditch, which is Idaho lingo for the same thing. Ditch water. We've got five bottles of MacNaughton's Reserve here, which is what you'll want to use. Add cold water from this container and the ice. Use the small cocktail glasses."

She continued, "I think Fred Searls likes old-fashioneds or manhattans. A perfect manhattan is a jigger of dry vermouth and about five jiggers of bourbon, plus a dash of Angostura bitters. Maybe a twist if that's what they ask for. An old-fashioned is about the same thing, but add a teaspoon of water and no vermouth. You can add a cherry on a toothpick or a small slice of orange for some color. Try not to fill the glass all the way to the rim. Leave about half an inch from the top.

"Now, the martini drinkers are a special case of purists. A normal martini is one part dry vermouth to about six of gin. Add a stuffed olive on a pick. Use the Gilbey's gin. They will have something in mind that ranges from a plain martini to a dry martini with about twenty variations along the way, only one of which will suit them perfectly. This will be the hardest part of your job. Listen to their comments so you can fine tune the refill. In any case, you won't have to mix more than two for anyone because of the effect they have. When they say 'dry' it means less vermouth. What you can do if they say a 'really dry martini' is just pour in the gin and dip the cork from the vermouth bottle in it for a second. It'll work. Trust me.

"Whatever you do, use these special martini glasses. This is crucial. We want them to think we know what we're doing. Oh, 'on the rocks' means over ice."

"Sure, you bet. I think I can remember all that."

"Don't fuss about it. If you get in trouble, hunt me up and I'll help. OK, I think we're ready."

The guests were to arrive at 6:00. At 6:01 the doorbell chimed. So much for fashionably late. Doris flew across the room with the energy of an Olympic gymnast vaulting onto uneven parallel bars.

"Plato and Fred, do come right in!"

"Plato" was Plato Malozemoff, president of Newmont Mining. "Fred" was Fred Searls Jr., Newmont's chairman. A large percentage of the mining savvy in the United States had just walked through the door.

These guys, like the managers of other mining outfits, gambled the entire company every time a decision was made to turn a raw prospect into a producing mine. The ratio of prospects to producing mines runs about 550 to 1. Some of the prospects lay offshore in the Philippines or Southwest Africa, others in neighboring Canada. And there was San Manuel, a heavyweight copper mine near Superior, Arizona, that no company in the world considered worthy of a second look until a Newmont geologist, John Gustafson, drilled a 1,500-foot-hole beneath an outcrop of oxidized copper the size of a desk—paving the way to a 462-million-ton ore body in production since 1944 and still going strong today.

Malozemoff wore an impeccable dark blue, finely tailored suit over a starched white shirt and a necktie that had an intricate crystallographic pattern. His thin hawkish face resembled the actor Gary Cooper in a businesslike way. He greeted Doris with a reserved smile, warm but cordial. A receding hairline accentuated laser-gaze eyes sizing up the surroundings. My first thought was that this guy makes lots of decisions, and they stick. Second, I sensed that he was careful and precise, a good listener perhaps but one who does not suffer fools gladly.

Wallace Woolf rounded the corner from upstairs and extended his hand in greeting. "Good to see you again. How are you both?" He too wore a conservative suit and white shirt, with a brilliant maroon tie, every inch the professional manager with his trim salt-and-pepper mustache and his polished black wing-tip oxfords.

"We've invited Rollin Farmin from Day Mines and Don Springer from A. S. and R. and Tibor Klobusicky. Joe Gordon, our manager of mines, will be here, and Ted Olds, the Bunker Mine superintendent. Do you remember Al Lenz and Veral Hammerand from our exploration staff? I think they're coming. Their wives too."

"Yes, yes, excellent," Searls replied. "I want to find out if they've looked into the uranium deposits over on the Spokane River. We're going down there tomorrow."

Fred Searls's looks were point and counterpoint to Malozemoff. His hair spread out across a wide brow like harvest straw loosed from a field and scattered by the wind. Combing it might have been an afterthought. He wore a very dark double-breasted suit with a pen stuck in the outside pocket. I had the feeling Mr. Searls was out of uniform. Like most exploration guys, management or not, khakis and field boots fit better and felt better than business suits and bowties. But social occasions provided a chance to find out what was going on, more productive than a meeting in the front office. Immense chicken scratches decorated the margins of each eye, the result of squinting into a multitude of desert suns. He had huge hands. His gravelly voice boomed across the room, more affable and charismatic than Malozemoff's.

Many years after the Woolfs' cocktail party I came to the conclusion that these two men made a strange but effective combination: Searls, the operator, full of geologic facts and data, more at home on a silica outcrop overlooking some remote valley, unpeopled and still; Malozemoff, the relentless problem solver, working stock prices, finding unique financing ploys, different ways of cutting deals.

The living room, with light gray walls and blue carpet, was all decked out with vases of cosmos and delphiniums. A vestige of early evening sunlight filtered through the study windows, highlighting the dark mahogany furniture and a striped sofa. It was eighty degrees outside. Doris opened the study windows, letting in fresh mountain air, for a north wind had conveniently showed up, moving the smelter fumes away from town. The atmosphere was festive but not overboiled. A common thread of past experience and shared lives ran through the group. The conversation never stopped. Everyone knew each other or knew someone who had worked at Grass Valley, Tonopah, Cripple Creek, Ouray, Telluride, Leadville, or Butte.

Doris took the time to introduce me to the group as the summer's student guest and occasional bartender. I shook hands with a few of the great men nearby, finding myself halfway nervous about the evening's prospects. I remember thinking, I wish I knew what I was doing. What will these guys talk about? How do you get to be president of Newmont? Were they just smart? What did it take? What will the women talk about?

The doorbell rang continuously for fifteen minutes as other guests arrived. I got glasses ready and laid out my booze bottles in alphabetical order. I had a round green tray with a cork-lined bottom to keep the drinks from sliding, and a towel.

Folks seemed thirsty. I acquired a long list of drink orders in no time, and the noise level crescendoed like a Rossini overture. I launched the first round of drinks with some panache, gaining confidence as the right drinks arrived in the right hands. I kept track of who was drinking what on a notepad next to the bar adding words like "dry" next to the order column for extra precision. "Pink dress / G and T. Gray suit, bald / bourbon and water. Tall guy / old-fashioned."

The women gathered around a love seat and sofa. The men preferred to stand, circling up in small flocks around the room. They seemed anxious to start moving tons of this or that around the world, or to tell the story about the last round shot in the Carlton tunnel at Cripple Creek in 1941. Water poured out of the old Portland mine at the rate of 125,000 gallons per minute, sending a three-foot wall of water tearing through the bore toward the portal six miles away. I had a tough time eavesdropping and mixing drinks at the same time.

"Is Woody Latvala still at Con Copper in Ely?"

"Is Renouard still manager of mines at Anaconda?"

"Where's Ken Nobs?"

No sports. No politics.

Someone asked Searls about Newmont's Tsumeb mine in South West Africa.

"Well, for one thing," he replied, "it's 335 long miles by rail northeast of Walvis Bay—about as desolate a countryside as there is anywhere on the planet. But the mineralization was, and still is, incredible. We didn't see the original outcrop of course because it was glory-holed before we took over. But they say it looked like a painter's palette sticking up forty feet above the surrounding plain, the colors of every metal oxide known to man. Milky quartz shot through with malachite and azurite, chrysocolla. Fissures of solid galena running everywhere."

Malozemoff added another insight. "Our biggest problem has been that the run-of-mine product to the mill is so rich it overloads the flotation circuits. Imagine this. When we sampled the dump left behind when the Germans abandoned the property, the *dump* ran 5 percent copper and 16 percent lead! And now we've discovered there's enough germanium in the ore body to be recoverable. No one knows a whole lot about germanium, but there's a market developing because of this new electronic gadget called a transistor, I believe."

I continued to prey on the conversations, lingering around the fringes rearranging the celery and cheese sticks.

"Here ya go, son. Might as well gimme a refill on this one. B and B."

"Sure, you bet."

Doris was everywhere. She'd leave the women's group and explode into the midst of the men's huddle from underneath—standing in the center of the circle completely unaffected and admonishing the guys to quit being so stodgy and get their wives involved in the conversation. They tried to smooth her over. She didn't give up, told a joke or two. Wallace stood aside, enjoying the interruption. He had seen his good wife in action before and knew she was an expert at stirring things up, making sure they were all having a good time.

I decided to snitch a shot of MacNaughton's during a lull in the bartending action. Of course, the bartender is never supposed to get snapped, but I thought just a wee dram wouldn't hurt. How to pull it off unnoticed? As I bent over to get toothpicks from a shelf under the sink, I took a shot glass with about two fingers of 100 proof with me and let 'er go. The depth charge took my breath away for an instant and warmed me thoroughly from the inside out. Not bad. Not bad at all.

In a few minutes Doris stopped by for a status check.

"How's it going?"

"Not bad, not bad at all."

"Pour yourself a drink before we break up for dinner. Nice job. Things are going fine."

The combined effect of the MacNaughton's and my need to know how to find more ore in the world got the best of me. I started paying more attention to the conversations than to filling drinks and keeping the canapés fully charged. The exploration group moved in closer to the bar. "Fred," a voice asked, "how did the Idarado project go in Colorado. What made you think it would work?"

"To tell the truth, it goes clear back to when I was with U.S. Smelting. I'd taken a look at the old Black Bear property, which is on the west side of the Uncompahgre near Telluride. As you know, it was high-grade silver but started zoning into lead and zinc as they went down on the vein. But the vein was hell for strong when they quit. I got to thinking if we could go around and extend the Treasury Tunnel from the Red Mountain side, we should pick up the vein's downward extension and explore all that country in between. So we took the chance. That was over ten years ago. We brought in Long John Austin from Denver to do the tunnel work. He did a fine job—drove seven thousand feet in about ten or eleven months—three shifts a day, six days a week. We cut the Black Bear vein a thousand feet below the old workings, and Sunshine Mining, the Idaho company, drove a raise up there and we were in ore all the way.

"When it comes to driving tunnel," he continued, "you never saw anything like Long John. I think he stood about six foot eight or ten. He was either up in the heading all day or on the phone ordering supplies. He pushed that crew. Wore canvas pants that looked like wind socks about five feet long, and size fifteen or sixteen rubber boots. Moved like a giraffe, in slow, graceful strides."

Veral Hammerand, Bunker Hill's chief geologist, entered the conversation. "We thought the upper Bunker workings were mined out too. You'd think that in a property that's been in production since 1885. But Al [Lenz, the diamond drill boss] has some core from holes we just drilled in the Roger-Orr area, clear up on Levels 9 and 14. The crew has a five-hundred-foot drift going, and it looks pretty good. Spotty high-grade."

I was as busy as a long-tailed cat in a room full of rocking chairs, serving drinks to about twenty people and the party only under way forty-five minutes. I approached the lady's group from time to time and found the reception warm and a great deal less serious.

I responded to a litany of those social niceties that have no place in a young man's world: "Well, *you're* all decked out." "Do you know my daughter, Linda?" "You should meet Valerie. She's the pro's daughter at the golf club in Pinehurst."

All I could muster up was, "Yes ma'am," and "I'd like to."

The women looked crisp in flared skirts or shirtwaist dresses hemmed an inch or so below the knee. I took particular notice of a scoop neck with fitted bodice, age differential notwithstanding. Mrs. Lenz asked for a gin and tonic with a twist of lime. A confusing mixture of perfumes sat on the air—probably Chanel No. 5 and a concoction called Tabu. A few spike heels, flashy red or blue, and clip-on earrings added a touch of elegance to the scene. One black cocktail dress and string of pearls. No hats.

Business slacked off after the second round of drinks.

"That was a fine martini you made, son, a damn fine martini!"

"Yes sir, 'dry' I think you said. Very dry indeed."

Then I decided to have just another little snort of Mac-Naughton's, at about the same time Doris announced, "We're ready to eat. Everyone come sit."

Ted Olds grabbed my arm as he passed by. "Give me a call when you're through at New Mexico." So I stood back and wistfully watched all those years of experience walk into the dining room: managers of change, men who had been humbled by the tricks and turns Mother Nature threw into ore deposits but who still had the courage of their convictions. "Let's drill just one more hole over there and see what happens."

Plato Malozemoff led Newmont Mining as president and chairman of the board all through the 1960s and into the 1970s. He's an interesting study. My impression of him at the Woolfs' party wasn't far off track. He was tough as diamonds, intimidating and fearful to some staff, yet no one worked any harder for the company or put more energy into the great corporate question—getting an answer to stand the test of time. I think much of what he brought to the company had roots in the early years.

His father was also a mining engineer and, though it sounds like a contradiction, suffered under the Stalinist regime for operating the only profitable gold mine in Siberia. His mother was well educated. By 1929 the dual affronts to the Communist paranoia of education and profitability earned the Malozemoffs persona non grata status. When his father went to New York on business, the government seized the gold mine. No one understands how it got through, but the elder Malozemoff was able to wire his wife instructions to get out of Siberia as fast as possible. The desperate family made it as far as the border of Outer Mongolia, where the Cheka secret police summarily placed them under house arrest. Months went by during which time neither parent knew where the other one was, or whether the other was even alive. Finally, Plato's mother thought up a ruse that got them across the border into Mongolia, only to land in the middle of the Chinese-Mongolian War. All means of travel and communication were blocked off. She must have displayed a single-mindedness greater than the local authorities could deal with, or perhaps money changed hands and greased the gates to freedom, but she and her sons were given permission to leave after a few days' detention.

They were lucky. The day following their departure, an insane former officer of the Russian Imperial Army proclaimed himself emperor of Mongolia, savior of the yellow race, and ordered the execution of all Russian nationals remaining in the area. By this time the mother and her two teenage sons were making their way toward Peking, a thousand miles away on mules or on foot. The family was reunited in Peking and finally arrived in the United States just in time for the Great Depression.

Plato attended the University of California, then did graduate work at the Montana School of Mines, where he earned highest honors. He supported the entire family for a while by working nights for the Works Progress Administration in Butte. Later on, his precise analysis of mineral properties for the War Production Board during World War II gained the attention of Phil Kraft at Newmont Mining, and Malozemoff's long association with that company began when he became staff engineer in October 1945.

♠ ♠ ♠ ♠ 24

A Fight

Closing hour at the bars might have been noisy affairs, but for the most part they were surprisingly peaceful. The bars provided a setting to socialize, to gossip, to discuss the latest union contract or upcoming strike, and to find out who was sleeping with whom. Things aren't a whole lot different today. It was something to do, a ritualistic close to a week of hard work. Married couples had a few drinks, cashed their paychecks at a virtual bank named the Last Chance tavern in Smelterville, and went home—a five-minute drive at best. But sex and booze, or ethnicity and booze, were lightning rod issues guaranteed to ignite an occasional brushfire. Take two drinks, call someone a Wop, a Dago, a Finn, or a dumb Swede, and you had a fight on your hands. Take two drinks and fall in love with some guy's wife or girlfriend, and you had a fight on your hands. The trouble with these passionate outbursts is that the start of the dispute tended to empty the dugout. A lot of people who couldn't care and didn't care about the outcome wound up in the middle of a free-for-all, no holds barred. Whose side you wound up on didn't matter either. But I would find that out later in the evening.

The fights didn't last long because whoever got hit was going to spend a lot of time and money in a dentist's chair. And whoever happened to connect with a haymaker punch was bound to wake up the next morning to find all twenty-seven bones in his hand hurting beyond belief, some broken, and with ligaments and tendons in new arrangements. He wouldn't want to pick up anything heavier than a paper clip for six months. This is not a good thing in a place where that selfsame hand is how you earn a living. But people do like to make speeches. The messenger never quits until the message is delivered, and the message could have some heat behind it.

Being something of a pacifist—*chicken* may be more correct—I sought ways to avoid violence, upset, and turmoil. Sometimes you get swept up in a story line in which you had no intention of playing a part. That's what happened when I met a guy from the Missouri School of Mines in Rolla. He, Don, suggested we meet on a Friday night at the Korner Klub and have a beer. I thought, why not? and agreed to see him there.

The Korner Klub was crowded when I arrived around ten o'clock. My friend was nowhere in sight. So, having made the effort to get there, I ordered a short beer and sat down on a barstool. I felt some uneasiness about his absence, since if trouble starts it's nice to have at least one person on your side.

Well, someone must have dropped the gauntlet, because no sooner had I taken a sip of ale than emotion-laden voices broke into shouts several decibels above the background chatter. Things began to unravel. Through the haze of blue-gray tobacco smoke I noticed a table with three couples close by my left side. Two of them seemed to be the center of whatever was about to happen.

A great big guy—I'll call him Merle—said, "You by-god sonofabitch, she came here with me and she's leavin' with me!"

The other guy, "Jake," put down his beer and rose up a little in his chair. "That's bullshit and you know it! We may be not gettin' along but we're still married, by damn. Dottie's still my wife until the ink's dry on them papers we had signed. You better stay out of the picture."

Dottie: "I ain't spendin' another night under the same roof with you, you cheatin' bastard. Don't go pullin' that 'She's still my wife stuff.'"

Jake: "Y'are too."

Dottie: "Am not."

Jake: "Y'are too."

Dottie: "Am not. You should've thought of that before you shacked up with Vivian and that other woman. Leastways, Merle's nice to me."

Merle: "C'mon, hon, let's go."

Jake: "You ain't goin' nowhere with my wife!"

The conversation seemed to have reached a fulcrum of some sort, headed downhill regardless of which side of the teeter-totter you happened to be on. It was a confusing argument. Why were these couples sitting at the same table having a drink if Merle and Dottie were sleeping together and Jake and Dottie were married? Truth be told, you don't have to go to a mining camp in Idaho to find a web as tangled as that. The rest of the crowd, not paying attention up to this point, began to take notice. Tension replaced chatter.

Then it started.

Merle: "Well, we'll just see about that." He reached across the table as if to help the loved one with her sweater, landing instead a sucker punch that glanced off Jake's forehead. Jake knocked his chair over backward getting to his feet.

Dottie screamed, "Oh my god! Stop the fight. They'll kill each other!"

Then, to my bewilderment, everyone in the room took sides. Two red-faced guys at the next table grabbed each other by the shirt collar and shoved one another against a wall. A complete stranger came up to me and said, "Damn you anyway!" He took a swing. I stepped back in defense and got hit on the arm. I shouted back, "Hell, I don't even know you!"

It didn't make any difference, if it registered at all.

I grabbed my assailant's arms above the elbow and hung on. At least he couldn't hit me while we were dancing between the tables in the general direction of the door. He tripped over someone on the floor and we went down together. I happened to land on top. It looked like a good opportunity to leave. I left.

A couple minutes went by. I checked my body parts for fit and function. Everything seemed to be where it was when I started. The melee inside subsided, but the fight between Merle and Jake spilled out on the street, heading downhill until it reached the sidewalk in front of Emmett's Cigar Store. About that time Charlie Biotti, the swing-shift cop, and his partner, Harry Breeden, showed up. Things quieted down. They separated the puffing, out-of-breath combatants. Charlie knew what to do. He said, "You two want to go down to the railroad tracks and finish this business up, or not?"

Merle, bruised and in a notably calmer frame of mind, said, "Aw, hell no. He's my best friend."

Jake said, "Yeah, that's right. Let's forget it."

Out came the handcuffs. "Okay. Save your story for Chief Gilbreath in the morning. You can bunk in the same cell tonight and be best friends."

Charlie Biotti worked two jobs for thirty years to raise a family and pay the bills. During the day, he hauled concentrate gondolas up the lonely grade leading from the mill to the smelter on the highline railroad. Then he pulled the three-to-eleven shift on the city police force. That's somewhere in the neighborhood of fifteen thousand eight-hour shifts.

25

Shorty

An operation in which danger stalks the strandlines every minute needs and profits from the one person who can loosen things up. That's true for logging, fishing in the Gulf of Alaska, high-climbing steel, and certainly for underground mining. The Bunker Hill crew was lucky. We had Orval "Shorty" Drapeau, alias "Lyin' Shorty." Standing 5 feet 3 inches with boots on, he was so short that when he tried to get a job at the Kaiser Aluminum works in Spokane during a 1950s strike at the mine, they said, "Well, we know you can do the work, but we won't hire you."

Shorty said, "Why not?"

"Because you're too short."

"That's not a reason."

"It is now."

And they call it the Human Relations Department.

I asked Shorty recently why it was Lyin' Shorty instead of plain old Shorty. He said that the nickname stuck after a conversation with some fellow miners and a guy named Louie. "I told 'em a big yarn about living on the side of the hill up there, that my wife had to pack water from the creek every day to do the washing. Our cabin didn't have no floors in it, I said—just big saw slabs on the sides and roof. It took me an hour and a half to tell 'em. So Louie says, 'I'm going over to Spokane and buy you an electric plant and I'll come down and wire your house. You can pay me back at five bucks a month.' I said, 'Gosh, I can't afford even that right now, we're so poor.' They asked me how she does the washing. I said, 'Well, I got her a bucket.' 'What does she do in the winter?' they asked. 'I buy her a hatchet to break the ice.' They believed that. And that's how I got the name Lyin' Shorty."

Shorty started out as a shoveler in the stopes in 1952, then he got a job as motorman, later as skip tender. The hoistman and the skip tender worked together all day, each on separate ends of the long wire rope running up and down the shaft. They put all the supplies down into the mine and loaded the ore out—not to mention everything from dynamite to portable potties and garbage. He worked under Curly Seufert in the Service Raise and under Virl McCombs in the #1 shaft. Curly ran the hoist, and Shorty did all the unloading, sliding packs of timber off the skip at each level, then riding behind the rest of the load down to the next destination. If the hoistman didn't know what he was doing, the skip tender was dead meat. But they worked as a team, with horns and bells for signals.

A lot of the mine's folklore starts and ends with Shorty Drapeau. He told me one day that he had told a fellow at lunch that he only had one pair of pants, that he had to go to bed when his wife washed them, even if it was daylight outside. One day the guy brought him three brand-new pairs of pants in a grocery bag. "Don't tell anybody I got these for you. It's just between you and me." Shorty said, "I didn't have the heart to tell him anything different."

I wasn't in the vicinity for his next escapade, but it spread quickly all through the crew. Jim Cantrell was a well-known shift boss. One day he came up to Shorty and said, "Gosh, I've got a kind of headache. My neck is sore. Would you rub my neck just a little bit?"

"Sure. Just step over here by the shaft." Then he phoned Curly Seufert, riding the hoist. "Hang me a skip real close to the station because I think I'm going to need it in a hurry."

Uunbeknownst to Cantrell, Shorty reached over and grabbed a handful of black gooey cable grease and started rubbing it into the boss's back. "Oh, oh, that feels good. Keep rubbing right there."

Then Shorty escaped in the skip. A few hours later another boss asked Cantrell, "Jesus Christ, Jim, what's that awful black stuff you've got all over your neck and shoulders?"

"Why that little son of a bitch! I'm going to can that Lyin' Shorty when I catch up to him!"

A while later Shorty took a timber chain and ran it through the sleeves of a dozen jackets hung on pegs at the landing on Level 26. Then he drove 60-penny nails through the chain links into the two-by-eight holding the jackets and bent the nails over. The jackets were there a long time. Everyone knew who'd done it. But nothing happened. A kind of uneasy quiet surrounded our court jester as he went about his business. Weeks later, around Christmastime, Shorty substituted on the hoist for a day. He told me, "Well, we cleared the shaft, and everybody was up on top waiting to get on the train. I shut everything down on the hoist and got ready to come down out of the chair. Here they come after me. The whole crew. They grabbed me and took cans of spray paint and sprayed me all over with fluorescent paint— called me names all the time they was painting me. I looked like a tie-dyed T-shirt. And then you know what, after I got to the dry house they gave me a watch. They handed me this present all done up, and I was afraid to open it 'cause it might explode or something. But inside was a brand-new Timex. When I got home, Ethel said, 'What in God's name happened to you?' 'Oh, they just pick on me 'cause I'm small.'"

Ethel told me that one summer Shorty took off two weeks for a vacation. When he returned to work, the other skip tender had penciled in on the calendar: "Come back, Shorty. Come back." All fourteen days.

Shorty worked in the Bunker Hill shafts thirty-one years. One afternoon I asked him what it meant taken all together. "Well, it was a steady paycheck, and you never got bored for one minute, never. I worked with some top hands. It fed the family. We got the house paid for. Now if we can just keep the federal government out of our pockets."

26

Joe Gordon

J oe Gordon was a mustang, working his way through the herd to become manager of mines. That position was the top of the heap in terms of mine operations. He oversaw all the Bunker Hill production, as well as leases outside the valley, like the Nancy Lee in Montana and the Sullivan near Metaline Falls, Washington. Joe was a local boy. He graduated from Kellogg High School in 1930 and worked underground for ten years to help support five siblings. He put himself through the University of Idaho's mining engineering program and returned to the Silver Valley. Joe started in management as a shift boss, then division foreman, mine superintendent, and finally, by the time I arrived, manager of mines. He knew the Bunker Hill upside down and backward. Joe took mining seriously. When it came to taking care of the men, he said what he meant and meant what he said.

Doukhobor Sam's real name was John Doukhobor. John's mental acuity was impaired, but he got along and worked hard, caused no trouble—qualities welcome on any crew. I think he was a roustabout underground, cleaning up after the bigger boys left, mucking track, pulling chutes, tramming cars. One day some guy with a smart mouth started abusing him with taunts and insults, pushing him around. Doukhobor looked confused and angry but immobilized, unsure of what to do.

Joe Gordon, standing unobserved a few feet away, happened to overhear the situation. Having seen enough, he approached the tormentor and said, "Leave this man alone and don't ever bother him again!"

Uninformed and unaware of who he was talking to, the man asked, "Why should I?"

"Because I said so."

"Who the hell are you?"

"I'm the mine boss."

Chris and I broke a drill steel midway through the shift. We knew of another crew working a few minutes away and hurried over there to find a replacement. Joe Gordon had arrived a few seconds before we did during his daily rounds through the stopes. It was past noon, and these guys were still trying to get their timber in. They were obviously in a bigger hurry than we were. A third man, a helper, stood in a hole beneath an unprotected overhang using a drift pick to make room for a post.

Joe looked at the helper then flashed his light up at the overhang. He turned to the lead miner and said, "What do you have that guy down there for? Get him out of there!"

"Why? He's OK. We barred down this morning."

Joe was in no mood for dialogue. "Get him out of there. Here with the bar, I'll show you."

The helper moved back under protecting timber. Joe picked up the bar and wedged it into an innocuous-looking crack, wiggling it sideways just a little. The crack got bigger. In the space of two or three seconds—WHAM!—ten tons of muck slid out of the back onto the floor where the man had worked moments before. The helper made the sign of the cross and looked up. I can't recall what else was said. Joe saw something no one else saw. I guess the lesson, not only for working underground, but also for all of life was, never assume anything.

Many times since those events took place, I've thought about them and of the need for a Joe Gordon approach to corporate management. Plenty of managers seem willing enough to dictate this or that and delegate authority because of their position.

The country needs people with the courage of their convictions, able and willing to take care of situations in the workplace requiring immediate action and the decency to be evenhanded when the situation arises.

Middle managers have been forced to roll over, afraid to take command. We have been emasculated by the fear of lawsuits and the fear that executive management and the legal department will leave us swinging slowly in the wind—which they will. We are judged guilty until proven innocent. The feeling invades the atmosphere like a calumnious fog stealing unspoken through your office. We go to work, attend meetings, and go home. Responsible for everything; authority for nothing.

But there was a time when a manager could say without fear of being called on the carpet, "Leave that man alone and don't ever bother him again. Why? Because I said so."

27

$2.50

Bunker Hill labor relations manager James Blaisdell's comment to the Mine, Mill and Smelter Worker's Union before the big strike: "Your demands contain a cost bill that, on the face of it, would appear to be aimed at the destruction of the Bunker Hill company."

North Idaho Press, January 1960

I remembered to call Ted Olds after I graduated from New Mexico Tech in January 1960, and it wasn't long before I returned to Kellogg with a job. In a little over three months' absence, things had changed. I learned that Wallace and Doris Woolf were about to retire in Salt Lake City, the Bunker Hill heir apparent and CEO, John Bradley, had been killed in a car accident, and labor-management relations had turned sour.

Bradley's death was more than just another accident. As Fred Bradley's son, he had been groomed for the job certainly, but he represented a lot more than nepotism: he knew what he was doing, and the company was at a critical juncture. The Mine, Mill and Smelter Workers contract had expired and work was continuing on month-to month extensions. The mood was ugly, very ugly. The union bosses rattled their sabers at the same time the price of lead, zinc, and silver headed south. In newspaper articles company management wondered if the union knew where the payroll came from.

I rented an upstairs two-room apartment in a tiny house at 507 Second Street. I had all 240 square feet to myself. It had a nice view from one window facing east and another facing west.

The day after my return Chris came into the dry house at the end of the day shift while I was hanging up my diggers. "Well, if it ain't me old partner. You're an engineer now, and you still want to go break rock down there? I guess I better be nice. You're gonna be a boss before long."

"Don't give me that old jazz, partner. It's like you always said, Chris: 'Take 'er slow.'"

"They got me on timber repair again. Must be good at it. Been doin' it ever since you left last fall. Jim Cantrell said you could start out with me again if you want."

"Just right. I was hoping for that."

So we got back to the same comfortable routine. But winter in northern Idaho turned out to be less fun than summer. It was dark when we went to work, dark all day in the mine, and dark by the time we showered and dressed. It snowed every other day. The thermometer went down to around twenty-five degrees and stayed there. I had the advantage over the folks on the lower floor of my little house because all their heat went up through the cheap ceiling joists into my apartment. You hunker down and hole up. You look for the wood stove's radiant heat, and the smell of smoke. At night, for something to do, I went out and walked around in the snow. Porch lights glistened like diamonds. The yellow cone descending from each streetlight indicated how much snow was falling, and how the next day's weather was going to turn out. Big flakes meant it was warming up, little ones meant colder. I listened to Marty Robbins's *Gunslinger* album with the hit tune "El Paso": "Out in the west Texas town of El Paso, I met a beautiful Mexican girl . . . " All the Johnny Cash tunes: "I Walk the Line" and "I Got Stripes Around My Shoulder."

Chris and I had worked only a week or so when Paul Sloan came down the drift one day during lunch. He said, "Ted Olds wanted me to offer you a chance to be lead man if you want. You still know how to run a jackleg?"

"Sure."

"You remember how to do your powder?"

"Sure."

"What's the last thing you say when you leave the round?"

"Fire in the hole!"

"What about your timber? What do you want to do with your timber?"

"Keep 'er tight. Use lots of wedges. Get it straight and true."

"You pass. See me Monday morning. I'll get you to the new stope we're opening up. It's big."

After Paul left, I told Chris I thought I could do it.

"You'll be OK. Just don't let anyone push you around. Don't get hurried by some shifter. You'll be OK."

So Monday morning I got a pay raise: 13 cents per hour, to $2.50. Over an eight-hour shift, that's an increase of

$1.04. Four gallons of gasoline, or five loaves of bread. Enough by Wednesday to buy a new pair of Levis.

My newfound position as lead man entitled me to a helper. I've tried to forget this guy, but I can't. His name was something like Erskine. I think his surname was Hollings. I just called him Erskine. He had some problem with his teeth falling out, so I had a hard time understanding what he was trying to say. He had never worked underground before. If ever there was a guy who didn't know up from around the corner, Erskine was the man. I say this at the risk of sounding pretentious. It wouldn't have been so bad if he had had an ounce or two of ambition, but I was constantly thinking of what he was supposed to be doing in addition to what I was supposed to be doing. And you would think that after three weeks of stope mining, doing the same thing day after day, he would have gotten some clue as to what came next. But he didn't. I will say on Erskine's behalf that he took directions well, and he was strong, which helped a great deal.

The entire day's conversation went something like this:

"Erskine, we need to bar down. Hand me the bar."

Later: "Now we need to bring the timber down. But first we need room for the timber. You dig there and I'll dig here. OK?"

Later yet: "Now it's time to drill the round. Drag the hoses over here so I can set the drill up. OK?"

Still later: "Hold the bit so I can start each hole. OK?"

Nearing the end of the shift: "Now it's time to load the powder. Hand me the sticks and I'll do the tamping."

The worst of it was, having so little in common, there wasn't much to talk about during lunch. So the conversations were dreadfully short and not very entertaining. I hoped Chris would stop by and tell the blond gorilla joke. In any event, things went along tolerably well through January 1960 and on into mid-February. A few changes in technology had taken place in my absence during the fall of 1959. The knock-on drill bits and multiple changes of drill steel had been replaced by one-piece steels with an integral bit. The bit's tungsten carbide inserts made it possible to drill several rounds without sharpening. Igniters crimped on the end of each fuse and tied together by a burning wire called Quarry Cord made it possible to time the round perfectly and not have to stand there with a spitter in your hand wondering if you'd got them all lit before something went wrong. Just light one end of the cord and leave. It was a vastly safer system.

For some reason, the bosses decided that the new stope was going to produce a bundle. It must have been high in silver. It didn't take long to open up a lot of ground—about ten square-sets across and four or five sets high. Guys were drilling off platforms all over the place in every direction. I cornered one of the mine geologists, Al Lenz, and asked him where we were. He said, "This Emery vein is big. It lies under the Cate fault. There's going to be trouble unless they backfill some of this open ground."

One day I drilled out the standard round and loaded each hole with the customary six sticks of powder. I lit the quarry cord and we left. The next morning when I got into the stope I looked into the cavity opened by the blast.

A backhole in the top right corner had apparently done its job and then some, because a feature roughly resembling an avalanche chute had caved about twenty-five feet high. All I could imagine was that I had drilled into a fracture zone of shattered quartz. It kept falling as we stood there looking up. Each time something came down it sounded like a baseball hitting a plate glass window.

I looked at Erskine. "Ahhhhh shit."

"Yup."

About this time Bill Lathrop showed up. This was his week to be relief shift boss. Bill got pretty excited. He looked at the hole in the mountain, started rolling his toothpick around so fast I thought he was going to swallow it, and stuttered, "Jesus Cccchrist. What'd you do that for? Don't you know how to blast? You could get canned for this. You could get canned. You could draw your time. Too much ground. Too much ground open. Caved clear up there. Got to catch this up right away. Jesus H. Christ, never seen . . . Jeeeezus."

Well, I didn't understand what all the fuss was about. Things like that must have happened once in a while. Surely there was a way to fix it. I was equally sure I didn't want to get fired on the first job of what I expected to be a long career.

I didn't feel like the mess was entirely mine. I couldn't see any farther into the earth than Bill could. There was no way of telling what was behind that hole when I drilled it. "Well, it didn't look any different to me than any other round. If I'd loaded that hole with only two sticks for some reason and the corner didn't pull you'd be all over my case like a bull's ass in fly time. That's a shear zone. Al Lenz told me."

Bill wasn't interested in explanations of the local geology or excuses. All he knew was that the whole thing could come down at any minute. But I didn't know that.

"Goddam, Jesus Christ. Got to fix it right away."

"OK, OK. I'll need some help."

We threw timber in that hole all day. Another crew crawled up above and drove some spiling (pointed timber planks) into the ground at the very top. That kept most of the stuff from falling, but it was shaky. It looked better when we quit that day than when we came in. That's about all I can say.

I came to work the next day all fired up and full of ideas about how to catch up the ground. But there was a big problem. The Mine, Mill and Smelter workers had struck. Pickets guarded the road to the dry house. An angry group stopped Red Morgan and one of the other bosses trying to make their way to the mine office. A terse conversation took place. After a minute of tough talk, the pickets let them through, which they were obliged to do anyway since the bosses were management. Chris saw me taking in the scene and came over.

"Don't try to cross that picket line. Best thing to do is stay out of the way."

Fixing the cave-in would have to wait. A long time, as it turned out.

Well, I felt pretty bad. First, I would be broke in no time, and second, I hated to leave a half-baked job undone down in the mine. I wandered around town all day listening to the strike talk. If I had it right, it sounded like the union's management and a few shop stewards were working hard to stir up sentiment for the strike. I heard someone say, "I'd rather have the company offer and a job than more money and no job." Others disagreed.

That night the phone rang. Woody Latvala, chair of the mining department at New Mexico Tech, was on the line.

"Say listen, I just got a call from a guy I used to work with at Consolidated Copper in Ely. Name's Jim Perkins. Jim is superintendent of a brand-new open pit operation in Wyoming—uranium out in the Gas Hills. He's looking for a foreman to start in two weeks. I told him I'd give you a call and see if you'd be interested. Jim's a good guy. You'd get along fine."

"Well, the Mine, Mill union just went on strike today and it might last a day or two or a year or two. I hate to bail out, but I'm stuck."

Woody gave me Perkins's phone number in Riverton.

Five minutes later the phone rang again. The voice on the other end said, "This is Ted Olds. I'm wondering if you could stop by my office tomorrow morning for a chat. Nine o'clock.

"Sure, you bet," I muttered back, heavyhearted, fearful.

Coeur d'Alene is a French term. A literal translation "heart of an awl," or, for all practical purposes, the point of an awl. Mr. Olds must've found out I'd blown up the big stope, I thought. I felt the *coeur d'alene* ironically probing my conscience. "This is it. Failure on the first job." I knew I was going to get canned. I took some comfort in the thought that I had only done what I had been trained to do. So I thought, Piss on old Bill Lathrop. Scream and shout, wave your hands and run about. Swallow that toothpick if you want, for all I care.

At nine o'clock the next morning I walked into Mr. Olds's office (now I was thinking of him as Mr. Olds instead of Ted) with my heart in my hand and as great a mea culpa as any orator ever thought up running through my mind.

Through the glass and mahogany-sided office, I saw him sitting at a desk. His secretary said he was expecting me. I thought, Oh great, of course he's expecting me. He has the "you're fired" speech all cooked up.

But Olds looked up over his horn-rimmed glasses, smiled, and said, "Thanks for coming. I wanted to tell all the college grads what we are up against with this strike so they can start planning for what comes next. That goes especially for guys like you who are mining engineers working in production."

I must have sighed a big sigh, for I wasn't about to get fired. The man was simply taking care of business.

He went on, not pausing for my speech, which wouldn't have made much sense at this point in any event. "The union leadership is grandstanding to a high degree, and I think we've made the best offer we can make and still keep things running in a time of lousy metal prices. We considered shutting down the whole operation months ago, strike or no strike, but decided to keep going and sending paychecks out to as many of our longtime employees as possible, for as long as possible. But the union has taken a hard line that will have a huge impact on the company and the community if the strike lasts more than a month or so. In my estimation it's going to go on a long time. A long time. My advice to you is to leave and then come back if and when things improve. You'll always have a job here."

I told him about my job offer in Wyoming. "Hell's fire, I know Latvala and Perkins from Ely. I worked there too. They're fine. Take the job."

So I did.

The next day I drove out to Pinehurst and caught Chris and Lucille coming out of the Lutheran church. "Chris, I got a job in the uranium patch, so with the strike and all I guess 'she's deep enough for me.' Just wanted to stop by and thank you for all you taught me, and for being a good lead man. And truth be told, I liked your jokes too."

"That's good of you to say, partner. You was a good partner. Stop by when you come through town if ever you do. We may go up to Murray if this lasts too long. I got plenty of work to do everywhere I go. Lucille here, she keeps me going. We've thought about buying the old hotel up there. Pump a little gas. Pour a beer or two. We'll see."

Then I stopped by the boardinghouse and had the same conversation with Dora Tatham. Except she said, "Well, I envy you. You've got the whole world in front of you. We're stuck. This is about as far out of town as we git, and we ain't even left the city limits. Good luck."

After the Bunker Hill office closed for the day, I dropped by the Woolfs' house to say good-bye. Charlie Schwab, John Bradley's heir, had taken over the lion's share of the company's bargaining with the union, so Doris and Wallace were busy packing for the move to Salt Lake. The three of us sat in the kitchen and had two fingers of McNaughton's Reserve, straight up. The talk was all about the strike. Wallace said, "We had a long period of time, from 1910 until maybe 1950 or so, without much labor disruption. But this one is different. I'm afraid the differences of opinion will put a strain on a lot of relationships if it lasts very long—marriages, friendships, guys who worked together. There will be that much difference in how things are perceived. Who knows what will happen, but at the same time there is the reality. It happens."

I said, "Thank you both for being so generous to this greenhorn kid from Seattle. Someday I could write a book about this whole experience."

Doris said, "We'll miss this place. We've spent most of a lifetime here. But it's time to move on. Let us know how you're doing. We've got a place picked out in Salt Lake City. Our daughter Jackie is there. Keep in touch."

Kellogg was strangely quiet that night. Life seemed to be on standby, like the community's spunk and fire had been snuffed out. Obvious questions flew back and forth over family dinner tables: How long will the strike last? Is the union going to pay for anything? Will we lose the house? What will happen? Fear and anxiety on the loose.

I was fortunate. No wife, no kids, no responsibilities, and a job in the red-hot uranium fields. So the next morning I tossed Marty Robbins and Johnny Cash in the VW, told the landlord I was a goner, and pulled onto U.S. Highway 10 headed for a still-frozen Wyoming. As I approached the summit of Lookout Pass an odd feeling crept over me, one of those way-down-deep-in-your-guts feelings that slides in when something significant has changed, but you can't quite put your finger on it. I think it was the realization that I'd just left a tight-knit group of stoic, hardworking, honest folks. They were tough but at the same time kind in their own way. Having said that, I knew everyone in the community wasn't destined for singing in the choir, but I had been privileged to know the people who had crossed my trail. Wolff, old man, I thought, if you're ever around when trouble starts, these are the people you want on your side.

28

More Money, Less Fun

I can't say if the word *enjoyment* was applicable to my new job in Wyoming. Much of the year we worked six days a week, ten hours a day in subzero temperatures. The mine was an hour's feverish drive each way across the sage-paved desert on a winding gravel road sixty miles from Riverton. Occasionally the driver fell asleep and wandered off the gravel, blasted out through the shallow borrow pit, and emerged again into the sagebrush. He usually woke up when this happened. For the rest of us, dozing slack-jawed in the back, the trick was to show only mild surprise. Ho hum, we're off the road out in the desert again. That must be sagebrush rushing by the window. Sometimes it snowed two inches and the wind blew all of it into the shallow arroyos, which we hit at seventy miles per hour. It was like running into a cloud of goose down. For about five seconds no one knew where the road was, or when it would appear. The best strategy was to hold rudder amidship and pray that no one approached from the other direction.

The thermometer went down to fifty-five degrees below zero for weeks on end in the winter of 1961–62.

High-pressure arctic cold lay over the state like a frozen, sunny liquid. At night you could see Uranus with the unaided eye. Columns of chimney smoke rose up straight as a ribbon to ten thousand feet in the super-cooled atmosphere. We couldn't turn the diesel equipment off at night because the fuel turned to Jell-O. Nothing would start. My boss, Jim Perkins, said we had to be careful when we spoke outside because when the words froze and fell to the ground, it would be impossible to understand the conversation until it thawed out in spring. That's when the wind blew. It also blew in summer, fall, and winter. It sandblasted our pickup windshields so many times the insurance company dropped our comprehensive coverage. It snowed at the mine on July Fourth.

We had drill rigs going constantly trying to find more radioactive ore. One day a driller's helper climbed down off the tower and headed for the bus. I said, "Hey, Will, where ya going?"

He said, "I forgot my jacket."

"Let me know where it is. I'll get it for you."

"It's in Tennessee. Good-bye."

I had my own crew. We moved twelve hundred tons a day with a Caterpillar loader and a bunch of borrowed trucks. One of the things I learned as foreman was if you want authority, you have to earn it and then you have to give it away. The little people know how to do the work. The boss's job is to let 'em do it. Tough lesson. Open pit mining was like playing in a gigantic sandbox. But it wasn't as much fun as finding a gleaming face of silver staring you in the face each morning. A high school grad could have made money there. But you do what you do.

After a few years of duty not far from the aptly named Wind River Mountains, I got a bug in my head to go for a master's degree in a related field—the thought being no more complicated than to make more money. I knew a job in corporate America wouldn't be as exciting as blowing up quartzite in Shoshone County, but a wife, three kids, and a mortgage tend to focus a fellow's mind. In retrospect, I suppose it wasn't such a whimsical decision at that.

The degree in materials engineering led to a research job at a Fortune 500 aerospace company. For a while I had a wonderful time being an engineer in an engineer-run company. I worked on flaps and landing gear and found heat-resistant coatings for engine mounts as the engines got bigger and hotter. We worked Saturdays and Sundays with no thought of extra pay because it was so important and we all felt tremendous loyalty to the company.

Then someone suggested I take a job in management. That's when I began thinking about the value of my greenhorn days in the mine with Chris. "Fire in the hole" was easier to comprehend than the atmosphere I was about to encounter.

In one respect my aerospace career was fortunate; the men I reported to turned out to be top-notch managers. But outside the organization, it was turf war and politics. On the few occasions when I made presentations at the VP or director level, I learned soon enough that I was swimming with sharks. Their jokes were funny, even the bad ones. If you happened to crack one, and they thought it wasn't funny, there was blood in the water.

Corporate fear in management ranks was alive and

well, pervasive. It strangled creativity and morale, and those who advocated changing the way things were done did so at their own peril. Conformity was highly valued, conflict shunned. Most of the news going up the chain of command was good news, even though the data might have been given a massage to make it fit the "happy path." Sometimes opinions masquerading as data dictated the decision-making process. But a room full of opinions produces heat; a room full of data produces light.

Underground, under thousands of feet of rock, surrounded by things that go bang, even when our lights went out, I felt safe psychologically. But in corporate management it felt like you spent the day with one foot onshore and the other in quicksand.

The Bunker Hill experience helped me to see through it all, notwithstanding a few anxiety attacks of my own, but it helps to have something else in your life for comparison. A backboard to bounce the latest crisis against and see what comes back at you. I often thought about solving problems like the drift cave-in—where the solution was rock by rock, piece by piece, until it was all caught up, the new timber in place and safe once again. But I had a mandate to classify 40 percent of my staff people as layoff material even though few if any were layoff material because I worked hard at not hiring layoff material in the first place. It kind of wore you down, affecting good, hardworking, loyal people's lives.

So I came away with an interesting thought after twenty years at the corporate fount: It's the little people who make the company. They are the ones who bring home the corporate earnings. All management has to do is hand them a process that works. All they ask in return is to feel like their efforts are rewarded along with those of the CEO and CFO, and to feel somewhere along the way, even if only for a few years, that there is a shared destiny.

There is nothing quite like crawling into a wooden skip with twenty-one fellow miners, then descending a mile beneath the earth's surface to develop a sense of shared destiny—not only with your companions but also with the hoistman who holds the entire crew in his right hand. I think it's about trust. The phrase "we're all in this together" takes on a new meaning—the same meaning as that shared by attack submarine crews who know that everyone's well-being depends on what everyone else does or does not do.

So the hubris, greed and avarice, and corporate theft that surfaced in 2002 during the Enron and Global Crossing messes might have been different if those high-fliers had spent some time underground getting the piss kicked out of them. That is a place to learn humility in dealing with immovable objects like mountains, using cantankerous jackleg drills, and water pouring down your neck in ninety-four-degree heat.

Epilogue

I suspect when we look back to another place and time we tend to make everything just a little better than the reality. Friends were friendlier, more steadfast, more loyal; weather was sunnier, warmer, the air fresher; jobs and futures were more secure, predictable, comfortable. True or not, the absolute unassailable freedom that comes from being eighteen and on your own—whether ten years ago or fifty—lights up the psyche like few things. You remember only something of what happened, but you recall exactly without any qualification what it felt like. A time without a mortgage, kids in braces, a car payment, or an impending layoff when an unknown policy written by an anonymous voice holds sway over your entire life, or at least the life you think you recognize. A few years when you were the only thing you had to take care of, and no matter what happened there was time to recover, to recoup and start over. A time without fear. It passes quickly.

The tough part of recollection arrives in the dark of night, with the devil dancing on the end of your bed because you had assumed that the people around you would always be there, that there was no particular need to hurry to make fast the lines of friendship. I wish I had taken more time with Chris, Doris Woolf, Dora Tatham, and Old Bill Bradley. Maybe that's a reason to write a book, to put them on the map. Even things up a bit.

The big strike at the Bunker Hill mine lasted 205 days, almost all of 1960. Nothing at the company or in the community was quite the same after that. As the strike wore on toward Christmas, the men finally got together and formed their own union, the Northwest Metal Workers—the long, troubled disruption only a harbinger of things to come.

I stopped at Pinehurst Lutheran in 1964 on my way through Kellogg and ran into Chris and Lucille just as they were coming out the door after services. He said they had purchased a hotel in Murray built in 1888 and planned on doing something with it, maybe sell a few groceries and pour a few drinks from the old bar. As time went on I didn't forget about Chris, but after the arrival of three kids I was just too busy taking care of business to look him up.

Finally, in 1982, during a down-and-out January Idaho blizzard, I found myself staring at the ceiling of a room in the Stardust Motel in Wallace, wondering if Chris was still in Murray, if he was even alive. The phone book seemed to think so. I bought a six-pack of beer and drove back over the mountainous twisting road to the birthplace of Terrible Edith. It was a lonely dark landscape when I got to the Sprag Pole Inn about 6:30 P.M. A few local citizens chatted quietly at the bar. The lights were on. It was warm inside. Everyone glanced in my direction when I opened the door—as if to say, "What's this guy, a nut or something? Who'd be out sight-seeing on a night like this?"

"Looking for an old-timer named Chris Christopherson. Lived here years ago. Anyone know him?"

The proprietress said, "Of course I know him. We all know Chris. He lives at the end of the street in a yellow house with a green roof. If you drive into the woods, you've gone too far."

I knocked on the door. Chris answered.

"Don't know if you remember me, Chris. I'm your old partner from the Oakie stope and timber repair days."

"Well, son of a biscuit, by golly. Sure. Come right in."

Chris wore a green plaid shirt, and his hair was all messed up. He looked a little older. So did I. Lucille did too. She wore a bathrobe. I wasn't sure if she was just getting up or was getting ready to go to bed. It appeared to me that even a pinnacle of Lutheran churchdom might have acquired a taste for a flagon of nut-brown ale. So we talked for quite some time. At about the end of my six-pack and the beginning of theirs, Chris said, "Say, I've got something you'd like to see."

He opened the pantry door and came back with a one-gallon French's mustard jar full of gold nuggets. He could hardly lift it.

"Christ in the foothills," I said. "Where did that come from?"

It was a long story.

"We did OK with the hotel when we moved back, mostly sellin' beer and gas. But one day I was out plantin' tomatoes in the back toward Prichard Creek and I kept finding these little nuggets and flakes of gold. I didn't think too much about it until Ike Hinkle—foreman on the old dredge—showed up."

Hinkle told Chris they had pulled three hundred and fifty ounces of gold in *one day's cleanup* from a hole in the gravel about twenty-five feet south of the hotel. If you're a miner and you own a hotel over bedrock that gave up a hundred thousand dollars in gold, it starts working on you at night.

Chris continued: "I got this idea if I took up the floorboards in the bedroom and sunk a shaft, I could have a roof over my head while I worked and a place to store my tools. So that's what I did. And that's where all this in the jar came from."

Everyone thought he was crazy until one afternoon in July 1973 he brought up a half-pound nugget. The whole town got drunk and stayed that way for four days.

He opened up a little stope thirty-five feet down a perfectly timbered, two-compartment shaft, hoist and all. The stope was about three feet high. It was wet and cold. Water poured down through the gravel. He worked on his hands and knees to excavate a bucket at a time, cleaning gold out of tiny riffles in the slate bedrock. He drove top spiling in the back, like we did on timber repair, to keep it from running-in and kept a pump with him all the time.

In April 1974 the producers of the Garry Moore TV show *To Tell the Truth* called. They wanted Chris to fly to New York and try to stump the panel with his crazy story about the Bedroom Goldmine. He told them, "I ain't goin' to no New York and be on no TV show." But Lucille had a different idea. She said, "I'll go." The panel was stumped until the very last instant, when longtime panel member Kitty Carlisle guessed the truth.

The first Viking invasion of North America took place sometime in the eighth century. The second occurred in 1974 when the Minnesota Vikings Investment Club, led by tight end John Beasley, showed up in Murray. The entourage included Benchwarmer Bob Lurtsema, Jim Berry (one of the first black quarterbacks in the NFL), and Bob Marshall. They bought the Golden Chest lode mine about a mile east of Murray, just below the Terrible Edith. The Vikings set up camp. The beer flowed and the stories grew. The Golden Chest adit needed eight hundred feet of retimbering, so Chris took it on. A picture of Chris in his diggers posed with the football pros appeared in an issue of the NFL's 1974 season program.

Fifteen years after my visit in the blizzard, in the summer of 1997, my wife, Mary, and I stopped by once more to see Chris. Lucille had died of liver complications in 1993. The light had dimmed. I asked Chris, I guess facetiously, if he'd decided to get married again. "No, never even crossed my mind. I'd never find anyone as good to me as Cile was. We had quite a time."

Mary asked, "What's your cat's name?"

"I don't know for sure. He just moved in and never told me who he was."

Chris didn't look very well. I said, "You ever think about seeing a doctor?"

"I did see one once. My army physical in 1941. I don't care for 'em much."

His niece, Edith Helfer, and her husband, Ed, lived down the road in Prichard. They looked after him with great care until he passed away. Chris died on April 29, 1999—on my son Andrew's birthday.

Betty Lou Arens née Tatham, in 1958 the best-looking fourteen-year-old in the state of Idaho, escaped from Kellogg after high school. She earned a degree in anthropology at the University of Washington and worked at the Smithsonian Institution. Years later, she qualified for a fifty-ton sea captain's rating and sailed charters around the Caribbean.

Dora Tatham, her mother, the cook who kept me fed, watered, and advised, was interviewed on national television in 1973 as the owner-operator of the only full-service boardinghouse left in this country. She said the TV guys just showed up one morning and started filming. The clientele changed rapidly afterward, and that was the end of Pat's Boarding House. Dora said the old regulars drifted off or died, and the tramp miners coming in were into drugs and slept in their diggers with their muddy boots on. It was too much to put up with. She and 'Tater bought a stump ranch near Lake Pend Oreille. I asked her if she missed getting up at four in the morning and cooking meals for fourteen hours after all those years. "Not really," she said. "I'm just plain tired."

"Do you have any idea how much that food meant to us working stiffs?"

"No one hardly ever thanked me. But I think some appreciated it. I done the best I could and raise a family the same time."

The Lux Rooms in Wallace turned into the Sixth Street Melodrama Theater, a tourist trap of a different sort. It features players like Craven Sinclair and Lilly Fairweather in productions such as "Alias Smedley McGrew."

In one comforting sign of permanence, the Pennaluna and Company stockbroker's office continues daily operations on Sixth Street, not far from the Melodrama Theater, in the same location with the same sparkling high-grade silver ore perched in the huge plate-glass window surrounded by the same Kelly green trim. Broker Jerome Bunde and I chatted about the old days and the new days for a few moments. "What about silver? Will the price ever go up to where it should be?" I asked. Quick as a cat, he replied, "Well, silver is a nonrenewable resource, and as far as I know God only planted one crop."

In 1988 a penurious FBI showed up and chased every prostitute out of Wallace and Kellogg and arrested the sheriff. I don't know what happened to him, but I hope he lived to see another day. This country can get hypocritical at times. Houses are legal in Nevada but not in Idaho. I don't know, what's good and what's bad gets kind of confusing. The girls had about five minutes' notice to either gather up their clothes or put them on, as the case may have been, and leave town. The U and I house above the Miner's Club must have burned. I think a muffler store stands on the property.

In 1968 Bunker Hill stock sold for about $44 per share. Gulf Resources and Chemical Company, a Texas-based outfit one-tenth the size of Bunker Hill, cooked up a hostile takeover offer at $56 and in one stroke grabbed a complex hardrock mining and smelting operation they knew little about. When the deal was finally approved by the Federal Trade Commission in June of that year, Bunker Hill's seven thousand stockholders owned stock in a company they hadn't asked for.

The Bunker Hill was declared a "listed" superfund site. The huge dune left by the smelter's slag pile was covered with topsoil and planted with grass. The mill's enormous tailings pond was drained and covered. At a permanent treatment plant below the portal, the mine drainage from the Kellogg Tunnel is neutralized with limestone. The smelter smokestacks were brought down in May 1996. The smelter itself was dismantled and carted away. Same with the Sullivan zinc plant.

A miner's miner named Bob Hopper bought the rights to the Bunker Hill in 1991 after every piece of equipment not bolted down had been sold and the mine allowed to flood. He made a living mining high-grade zinc ore left in the upper workings and selling rare pyrolusite crystals to collectors. More important, he sandblasted the soot off the walls of the hoist room and Kellogg Tunnel terminal and rebuilt the beautiful hoist sitting atop #2 shaft made by the Coeur d'Alene Hardware Company. It's painted white and has been restored to pristine operating condition. When he was kind enough to show it to me in the summer of 1999, I didn't want to walk across the floor for fear of muddying it with my boots.

The Oakie stope is under two thousand feet of water. The lowest level, 31, was in good ore when Gulf Resources quit the mining business. No one knows where the end of the Bunker Hill ore body lies.

Today, the South Fork of the Coeur d'Alene River flows crystal clear. The mouse-colored lead water is gone. Hecla, Sunshine, and Dayrock, along with the Bunker Hill, changed their operations in the 1960s and 1970s. Impoundments captured mill tailings, some of which were dewatered and pumped underground to backfill empty stopes. Although fish may still be at risk in the lower reaches toward the lake because of zinc and copper levels, hooded mergansers and wood ducks can be seen in wetlands surrounding the Cataldo Mission, the site of the famous Bunker Hill dredge. Not a complete picture but an indication that things are better.

Mining caused some of the pollution problem, but early-day clear-cuts compromised the land's ability to retain rainfall. The term "100-year flood" has become something of a fiction. A standing forest would have held a lot of water that now cascades uninterrupted into the river. It rushes downstream and churns the historic mill tailings, releasing contaminants that could have remained buried. Now there's a big lawsuit, and the most common sign in the Silver Valley is one marked "EPA."

Are there elevated levels of zinc in Lake Coeur d'Alene? Sure. Given the nature of geochemical processes and one hundred million tons of mineral cropping out upstream, there were elevated levels in the lake when Stonehenge was erected too. Earl Bennett, a department chair at the University of Idaho, made an interesting comparison: "Do you take Centrum vitamin tablets? If so, you can get the same amount of zinc for your prostate, if you have one, by quaffing eight gallons of lake water every day."

At Sam's Cafe in Kellogg you see things on the menu like "The Mother Lode" breakfast assortment for $5.29. That'll get you two eggs, hash browns, toast, coffee, and bacon or sausage. The "Big Strike" is similar, except biscuits and gravy are added. I suppose to the tourists the Big Strike breakfast is a reference to Noah Kellogg's big silver strike in 1885. To me and all the locals having breakfast, it means the labor strike of 1960. The coffee supply never ends. Refills are free. It's likely your waitress will be a twenty-something Kellogg native, probably blond, friendly, cute, and named Gloria. She's all business. Chances are you'll see a couple of ex-miners or smeltermen having breakfast together on a Sunday morning. In all probability they will wear flannel shirts, blue jeans, white socks, and black shoes. If you happen to mention ever having worked at "Uncle Bunker," you will have an instant conversation on your hands about when, who you knew, and who the shift boss was.

A new high-speed gravel road bypasses the settlement of Murray. So you can drive sixty miles per hour to Thompson Falls instead of twenty. That's progress. At the Sprag Pole Inn, which serves the best cheeseburgers on this planet, proprietress Connie Roath said, "Yes, the highway went right over the old dredge piles, and the dredge went right over the old red-light district. That's all been gone for many years, of course. But there's still some around who don't charge."

Doris and Wallace Woolf moved to Salt Lake City near their daughter, Jackie Rosenblatt, in April 1960. Doris and I corresponded for several years afterward. She wrote long notes filled with funny goings-on in their retirement lives, and as always full of new ways of thinking and great thoughts about the world politic. I wish I had kept them. She contracted throat cancer and passed away in 1971. If I had known, I would have done something to help, but of course there's nothing to do for anyone but let them know. Doris was a role model.

Wallace Woolf celebrated his 100th birthday on March 9, 1990. In 1978, at the age of eighty-eight, he stood on his feet for four hours, greeting every person who came to the fiftieth anniversary of the construction of the electrolytic zinc plant that he designed and managed. He not only said hello but also hailed everyone on his watch by his or her first and last name.

Three of the best miners who ever rode a hoist, Virl McCombs, Curly Seufert, and Gary Hoffman, still live in the Silver Valley area. Lyin' Shorty Drapeau and his truthful, honest wife, Ethel, live at Post Falls in the same home as when he worked at the mine. He remembers all the old stories and keeps busy making up new ones.

Forty years almost to the day from that sunny afternoon in 1959 that I spent exploring the Terrible Edith mine, my friend Paul and I stood in the middle of the Murray cemetery surrounded by one hundred resting souls. How many full-length novels, I wondered.

I searched for Edith's marker, hoping to find some clue as to her final acknowledgment by the world. The cemetery is on a high slope overlooking town. It is a triangle tucked away on the forest edge, not more than one hundred feet on a side. It has the appearance of moving slowly downhill, but I don't think that's the case. The cemetery committee has added a location roster, gates, and gravel pathways. Here and there Douglas fir and hemlock seventy-five feet tall stand watch over a patchwork quilt of eternity. Their roots tilt the headstones at odd angles. The markers for most of these good people are not fancy. The wooden ones are virtually unreadable, even from the 1930s, because of the harsh winters.

Finally, Paul looked up and pointed. "There she is." A few feet away, in the center of the cemetery, stood a

MINER'S CABIN
MURRAY, ID.

M MCCANN©

brand new plywood marker done up in reddish brown enamel and neat, white capital letters:

EDITH MCCORKENDALE 1882–1905
KNOWN AS TERRIBLE EDITH
OF THE MURRAY RED-LIGHT DISTRICT

It was a glorious September afternoon. While we wandered around, the temperature nipped down into the low fifties and the forest shadows lengthened out across the grass. A crow flew over. A wisp of fog drifted down through the treetops, hit some warmer air, and evaporated. All I could think of to say was, "Well, Edith Bergoine Arnberg McGongil McCorkendale, you have certainly provided this old miner with a long, long entertainment. I thank you for that and wish peace upon your soul."

Over in the northwest corner an engraved granite head-
stone reads:

CHRIS CHRISTOPHERSON—A MURRAY GOLDMINER

1910–1999

Beneath that stone does lie, as much a miner as could die.

PROMISE

The years slide by
  We was too soon old and too late smart
Fold into one another
  Times goes by so fast you don't pay no attention to it
Lost within the details
  There comes a time . . . and you live with the memories

Who will speak for us
When we are gone?

I will tell my story
I will speak of my forefathers and mothers
I will hold the daily, the usual, close to my heart

I will pass it on
Before it's gone

Rita Helene Levitz, *Images and Voices of Lighthouse Country*

Notes

1. Patricia Hart and Ivar Nelson, *Mining Town* (Seattle: University of Washington Press, 1984), 38.

2. Letter, V. M. Clement to John H. Hammond, 12 September 1892, Bunker Hill Mining Co., Manuscript Group 367, Special Collections, University of Idaho Library, Moscow. (Hereafter cited as Bunker Hill MSS.)

3. Report, C. R. Corning to Bunker Hill and Sullivan Co., President and Board of Directors, 14 May 1894, Bunker Hill MSS.

4. Report, C. R. Corning to General N. H. Harris, 14 July 1896, Bunker Hill MSS.

5. Ibid.

6. Report, Frederick Burbidge to F. W. Bradley, 29 October 1897, Bunker Hill MSS.

7. Charles Kelly, *The Outlaw Trail* (Lincoln: Bison Books Edition, University of Nebraska Press, 1996).

8. Report, Burbidge to Bradley, October 1897, Bunker Hill MSS.

9. Report, Burbidge to Bradley, 7 December 1897, Bunker Hill MSS.

10. Report, Burbidge to Bradley, 15 December 1897, Bunker Hill MSS.

11. Manager's fiscal-year-end report, 31 May 1899, Bunker Hill MSS.

12. General Correspondence File, folders 93–99, Bunker Hill MSS.

13. J. Anthony Lucas, *Big Trouble: Murder in a Small Western Mining Town Sets Off a Struggle for the Soul of America* (New York: Simon and Schuster, 1997), 112.

14. Cover letter for manager's fiscal-year-end report, 31 May 1899, Bunker Hill MSS.

15. Report, Burbidge to Bradley, 30 October 1899, Bunker Hill MSS.

16. Report, Burbidge to Bradley, 16 February 1900, Bunker Hill MSS. Emphasis added.

17. Report, Burbidge to Bradley, 25 May 1900, Bunker Hill MSS.

18. Report, Burbidge to Bradley, 22 June 1900, Bunker Hill MSS.

19. Manager's fiscal-year-end report, 31 May 1901, Bunker Hill MSS.

20. Stanley A. Easton, taped interview, Stanley Easton Papers, 21 October 1957, MS Group 5, University of Idaho Special Collections, Moscow: "Late in the summer or mid-fall of 1902, I reported to Kellogg to take over. The situation was as follows: the tunnel on the valley floor level started by Clement back in the '90s had been gradually extended until it had cut the structure at which ore could be expected to be found. All of the orebodies in the upper levels indicated a strong westerly trend and the tunnel had been projected to cut this point, but unfortunately, when the tunnel reached the indicated area, the rock *structure* was found but there was no ore" (emphasis in original). Also, personal observation, 1956.

21. Report, Al Burch to Bradley, 21 December 1901, Bunker Hill MSS.

22. Manager's year-end report, 31 May 1902, Bunker Hill MSS.

23. Report, Operative #15 to Stanley Easton, 13 January 1906, Folder 1578, Bunker Hill MSS.